The Ultimate Christmas Song Guide

Steven Mandeli

Nothing But the Truth

DEDICATION

For My Parents
For making me who I am, may they rest in eternal peace

For My Brother and Sister
For always being with me

For My Family
My wife, my girls, my grandchildren
For being with me now

And for my best friend, Erica
For always being a best friend

"The best way to spread Christmas cheer is singing loud for all to hear"
- Will Farrell, in *Elf*

TABLE OF CONTENTS

FOREWORD

On March 18, 2024, I had a total knee replacement. The operation went well, performed by a highly skilled surgeon aided by a robotic apparatus of some kind. Recovery was the hard part. I spent a of of time in bed, at times feeling very depressed.

My family and friends were very supportive but being essentially bedridden for a long time made me sad. I killed time by reading voraciously and utilizing all the features of my phone, including listening to music. Music helped in my battle against depression. Thank God for music streaming services! I found the most uplifting music to be Christmas music. Christmas music is uplifting by nature and made me think of my favorite time of year: Arbor Day (actually, Christmas). And Christmas represented happiness.

I searched for all kinds of Christmas music, old and new, and added them into a playlist. At over 800 songs and more than 2000 renditions I slowed down a bit. Even as I healed and became mobile again, I kept on listening and looking for more.

And then it hit me: I know a *lot* about Christmas music. What about writing a book about Christmas music? Was there anything out there of a comprehensive nature about Christmas music?

The answer was no. So I went through my playlist, now at 850 songs with over 2200 renditions, and entered all of it into spreadsheets. The streaming service provided basic information, like composers, albums the songs were from, and dates. But as I proceeded, I noticed discrepancies in dates. So, I searched for a website that could give me accurate dates. I found it: it was *secondhandsongs.com*. It listed almost all the songs, all the renditions it was aware of, and accurate release information. Sometimes information was missing, and I found a site called *discogs.com* that actually had pictures of records. If I didn't have composer information, I could just literally look at the record and read it off the label.

Of course, I didn't want just titles, authors and release info of the more popular songs. I wanted the stories behind them. For this, I just googled the internet. It was like mining for gold, and my background in research in Electrical Engineering helped.

After many weeks I completed my spreadsheets. But they weren't a book. I came up with a format for a book and did a *lot* of copying and pasting. It turned out to be more than that, though—in the process I learned more and more, and the resultant book had not only more information but more *accurate* information. The few books I saw out there had no references, so I made a point of including references in mine. I split the songs into four periods: traditional (pre-20th century), first half of the 20th century, the latter half, and the 21st century so far. I created summaries for each chapter that together provide a good history of Christmas music, I think.

How did I choose what songs to include? First, I had to *like them*. But I kept in mind that I could not be narrow-minded about this thing. I considered the broad appeal of the songs, and included all genres, from classical to modern Pop. Fortunately, when it comes to Christmas music, I am quite broadminded. I tried to include everything popular at some time and every song I considered "Important." There are many songs included that are not so well-known but are *good*.

I wish I had this book to find Christmas songs that were out there. You are lucky—you hold this book (or e-reader) in your hands. Look around, find something you like, and find it on your music streaming service. Almost literally 100% of each song rendition listed here can be found on any streaming service.

An important point that I'd like to make is that Christmas is the Christian celebration of the birth of Jesus Christ. Many Christmas songs, especially the earlier ones, embrace this celebration; many are secular and do not. Both types of songs are included here. I describe the religious ones as a "believer" would, as this makes the explanation easier. If I described everything from a secular lens, I would be writing things like "a song about Mary, whom Christians believe is Jesus' mother." Instead, I write "a song about Mary, the mother of God." You don't have to have Christian beliefs—and I am certainly not imposing them on anybody. I just explain what the song was meant to be about by its author.

For those who haven't been around nearly as long as I have, I need to explain something. A "single" used to be a record with two sides, a different song on each side. Prior to the 60s, these were 10" records (played at 78 RPM) and then later 7" (played at 45 RPM). Songs released as singles actually had two songs on the record, one on each side. The primary song, the one you bought the record for, was considered the "A" side. The "B" side song just came along for the ride. Sometimes, the "B" side turned out to be more popular than the "A" side, and other times both were hits. As for albums, these were on a 12" record, known as an "LP" (Long Playing) record. It utilized both sides as well, to fit all the songs.

Please use the guide on the next page when looking at the song entries.

That's it. Enjoy. Please feel free to contact me at smandeli1701@gmail.com.

Steve Mandeli
December 25, 2024
(*really*)

Song Title (and alternates)

Composers   **Year written or first released, whatever is sooner**

First Release Performers   *First release album* or "Single" (First release Year)

Song discussion, with citations. Background stories of many songs.

Discussion of renditions below, referenced by letter (a), (b), (c) etc.

a	Year	Artist	Album
b	Year	*Artist*	*Album (in italics if it is an Instrumental)*

1 Traditional Music (Pre-1901)

Christmas music before the 20th century features a rich tradition rooted in religious and folk customs. These pieces include hymns, carols, and compositions that celebrate the Nativity and festive spirit of Christmas.

Christmas music before the 16th century was dominated by sacred chants, hymns, and carols that blended reverence with communal celebration. The use of Latin and vernacular languages allowed these songs to resonate across social and linguistic divides, creating a foundation for the more elaborate carols and hymns of later centuries.

One of the earliest pieces of Christmas music that survives today is "O Come, O Come, Emmanuel," then known as *Veni Veni Emmanuel*. The lyrics come from a 7-verse poem that dates to possibly the 12th century, though the verses may be of 8th century origin. Music was added in the 15th century but may also have 8th century origins. It was used in a call and response fashion during the vespers, or evening, service and was particularly appropriate for the Christmas Advent season. The first English translation was made in 1851.

The melody of "Good King Wenceslas" came from a 13th century spring carol *"Tempus adest floridum"* ("Eastertime Is Come"). This was found by English hymnwriter John Mason Neale and his music editor Thomas Helmore in a 1582 Finnish song collection. They wrote the lyrics of the legend of King Wenceslas to fit the song in 1853. According to the legend, King Wenceslas and his servant had trudged through cold and snow to bring provisions to a poor man and his family.

"In dulci jubilo," Latin for "in sweet rejoicing," is a German-Latin carol blending joyous lyrics and devotion to the Nativity originating from about 1328. It was translated into English in 1853 and came to be known as "Bell Carol (Good Christian Men, Rejoice)." It is a "macaronic" carol as it originally combined two languages. The vernacular language, German, made it accessible to common people while Latin preserved its sacred nature.

The English "Coventry Carol" from the 15th or 16th century refers to the Massacre of the Innocents from the Biblical story of an event described in the Gospel of Matthew. In it, King Herod orders the execution of all male children in Bethlehem under the age of two based on information received from the Three Wise Men (on their way to visit the infant Jesus) that a baby had been born who would become king of all Jews. The song is a lullaby supposedly sung by the mothers of Bethlehem to their doomed sons.

Christmas songs of the 16th century are deeply rooted in both religious traditions and folk customs. This period, spanning the late Renaissance, saw the rise of polyphonic choral music and the continued popularity of carols that celebrated the Nativity.

The German carol "*Es ist ein Ros Entsprungen*," literally translated as "a rose has sprung up," is a devotion to the Virgin Mary, the rose in the German text being a symbolic reference to the Virgin Mary. The lyrics to this song were first printed in 1599 and the music is from 1609. The song became known in English as "Lo How a Rose E'er Blooming."

"God Rest Ye Merry, Gentlemen" has its origins in the 16th century, though developed further in the ensuing years. The first printed edition of it is dated about 1760. The full current melody was published in 1855.

The origins of "The Holly and the Ivy" are uncertain and may predate the 16th century. The melody for this popular carol is an old English folk song. The lyrics date to at least the early 18th century, and there is evidence that some lyrics may have been from Chaucer's *Canterbury Tales*, which dates to the late 14th century.

"Greensleeves" is not a Christmas song, but its melody was later used in one, "What Child is This?" "Greensleeves" itself was published in 1580.

"Ding Dong Merrily on High" first appeared as a secular dance tune written by a French cleric, composer and writer in the 16th century. The familiar words to it would not be published until 1924.

"Bring a Torch, Jeanette, Isabella" got lyrics in the 16th century, to a tune that dated back to the 14th century.

The melody for "Deck the Halls" came from about the 16th century, from the Welsh winter carol, "*Nos Galan*" (English: "New Year's Eve"). The song would not become familiar to us until the 19th century, when English lyrics were written.

Christmas songs of the 17th century emerged during a time of significant religious and cultural change. The period saw the development of sacred hymns, carols, and folk songs that celebrated the Nativity and festive traditions. Some of these songs became enduring parts of Christmas music traditions, reflecting both solemn devotion and joyful celebration.

"Angels We Have Heard on High" is derived from the French song "*Les Anges dans Nos Campagnes,*" which is believed to have its origins in the 17th century. It was translated into English in 1862.

"The First Noel" has words and music that come from a traditional English carol of the 16th or 17th century, but possibly dating from as early as the 13th century. The final combination of tune and lyrics first appeared in the early 1800s.

In the 17th century "Here We Come A-Wassailing" was being sung in rural England, but its origin may go back earlier. The word "wassail" comes from the Middle

English toast, "*waes hael,*" meaning "be thou hale," which in turn means "be in good health." The phrase "*waes hael*" dates to pre-Norman [Norman Conquest, 1066] times. Bands of beggars and orphans used to dance their way to homes of the more fortunate, offering to sing good cheer and to tell good fortune if the house-holder would give them a drink from his wassail bowl. This wasn't always done politely.

"I Saw Three Ships" came out of the 17th century. The modern lyrics are from an 1833 version by the English lawyer and antiquarian William Sandys.

Christmas songs of the 18th century reflect the era's musical and cultural diversity, blending sacred hymns with early secular traditions. Many of these pieces have roots in liturgical music, folk traditions, and classical compositions, often performed in churches or at community gatherings.

The lyrics to "Joy to the World," the most-published hymn in North America, were written in 1719 by Isaac Watts. Watts didn't write this song originally to be a Christmas carol, as the lyrics do not reflect Jesus' birth, but rather Christ's Second Coming. Lowell Mason designed the orchestral arrangement in 1848. Mason's tune is called "Antioch." The tune has some notes in common with Handel's "Messiah." For this reason, it has been described as "arranged from Handel." Nowadays, how-ever, Handel's scholars seem to agree that the resemblance is accidental.

The lyrics to "Hark! The Herald Angels Sing" were written by Charles Wesley in 1739 and sung to a different tune than today. The music we know was written by Felix Mendelssohn in 1840—the "God is Light" chorus from the "Festival Song" cantata celebrating the 400th anniversary of the invention of the printing press. Words and music were brought together by William Hayman Cummings in 1855.

Evidence indicates that the hymn "*Adeste Fideles*" was composed by John Francis Wade, an English hymnist, sometime in the first half of the 18th century. The earli-est existing manuscript (c. 1743) shows both words and tune. In 1751 he published a printed compilation of his manuscript copies. Wade had composed four stanzas, in Latin. Three more stanzas in Latin were probably composed by the French Catholic priest Jean François Borderies. The song was translated by two men, and the result was printed in 1884.

The "Hallelujah Chorus," known as "For unto Us a Child Is Born," was composed by George Frideric Handel in 1741, being from Handel's *Messiah Part II.*

Christmas songs from the 19th century reflect a mix of traditional carols and newer compositions that became staples of holiday celebrations. This era saw the rise of many beloved songs we still sing today, often inspired by both religious themes and festive cheer.

The lyrics for "Silent Night" were written in 1816 by Joseph Mohr, and music was written for it in 1818 by Franz Gruber. This Austrian carol, written for guitar, is one of the most famous Christmas hymns worldwide and is the most recorded Christmas song. The traditional story about a broken organ at St. Nicholas Church in Oberndorf, Austria is fiction from a story published in the US in the 1930s.

"Ave Maria" or *Ellens Gesang III* was written by Franz Schubert in 1825, based on Walter Scott's 1810 narrative poem "The Lady of the Lake."

"O Christmas Tree" (German: "*O Tannenbaum*") was written in 1819. The original lyrics were a sexist love song. In 1824 they were transformed into the Christmas song we know today. Incidentally, a *Tannenbaum* is a fir tree; the German word for Christmas tree is actually *Weihnachtsbaum*.

"O Holy Night" was composed in 1847 by Adolphe Adam with lyrics by Placide Cappeau. It was a French composition known as "*Cantique de Noel,*" based on an 1843 French poem. This song did not sit well with church authorities. Soon after it was written, the 1848 Revolution broke out in France, and Adam worried some observers by calling "O Holy Night" a "religious Marseillaise," referring to the 1792 song adopted as the Gallic national anthem.

"It Came Upon the Midnight Clear" started as a poem by Edmund Sears in 1849, with music added in 1850 by Richard Storrs Willis. The song is not about Christmas and the birth of Christ—which is not mentioned—but is a plea for peace after the Mexican-American War, which had just ended in 1848, one year before the poem the song is based on was written.

Another version of "Ave Maria" was written in 1853 by Charles Gounod. He superimposed over an only very slightly changed version of Bach's "Prelude No. 1 in C major," composed in 1722. This song is one of the first Christmas recordings made, in 1898.

"Jingle Bells" was written by James Lord Pierpont probably in 1850 but not copyrighted until 1857. It was written for a Thanksgiving program at his father's Sunday school. The song proved to be so popular the children were asked to sing the song again at Christmastime, and it has been tied to the latter holiday ever since.

"We Three Kings (of Orient Are)," written by John Henry Hopkins Jr. in 1857, is, like "Jingle Bells," one of the earliest American Christmas songs.

As noted above, the melody for "Deck the Halls" came from about the 16th century, from the Welsh winter carol, "*Nos Galan.*" In 1862 Thomas Oliphant wrote English lyrics for the song, as it is heard today. Also as noted above, "Angels We Have Heard on High," derived from the French song "*Les Anges dans Nos Campagnes,*" was translated into English in that same year, to make it the song we know today.

In 1864 Benjamin Hanby wrote one of the first secular songs to feature Santa Claus, in fact he called it "Santa Claus." The name was changed to "Up on the Housetop."

In 1865 William Chatterton Dix wrote new Christmas lyrics to the very old song "Greensleeves" and called it "What Child is This?"

"O Little Town of Bethlehem" was written by Brooks (lyrics) and Redner (music) in 1868. The song was inspired by a trip Brooks had made to Bethlehem in 1865. Strangely, a Reverand who had asked permission to print it in his Sunday-school hymn and tune book christened the music "Saint Louis" and the name stuck. In 1903 alternative music was written, called "Forest Green" or "Ploughboy's Dream." That music is used for the song in the UK and the Commonwealth, and sometimes in the US, especially in the Episcopal Church.

"Away in a Manger" was usually ascribed to Martin Luther and a German source. Evidence now indicates that Luther had nothing to do with it, and that it was written in the US circa 1887 by Charles H. Gabriel and James Murray. In the UK the lyrics are usually set to the tune "Cradle Song," written in 1895 by William J. Kirkpatrick.

Two songs usually associated with Christmas that were written in the 19th century are "Dance of the Sugar Plum Fairy" and "March from The Nutcracker," both written by Pyotr Ilyich Tchaikovsky in 1892.

Adeste Fideles (O Come All Ye Faithful)

Latin: John Francis Wade & Jean François Borderies
English translation: Frederick Oakeley & William Thomas Brooke

1751 (first printing)

John McCormack (in Latin)　　　　　　　　　　　　Single (1915)

Evidence indicates that the hymn was composed by John Francis Wade (1711-86), an English hymnist, sometime in the first half of the 18th century. The earliest existing manuscript (c. 1743) shows both words and tune. In 1751 he published a printed compilation of his manuscript copies. Wade had composed four stanzas, in Latin. Three more stanzas in Latin were probably composed by the French Catholic priest Jean François Borderies. The suggestion is that Borderies heard the hymn sung while exiled in England in 1793 and wrote the three additional stanzas after he returned to France in 1794. The French form of the hymn with a total of eight stanzas was first printed in 1822, the additional stanza being of unknown origin. The translation to English is also composite. Four stanzas were translated by Frederick Oakeley (1802-80) in 1841 and printed in 1852. Three were translated by William Thomas Brooke and printed in 1884. One stanza has not come into general use in the English-speaking countries, so there is a total of seven in English.[1]

The following songs are listed as "Adeste Fideles": (b), (c), (e), (g), (h), (j), (s), and (z); the rest are listed as "O Come All Ye Faithful." Song (p) is a medley with "O Holy Night"; (y) is a medley with "Hallelujah Chorus"; and (ag) is a medley with "The First Noel."

Song (o) is the only known Christmas song by Art Garfunkel, and his excellent voice is perfect for this song.

Most of the songs below are performed in a traditional manner. The exceptions are the following: (p) is a Rock song; (s) is New Age and is sung in Latin; and (af) has a New Age sound.

a	1935	Bing Crosby with Victor Young and His Orchestra	Single ("B" side of "Silent Night")
b	1942	Bing Crosby with John Scott Trotter and His Orchestra	Single ("B" side of "Silent Night, Holy Night")
c	1946	Frank Sinatra – Orchestra under the direction of	Single ("B" side of "Silent Night, Holy Night")

		Axel Stordahl	
d	1948	Frank Sinatra	Christmas Songs by Sinatra
e	1958	*101 Strings*	*The Glory of Christmas*
f	1958	*Mantovani*	*Christmas Carols*
g	1959	Pat Boone	White Christmas
h	1960	Nat King Cole	The Magic of Christmas
i	1960	Bobby Darrin	The 25th Day of December with Bobby Darin
j	1962	The Everly Brothers	Christmas with the Everly Brothers and the Boystown Choir
k	1962	*The Philadelphia Orchestra - Eugene Ormandy, Conductor. The Temple University Concert Choir - Robert Page, Director*	*The Glorious Sound of Christmas*
l	1967	Ella Fitzgerald	Ella Fitzgerald's Christmas
m	1971	Elvis Presley	Elvis Sings the Wonderful World of Christmas
n	1988	Ann Murray	Ann Murray's Christmas Album
o	1990	Art Garfunkel	Christmas Hits; Acoustic Christmas
p	1996	*Trans-Siberian Orchestra*	*The Ghosts of Christmas Eve*
q	1998	Vince Gill	Breath of Heaven: A Christmas Collection
r	2002	Jose Feliciano	Previously Unreleased track from Feliz Navidad (1970)
s	2006	Enya	Amarantine (Christmas Edition)
t	2006	Celtic Woman	The Best of Christmas
u	2007	Olivia Newton-John	Christmas Wish
v	2007	Josh Groban (with the Mormon Tabernacle Choir & Craig Joseph)	Noel
w	2008	Elvis Presley with Olivia Newton-John	Christmas Duets
x	2008	Faith Hill	Joy to the World
y	2010	Mariah Carey (feat. Patricia Carey)	Merry Christmas II You
z	2011	*Andre Gagnon*	*Dans le silence de la nuit*
aa	2012	Richard Marx	Christmas Spirit
ab	2013	Susan Boyle (with Elvis Presley)	Home for Christmas
ac	2016	Sarah McLachlan	Wonderland

ad	2017	Elvis Presley & The Royal Philharmonic Orchestra	Christmas with Elvis and the Royal Philharmonic Orchestra
ae	2020	Carrie Underwood	My Gift
af	2020	For King and Country	A Drummer Boy Christmas
ag	2021	Nat King Cole	A Sentimental Christmas with Nat King Cole and Friends: Cole Classics Reimagined
ah	2022	*Boston Pops Orchestra & John Williams*	*Christmas Collection*

All Through the Night

Unknown   **1784**

Henry Burr   Single (1906)

Traditional Welsh song, "*Ar Hyd y Nos.*"

Song (e) is Celtic New Age. Songs (d) and (f) are different: song (d) is a standard version, while song (f) is a "reimagined" version, where the song is performed like a classic 1970s Olivia Newton-John song, using digital sampling of her voice.

a	1958	*101 Strings*	*Quiet Hours*
b	1960	The Kingston Trio	The Last Month of the Year
c	1998	Shawn Colvin	Holiday Sings and Lullabies
d	2007	Olivia Newton-John (feat. Michael McDonald)	Christmas Wish
e	2019	Caranua	A Celtic Christmas
f	2024	Olivia Newton-John (feat. Michael McDonald)	Angels in the Snow (Reimagined)

Angels We Have Heard on High (Gloria)

English lyrics by James Chadwick   **1862**

Joseph Saucier (in French)   Single (as *Les anges dans nos campagnes*) (1905)

A Christmas carol to the tune of the Hymn "Gloria," itself from a traditional French song called "*Les Anges dans nos campagnes.*"

The following songs are performed non-traditionally: (e) and (l) are a cappella; (f), (o) and (q) are New Age; and (i) and (r) can be considered New Wave Rock.

Song (n), performed by Lindsay Stirling on violin with orchestral accompaniment, is stunning. Even more so is her video[2] of the performance, wherein she plays the violin and dances in Utah Lake, a natural shallow freshwater lake. One of the best videos I have ever seen, it is breathtakingly beautiful.

a	1958	*Percy Faith*	*Hallelujah! [Repackaged as Music of Christmas, Vol. 2 in 1965]*
b	1962	Robert Shaw Chorale, Al Chernet & RCA Victor Symphony Orchestra	The Many Moods of Christmas
c	1967	Ella Fitzgerald	Ella Fitzgerald's Christmas
d	1989	*Royal Philharmonic Orchestra*	*Family Christmas: Favorite Carols and Holiday Songs*
e	1990	The Roches	We Three Kings
f	1995	*Mannheim Steamroller*	*Christmas in the Aire*
g	1999	Michael Crawford	A Christmas Album
h	2008	*101 Strings*	*101 Strings Christmas - 30 Greatest Orchestral Holiday Favorites*
i	2008	Sixpence None the Richer	The Dawn of Grace
j	2009	*Daniel Berthiaume*	*O Holy Hight*
k	2010	The Commodores	Stars Come Out for Christmas - Special Edition II
l	2012	Pentatonix	PTXmas
m	2016	Sarah McLachlan	Wonderland
n	2017	*Lindsey Stirling*	*Warmer in the Winter*
o	2018	*Christmas Candles*	*Relaxing Christmas Music 2018*
p	2019	Lea Michele	Christmas in the City
q	2020	For King & Country	A Drummer Boy Christmas
r	2023	Kascade & The Moth & The Flame	Kascade Christmas
s	2023	Karla Bonoff	Silent Night

Ave Maria

Charles Gounod   1853

W.D. McFarland (Instrumental)   Single (1898)

Charles Gounod superimposed over an only very slightly changed version of Bach's Prelude No. 1 in C major, composed in 1722.

I have found that the songs attributed to Gounod sound the same as those attributed to Schubert. After trying to separate songs that sounded the same, I present all of the Ave Maria renditions under "Ave Maria (Ellens Gesang III)," by Schubert, with apologies to Charles Gounod. [There is a totally different song called "Ave Maria" from 1970, which is in Chapter 3.]

Ave Maria (Ellens Gesang III)

Franz Schubert   1825

Jesse Crawford (Instrumental)   *In a Monastery Garden* (1949)

"Hail Mary" in English. Officially, "Ellens Gesang III," D. 839, Op. 52, No. 6, 1825. "Ellens Gesang III" translates to "Ellen's Third Song." Based on Walter Scott's 1810 narrative poem "The Lady of the Lake." The poem is set in a small island along a lake called Loch Katrine. It goes on to depict a clash of different clans, in a feudal world, where a lady named Ellen is caught in the middle of a family feud. She is often treated as a prize of conquest, with men fighting for her approval, without adhering to her thoughts. She and her family take refuge in a fortified island, which would later be called Ellen's Isle, which still exists in Scotland. While Ellen and her family take refuge in the island, Ellen looks up to the night sky and sings a prayer to the virgin Mary to look over her in those perturbed times. It goes on to describe how the vile men are trying to win her as a prize with great poignancy, and appeals to the maiden in the Virgin Mother, to look over them as they sleep through the night.[3]

One of the most moving pieces of music of all time, it is performed splendidly by all below. Song (l) is New Age, sung in a mixture of English and Latin. Songs (b), (e), (f), (h), (i), (j), and (k) are sung in Latin.

a	1958	Johnny Mathis (with the Percy Faith Orchestra)	Good Night, Dear Lord
b	1960	Bobby Darin	The 25th Day of December with Bobby Darin

c	1962	Eugene Ormandy, The Philadelphia Orchestra, Robert Page and Temple University Choir	The Glorious Sounds of Christmas
d	1968	Burl Ives	Christmas Album
e	1968	Perry Como	The Complete RCA Christmas Collection
f	1978	The Carpenters	Christmas Portrait
g	1998	Celine Dion	These Are Special Times
h	2001	Sarah Brightman	Classics
i	2007	Josh Groban	Noel
j	2009	London Philharmonic Orchestra, David Perry & London Philharmonic Choir	The 50 Most Essential Relaxing Classics
k	2011	Michael Bublé	Christmas
l	2019	Caranua (feat. Lynn Hilary & Alex Sharpe)	Celtic Dreaming

Away in a Manger

Charles H. Gabriel, James Murray & James Kirkpatrick

1887 (Murray)
1895 (Kirkpatrick)

Gabriel & Murray version: Robert Shaw and His RCA Victor Chorale
Kirkpatrick version: Mario Lanza

Gabriel & Murray version: *Christmas Hymns and Carols* (1946)
Kirkpatrick version: *Mario Lanza Sings Christmas Songs* (1951)

In many hymnbooks this lyric is ascribed to Martin Luther. But there is nothing corresponding to it in any of his hymns or in his other writings. Martin Luther had nothing to do directly with the writing of the words or the composing of any of the forty-one musical settings of "Away in a Manger." Martin Luther did not often appear as a gentle character. He was generally brusque and uncouth; yet it has not been considered an incongruity to ascribe to him this tender and lovely carol that for centuries, in the several tongues of many lands, has been the lullaby sung over the beds of countless children. In fact, upon study of the lyrics, it becomes apparent that the German form of the lyrics is the translation, not the English. Although Luther himself had nothing to do with the carol, the colonies of German Lutherans in Pennsylvania almost certainly did.[4]

The widest known version of the song uses James Murray's tune and lyrics, as well as the third stanza, which first appeared in the 1892 Charles Gabriel version. This version is also known as "Mueller," after a mysterious composer called Carl Mueller. To date, nothing has been found about his identity and his role in the composition. Nevertheless, there are several documents (especially from the 1920s and 1930s) that mention the song as credited to Martin Luther (lyrics) and Carl Mueller (music). It is likely that the false attribution to a "German" composer served as a sort of "proof" that the song came from Germany, where Lutheranism was born.

In the UK the lyrics are usually set to the tune "Cradle Song," written in 1895 by William J. Kirkpatrick.[5]

The following renditions are all so wonderful. Song (j) is a cappella. Song (e) is a vocal with chimes. Song (h) has a simple guitar accompaniment. Song (m) sounds like a chorus—though it is predominately only of one person, Linda Ronstadt. Song (n) has a Middle Ages sound to it. Song (s) is a beautiful New Age song by an artist called "2002." The Instrumentals are beautiful.

a	1952	Leroy Anderson & Leroy Anderson with His Orchestra	*A Leroy Anderson Christmas*
b	1960	Nat King Cole	The Magic of Christmas
c	1963	Andy Williams	The Andy Williams Christmas Album
d	1963	Leonard Bernstein, The Tabernacle Choir at Temple Square, New York Philharmonic & Richard P. Condie	I Love...Classical Christmas
e	1966	Joan Baez	Noel (Bonus Track Version)
f	1967	Ella Fitzgerald	Ella Fitzgerald's Christmas
g	1968	Ed Ames	Christmas with Ed Ames - Christmas is the Warmest Time of the Year
h	1979	Emmylou Harris	Light of the Stable
i	1982	Julie Andrews	Christmas with Julie Andrews
j	1990	The Roches	We Three Kings
k	1994	*Kenny G*	*Miracles - The Holiday Album*
l	1996	Glen Campbell	Home for the Holidays
m	2000	Linda Ronstadt	A Merry Little Christmas
n	2001	*Mannheim Steamroller*	*Christmas Extraordinaire*
o	2005	Carrie Underwood	My Gift
p	2006	Willie Nelson	A Country Christmas
q	2006	Celtic Woman	The Best of Christmas
r	2008	Faith Hill	Joy to the World

s	2008	*2002*	*Christmas Dreams*
t	2010	Aled Jones	Christmas Gold
u	2010	Kim Carnes	Stars Come Out for Christmas - Special Edition II
v	2012	The Galway Christmas Singers	Family Christmas: Favorite Carols and Holiday Songs
w	2012	*101 Strings*	*101 Strings Christmas - 30 Greatest Orchestral Holiday Favorites*
x	2016	Sarah McLachlan	Wonderland
y	2021	Matthew West	We Need Christmas
z	2022	Joss Stone	Merry Christmas, Love

Bell Carol (Good Christian Men, Rejoice)

Heinrich Seuse　　　　　　　　　　　　　　　**c. 1328**

Ukrainian National Chorus　　　　　　Single (1923) as "Poor Hawthorne"

English Translation of "*In dulci jubilo*" (Latin for "in sweet rejoicing") by J. M. Neale in 1853.

a	2008	*101 Strings Orchestra*	*101 Strings Christmas – 30 Greatest Orchestral Holiday Favorites*

Bring a Torch, Jeanette, Isabella (AKA Jeanette, Isabella)

Translated to English by Edward Cuthbert Nunn　　　　**Music: 14th century**
　　　　　　　　　　　　　　　　　　Lyrics: 16th century

Robert Shaw and His RCA Victor Chorale　　*Christmas Hymns and Carols* (1946)

This wasn't originally composed as sacred music at all, but as a lively court dance tune for the nobility. The carol, with both words and music, first appeared in a French book of Christmas Carols published in 1553. The song is about two peasants coming upon Jesus' manger and rushing back to town with torches to tell them the great news that Christ was born.[6]

Song (a) is titled "Bring a Torch, Jeanette, Isabella" and song (b) is titled "Jeanette, Isabella." Very pretty song.

a	1984	Louis Davis Jr. & Jackson Berkey	Christmas
b	2009	Tori Amos	Midwinter Graces

Coventry Carol

Unknown   **1500s**

Robert Shaw and His RCA Victor Chorale — *Christmas Hymns and Carols* (1946)

This English carol refers to the Massacre of the Innocents from the Biblical story of an event described in the Gospel of Matthew. In it, King Herod orders the execution of all male children in Bethlehem under the age of two. The story goes that Herod did this because he heard of the birth of a baby who would become the king of all Jews—news that was relayed to him by the Magi (or the Three Wise Men referred to in the carol "We Three Kings"). Joseph, having been warned by an angel, escapes Bethlehem with Mary and the newborn Jesus to Egypt. The song, then, is a lullaby supposedly sung by the mothers of Bethlehem to their doomed sons.[7]

Song (d) is titled "Candle: Coventry Carol." Song (f) is a cappella.

a	1975	John Denver	Rocky Mountain Christmas
b	1995	The Choir of King's College, Cambridge & Sir David Wilcocks	Essential Carols - The Very Best of King's College Choir, Cambridge
c	1995	Lareena McKennitt	A Midwinter Night's Dream
d	2009	Tori Amos	Midwinter Graces
e	2015	The City of Prague Philharmonic Orchestra & Crouch End Festival Chorus	The Greatest Christmas Choral Classics
f	2016	Pentatonix	A Pentatonix Christmas (Deluxe)

Dance of the Sugar Plum Fairy

Pyotr Ilyich Tchaikovsky   **1892**

Leopold Stokowski and The Philadelphia Orchestra — Single (1935)

From *The Nutcracker* ballet.

25

Song (a) is simply titled "Faeries." Song (b) is a wild violin performance backed up by an orchestra. Song (c) is a cappella.

a	2001	*Mannheim Steamroller*	*Christmas Extraordinaire*
b	2017	*Lindsey Stirling*	*Warmer in the Winter*
c	2014	Pentatonix	The Greatest Christmas Hits

Deck the Halls (with Boughs of Holly)

English Lyrics: Thomas Oliphant (1862)   **1500s**

William H. Reitz (Instrumental)   Single (1927) – "B" side of "Christmas Bells"

The melody is Welsh and belongs to a winter carol, *"Nos Galan"* (English: "New Year's Eve"). It was played on a harp with dancers circling around who would improvise lyrics in a game. While this tune is thought to date from as early as the 16th century, it was first found (untitled) in John Parry's manuscript "Twelve Airs for One and Two Guitars" (1781). It was then published in "Musical and Poetical Relicks of the Welsh Bards" by Edward Jones (1784) titled *"Nos Galan."* Welsh lyrics were added still later.[8]

Song (k) is titled as "Boughs of Holly." Song (p) is in a medley with "Joy to the World."

A number of Instrumentals below are not with standard orchestras. Song (i) is New Age, but has become pretty much a classic Christmas song, now over 40 years old. Song (j) features the fantastic guitar stylings of Ottmar Liebert. Song (k) is an excellent Rock rendition. Song (m) is a piano piece.

Song (n) is unique as it has a Renaissance sound.

a	1954	*Percy Faith & His Orchestra*	*Music of Christmas*
b	1960	Nat King Cole	The Magic of Christmas
c	1961	Mitch Miller	Holiday Sing Along with Mitch
d	1962	The Everly Brothers	Christmas with the Everly Brothers and the Boystown Choir
e	1962	Eugene Ormandy & The Philadelphia Orchestra	I Love...Classical Christmas
f	1964	Bobby Vinton	Kissin' Christmas: The Bobby Vinton Christmas Album
g	1964	Jo Stafford	Joyful Season
h	1972	The Singers Unlimited	Christmas

i	1984	*Mannheim Steamroller*	*Christmas*
j	1990	*Ottmar Liebert*	*Poets & Angels - Music 4 the Holidays*
k	1998	*Trans-Siberian Orchestra*	*The Christmas Attic*
l	2008	*101 Strings*	*101 Strings Christmas - 30 Greatest Orchestral Holiday Favorites*
m	2016	*Christmas Eve*	*Traditional Christmas Classics - Relaxing Instrumental Music for the Holiday Break*
n	2017	Blackmore's Night	Winter Carols
o	2019	Celtic Woman	The Magic of Christmas
p	2021	Nat King Cole & Johnny Mathis	A Sentimental Christmas with Nat King Cole and Friends: Cole Classics Reimagined
q	2022	*Boston Pops Orchestra & John Williams*	*Christmas Collection*
r	2022	*Lindsey Stirling*	*Snow Waltz*

Ding Dong Merrily on High

Words by George Ratcliffe   **1588**
Woodward (published in 1924)

The Young Americans   *Firestone Presents Your Favorite Christmas Music Volume 4* (1965)

The music first appeared as a secular dance tune written by the French cleric, composer and writer Thoinot Arbeau, pen name of Jehan Tabourot (1519-1593).

The following are very good renditions. I am most familiar with (b), which I have listened to for years on CD.

a	1974	Placido Domingo, Patricia Kaas, Alejandro Fernandez, Gumpoldskirchner Spatzen, Vienna Symphony & Steven Mercurio	I Love...Classical Christmas
b	1995	Roger Whittaker	The Christmas Song
c	2002	Blackmore's Night	Winter Carols

The First Noel (Nowell)

Unknown   **Unknown**

Tally-Ho!   Single (1902) as "The First Nowell"

The words and music come from a traditional English carol of the 16th or 17th century, but possibly dating from as early as the 13th century. The final combination of tune and lyrics first appeared in the early 1800s.[9]

Song (r) is in a medley with "Mary, Mary." Song (w) has a "Born Is the King" Interlude.

There are so many good renditions of this classic. Songs (o) and (u) are excellent New Age Instrumentals. Song (y) is a cappella. Songs (q) and (aa) have the same tempo, but different from the others. [Song (aa) is performed by John Farnham & Olivia Newton-John. Olivia Newton-John had a solo version of this song with that tempo that was very popular, but it is no longer available, unfortunately.]

a	1957	Frank Sinatra	A Jolly Christmas from Frank Sinatra
b	1958	Johnny Mathis	Merry Christmas
c	1958	*101 Strings*	*The Glory of Christmas*
d	1958	*Mantovani*	*Christmas Carols*
e	1960	Nat King Cole	The Magic of Christmas
f	1962	The Everly Brothers	Christmas with the Everly Brothers and the Boystown Choir
g	1963	Jackie Wilson	Merry Christmas from Jackie Wilson
h	1963	Andy Williams	The Andy Williams Christmas Album
i	1967	Ella Fitzgerald	Ella Fitzgerald's Christmas
j	1970	Jose Feliciano	Feliz Navidad
k	1984	Roger Whittaker	Tidings of Comfort and Joy
l	1987	Air Supply	The Christmas Album
m	1993	David Foster (feat. BeBe Winans & CeCe Winans)	The Christmas Album
n	1999	*Kenny G*	*The Classic Christmas Album*
o	2001	*Mannheim Steamroller*	*Christmas Extraordinaire*
p	2001	Joan Baez	Noel (Bonus Track Version)
q	2003	Whitney Houston	One Wish: The Holiday Album
r	2006	Sarah McLauchlin	Wintersong
s	2007	Juice Newton	The Gift of Christmas
t	2007	Josh Groban (with Faith Hill)	Noel
u	2008	*2002*	*Christmas Dreams*
v	2010	*David Tolk*	*Christmas*

w	2010	Mariah Carey	Merry Christmas II You
x	2012	Lady A	On This Winter's Night
y	2014	Pentatonix	That's Christmas to Me
z	2017	Elvis Presley & The Royal Philharmonic Orchestra	Christmas with Elvis and the Royal Philharmonic Orchestra
aa	2017	John Farnham & Olivia New-ton-John	Friends for Christmas
ab	2023	Karla Bonoff	Silent Night

God Rest Ye Merry, Gentlemen

Unknown   **1650s**

Meister Glee Singers   Single (1908)

Some sources claim that this carol dates as far back as the 16th century. Others date it later, to the 18th or early 19th centuries. However, there are printed editions from c. 1760 and November 1764. The full current melody was published in 1855.

Song (b) is within a medley with "Good King Wenceslas" and "Jingle Bells." Song (h) is within a medley with "Deck the Halls" and "Hark! The Herald Angels Sing."

I would classify this as a Bing Crosby (a) classic, but there are many other good renditions. Songs (j) and (m) are New Age Instrumentals. Song (n) is a cappella. A relatively recent (2005) popular rendition is (k), which gets a lot of airplay.

a	1942	Bing Crosby with John Scott Trotter and His Orchestra	Single - "B" Side of "Faith of Our Fa-thers"
b	1958	*101 Strings*	*The Glory of Christmas*
c	1959	Pat Boone	White Christmas
d	1959	Perry Como	The Complete RCA Christmas Collection
e	1960	Nat King Cole	The Magic of Christmas
f	1962	The Everly Brothers	Christmas with the Everly Brothers and the Boystown Choir
g	1963	Leonard Bernstein, New York Philharmonic & The Tabernacle Choir at Temple Square	I Love...Classical Christmas
h	1966	Henry Mancini	A Merry Mancini Christmas
i	1967	Ella Fitzgerald	Ella Fitzgerald's Christmas
j	1984	*Mannheim Steamroller*	*Christmas*
k	2005	Barenaked Ladies & Sarah McLachlan	A Winter's Night

l	2011	Bobby Fox	Season's Greetings - A Jersey Boys Christmas
m	2014	*Christmas Eve Carols Academy*	*Christmas Carols*
n	2016	Pentatonix	A Pentatonix Christmas
o	2017	Blackmore's Night	Winter Carols

Good King Wenceslas

Lyrics: John Mason Neale   **1853**
Music: Thomas Helmore

Svend Saaby Choir

Christmas Everywhere - A Selection of Christmas Carols from the Old and New World (1956)

English hymnwriter John Mason Neale wrote the lyrics in collaboration with his music editor Thomas Helmore to fit the melody of the 13th century spring carol *"Tempus adest floridum"* ("Eastertime Is Come"), which they had found in a 1582 Finnish song collection. The carol first appeared in *Carols for Christmas-Tide*, published the same year.

The legend behind the song is as follows: Wenceslaus I, Duke of Bohemia (the present-day Czech Republic) spotted on a bitter cold Winter night a poor man in rags. When he inquired Otto, his servant, about the man, he was told that it was "Rudolph the swineherd, he that lives down by the Brunweiss. Fire he has none, nor food neither: and he was gathering a few sticks where he might find them, lest, as he says, all his family perish with cold." Wenceslaus ordered that "the best" provisions be provided to the poor man, and that he and his servant travel to Brunweiss.

The servant protested because of the severity of the cold but agreed to accompany the King on the journey. The King carried wood for fire and the servant carried the provisions. The journey was arduous, and the servant wanted to go back. But the King ordered Otto to follow him, literally in his footsteps. The legend ends with "And so great was the virtue of this Saint of the Most High [Wenceslaus], such was the fire of love that was kindled in him, that, as he trod in those steps, Otto gained life and heat. He felt not the wind; he heeded not the frost; the footprints glowed as with a holy fire, and zealously he followed the King on his errand of mercy." This reportedly occurred on December 26, the Feast Day of Saint Stephen, as mentioned in the song. The duke was proclaimed a King after his assassination by his brother, as well as a martyr and a Saint.[10]

| a | 1968 | Morton Gould & The RCA Symphony Orchestra | The Most Fabulous Classical Christmas Album Ever! |
| b | 1972 | The Singers Unlimited | Christmas |

c	1990	The Roches	We Three Kings
d	2009	Tori Amos	Midwinter Graces (Bonus Track)

Greensleeves (What Child Is This?)

"Greensleeves": Richard Jones
"What Child is this?" Lyrics: William Chatterton Dix

1580 ("Greensleeves" publication date)
1865 ("What Child Is This?" Lyrics)

"Greensleeves" - Susan Reed
"What Child Is This?" - Saint Peter's Choir - Harold W. Gilbert, director

"Greensleeves" - Single (1947)
"What Child Is This?" - Single (1950)

"What Child Is This?" uses the tune of "Greensleeves" with lyrics written by William Chatterton Dix in 1865.

"Greensleeves" is a traditional English folk song. A broadside ballad by the name "A Newe Northen Dittye of ye Ladye Greene Sleves" was registered by Richard Jones at the London Stationer's Company in September 1580 and Shakespeare's "The Merry Wives of Windsor" (1597) has a reference to the song by that name.

"Greensleeves" was registered at The Stationer's Hall (England) in 1580. Despite arguments to the contrary, there is no proof that Henry VIII was the songwriter. Sources credit John Dowland (1562-1626) with the ballad version familiar to most of us.[11]

The following songs are titled "Greensleeves": (n), (t), and (ad). The first two are Instrumentals, so it doesn't matter if they are called that or "What Child Is This?" (ad) is a cappella, but with only vocalizations, no words. Song (ac) is called "What Child Is This (Christ the King)" and extends the song with new lyrics. Songs (b) and (n) are called "Greensleeves (What Child Is This?)" and the rest are simply called "What Child Is This?"

Of the Instrumentals, (g) and (p) are jazz. Song (ab) is a violin with orchestral background. Songs (r), (v), (z), and (ae) are New Age, with (ae) also being Celtic.

The rest are all beautiful but follow a traditional sound.

a	1952	Burl Ives	Christmas Day in the Morning - Yuletide Folk Songs Sung by Burl Ives
b	1958	Ray Conniff	Christmas With Conniff
c	1958	Johnny Mathis with the Percy Faith Orchestra	Merry Christmas

d	1962	The Everly Brothers	Christmas with the Everly Brothers and the Boystown Choir
e	1962	Eugene Ormandy & The Philadelphia Orchestra	I Love...Classical Christmas
f	1964	Al Martino	A Merry Christmas
g	1965	*Vince Guaraldi Trio*	*A Charlie Brown Christmas (Original 1965 TV Soundtrack)*
h	1965	Harry Simeone Chorale	The Little Drummer Boy
i	1966	Joan Baez	Noel (Bonus Track Version)
j	1966	The Lettermen	For Christmas This Year
k	1982	Julie Andrews	Christmas with Julie Andrews
l	1992	Mel Tormé	Christmas Songs
m	1993	Harry Connick, Jr.	When My Heart Finds Christmas
n	1994	*Kenny G*	*Miracles - The Holiday Album*
o	1995	First Call & Larnelle Harris	Beyond December
p	1995	*Oscar Peterson*	*An Oscar Peterson Christmas*
q	1996	Glen Campbell	Home for the Holidays
r	1999	*Krysna*	*Krysmas Joy*
s	2006	Sarah McLauchlin	Wintersong
t	2007	*101 Strings*	*101 Strings Christmas - 30 Greatest Orchestral Holiday Favorites*
u	2008	Faith Hill	Joy to the World
v	2008	*2002*	*Christmas Dreams*
w	2011	Tony Bennett	The Classic Christmas Album
x	2012	Rod Stewart	Merry Christmas, Baby
y	2012	Francesca Battistelli	"First Noel" Prelude
z	2014	*Christmas Eve Carols Academy*	*Christmas Carols*
aa	2014	Michael W. Smith (feat. Martina McBride)	The Spirit of Christmas
ab	2017	*Lindsey Stirling*	*Warmer in the Winter*
ac	2017	Casting Crowns	It's Finally Christmas
ad	2018	Pentatonix	Christmas Is Here!
ae	2019	*Caranua (feat. John Knudson)*	*A Celtic Christmas*

Hallelujah (Chorus)

George Frideric Handel   1741

The Sheffield Choir   Single (1926) - as "The Messiah -- Worthy is the Lamb"

The chorus from *Handel's Messiah Part II.*

Song (c) is New Age.

a	1954	Percy Faith	The Essential Percy Faith - The Christmas Recordings
b	1962	101 Strings	101 Strings Christmas - 30 Greatest Orchestral Holiday Favorites
c	2001	Mannheim Steamroller	Christmas Extraordinaire

Hark! The Herald Angels Sing

Lyrics: Charles Wesley　　　　　　　　　　**Lyrics: 1739**
Music: Felix Mendelssohn　　　　　　　　　**Music: 1840**

Columbia Male Quartet　　　　　　　　　　　Single (1904)

The original hymn text, wherein the hymn was known as a "Hymn for Christmas-Day," was from 1739, but in 1754 was changed, and the song title was changed to the current one. A final change was made in 1782.

Words of the song, originally titled "Hark! How All the Welkin Rings," were written by Charles Wesley in 1739. They were amended by at least two writers: George Whitfield in 1753 and Martin Madan in 1760.

The music was written by Felix Mendelssohn in 1840—the "*Gott ist Licht*" ("God is Light") chorus from the *Festgesang* ("Festival Song") cantata celebrating the 400th anniversary of the invention of the printing press.

Words and music were brought together by William Hayman Cummings in 1855. They were first performed by the choir at Waltham Abbey, where Cummings was organist.[12]

Song (j) is a medley with "The First Noel," "Come all Ye Faithful," "Deck the Halls" & "O Come, O Come, Emmanuel." Song (q) is a medley with "O Come, O Come, Emmanuel" and "We Three Kings." Song (r) is a medley with "O Come All Ye Faithful."

The Instrumentals are wonderful, with most having a classic orchestra. However, there are some that do not. Song (g) is performed beautifully with music box sounds. Songs (n) and (t) are New Age.

A non-standard vocal rendition is (k), which is jazz; song (w) is a cappella.

The rest are all beautiful but follow a traditional sound.

a	1954	*Percy Faith & His Orchestra*	*Music of Christmas*
b	1957	Frank Sinatra	A Jolly Christmas from Frank Sinatra
c	1958	*Mantovani*	*Christmas Carols*
d	1958	Petula Clark	A Christmas Carol
e	1958	*101 Strings*	*The Glory of Christmas*
f	1960	Nat King Cole	The Magic of Christmas
g	1961	*Rita Ford*	*A Music Box Christmas*
h	1962	The Everly Brothers	Christmas with the Everly Brothers and the Boystown Choir
i	1962	*Eugene Ormandy, The Philadelphia Orchestra, Robert Page & Temple University Concert Choir*	*I Love...Classical Christmas*
j	1964	Jo Stafford	Joyful Season
k	1965	Vince Guaraldi Trio	A Charlie Brown Christmas (Original 1965 TV Soundtrack)
l	1967	Ella Fitzgerald	Ella Fitzgerald's Christmas
m	1970	Jose Feliciano	Feliz Navidad
n	1993	*Mannheim Steamroller*	*A Fresh Aire Christmas*
o	1995	Roger Whittaker	The Christmas Song
p	1996	Glen Campbell	Home for the Holidays
q	1997	Judy Collins	Christmas At the Biltmore Estate
r	2002	Blackmore's Night	Winter Carols
s	2008	Natalie Cole (feat. London Symphony Orchestra)	The Magic of Christmas
t	2008	*2002*	*Christmas Dreams*
u	2009	Bill Ives & The Choir of the Magdalen College, Oxford	Carols by Candlelight
v	2012	Celtic Woman	Home for Christmas
w	2014	Pentatonix	The Greatest Christmas Hits
x	2016	Neil Diamond	Acoustic Christmas
y	2016	John Farnham & Olivia Newton-John	Friends for Christmas
z	2022	*Boston Pops Orchestra & John Williams*	*Christmas Collection*

Here We Come A-Caroling (AKA Here We Come A-Wassailing)

Unknown   **Mid-1800s (but is probably much older)**

Robert Shaw and His RCA Victor Chorale | *Christmas Hymns and Carols* (1946)

This song is an old English wassail song. The word "wassail" comes from the Middle English toast, "*waes hael*," meaning "be thou hale," which in turn means "be in good health." The phrase "*waes hael*" dates to pre-Norman [Norman Conquest, 1066] times. In days of yore, the Christmas spirit often made the rich a little more generous than usual, and bands of beggars and orphans used to dance their way through the snowy streets of England, offering to sing good cheer and to tell good fortune if the householder would give them a drink from his wassail bowl or a penny or a pork pie or, better yet, let them stand for a few minutes beside the warmth of his hearth. In its less sociable format, the singers would cross the threshold and make their gluttony known. "Figgy pudding" was a common craving, and the mob would further insist that, "we won't go until we've got some, so bring some right here." The wassail bowl itself was a hearty combination of hot ale or beer and spices and mead, just alcoholic enough to warm the tingling toes and fingers of the singers.[13,14]

Song (b) is a medley with "O Christmas Tree" and "I Saw Three Ships." Song (c) is a medley with "We Wish You a Merry Christmas."

Song (f) is titled "Wassail Song."

a	1954	*Percy Faith & His Orchestra*	*Music Of Christmas*
b	1959	*Arthur Fiedler & Boston Pops Orchestra*	*A Christmas Festival*
c	1959	Perry Como with The Ray Charles Singers	Season's Greetings from Perry Como
d	1962	Living Voices	Living Voices Sing Christmas Music
e	1966	The New Christy Minstrels	Christmas with the Christies
f	1972	The Singers Unlimited	Christmas
g	1990	The Roches	We Three Kings
h	2008	*101 Strings*	*101 Strings Christmas - 30 Greatest Orchestral Holiday Favorites*
i	2020	Blackmore's Night	Winter Carols

The Holly and the Ivy

Unknown | **Early-1800s**

The English Singers | Single (1928) – "B" side of "Corpus Christi"

The melody for this popular carol is an old English folk song, and the lyrics date to at least the early 18th century. But the sacred symbolism of holly and ivy extends even further back into medieval England. Holly and ivy are traditional rivals in the forest, representing masculine and feminine traits respectively, and they have been customary Christmas decorations since the late medieval period.

The lyrics for this carol interpret the holly's physical traits—blossom, berry, thorns, and bark—as parallel symbols of Mary and Christ. Given the ancient origins of the carol, it's not surprising that the phrase "merry organ" from the song's refrain is found in Chaucer's *Canterbury Tales*, which may be the original source for that lyric.[15]

The version which is now popular was collected in 1909 by the English folk song collector Cecil Sharp (1859-1924).

Song (b) is a medley with "What Child Is This?"

Song (e) is New Age. Annie Lennox (j) is well-known for her solo career but was originally part of The Eurythmics in the 1980s, which produced hit songs such as "Sweet Dreams (Are Made of This)" (1983) and "Here Comes the Rain Again" (1983). As a solo artist in the 1990s, she sang hits such as "Walking on Broken Glass" (1992) and "No More 'I Love You's'" (1995).

a	1958	Petula Clark	A Christmas Carol
b	1962	Bing Crosby	I Wish You a Merry Christmas
c	1984	Roger Whittaker	Tidings of Comfort and Joy
d	1990	The Roches	We Three Kings
e	1993	*Mannheim Steamroller*	*A Fresh Aire Christmas*
f	1994	Natalie Cole	Holly & Ivy
g	1997	Judy Collins	Christmas At the Biltmore Estate
h	2004	Vanessa Williams (feat. Cormac Breatnach & Martin Dunlea)	Silver & Gold
i	2006	Sam Stryke featuring Alice Peacock	Christmas
j	2010	Annie Lennox	A Christmas Cornucopia

Huron Carol

Jean de Brébeuf   **1642**

The George Mitchell Minstrels   *The Magic of Christmas* (1970)

Canada's oldest Christmas song, it is a hymn that re-imagines the traditional Nativity story, using early Canadian imagery, including Jesus being born in a "lodge of broken bark" and wrapped in a "robe of rabbit skin."

a	2016	Sarah McLauchlin	Wonderland

I Saw Three Ships (Come Sailing In) AKA There Were Three Ships

Unknown   **1600s**

Bing Crosby with Choir and Orchestra directed by Simon Rady (Medley with "Deck the Halls" and "Away in a Manger")

Christmas Greetings (1949)

The modern lyrics are from an 1833 version by the English lawyer and antiquarian William Sandys.

Song (f) is a medley with "Joy to the World."

The only instrumental below is by Lindsey Stirling (l), an incredible violinist and dancer who performs this song with orchestral accompaniment.

Song (m) is a cappella.

Song (h) is by the cast of Miss Saigon. *An original cast member of that play is Willy Falk, who was a Tony nominee for the play. Willy is a member of my family, and one of the sweetest and most talented men I know. When my family and I went to see* Mama Mia, *he arranged for us to meet the cast of that play and step on stage; this was a great experience, especially for my daughter Vicky who is a big fan of the play.*

a	1952	Burl Ives	Christmas Day in the Morning - Yuletide Folk Songs Sung by Burl Ives (first recording not in a medley with other songs)
b	1960	Nat King Cole	The Magic of Christmas
c	1991	The Chieftains with Marianne Faithfull	The Bells of Dublin
d	1995	Glen Campbell	Christmas with Glen Campbell
e	1997	Judy Collins	Christmas At the Biltmore Estate
f	1998	Michael W. Smith	Christmastime
g	1999	Dan Fogelberg	The First Christmas Morning

h	1999	Members of the Cast of Miss Saigon	Broadway's Greatest Gifts - Carols for a Cure 1999
i	2004	Barenaked Ladies	Barenaked for the Holidays
j	2006	Blackmore's Night	Winter Carols
k	2016	GENTRI	Finding Christmas
l	2017	*Lindsey Stirling*	*Warmer in the Winter*
m	2021	Pentatonix	Evergreen

In the Bleak Mid Winter (AKA In a...)

**Lyrics: Based on a poem by
Christina Rossetti
Music: Various, most notably
Gustav Holst and Harold Darke**

**Lyrics: 1872
Music:
1906 (Holst)
1909 (Darke)**

Cliff Richard

Carol Singers (1967)

The poem describes the winter cold, the coming of Christ, the description of the nativity scene and, finally, a "What shall I give him?" moment of self-reflection. It has been set to music several times. Two settings, those by Gustav Holst and by Harold Darke, are popular and often sung as Christmas carols. Darke's arrangement, which begins with a single voice rather than a full choir, was voted in 2008 as the best Christmas carol of all-time by 51 directors of music in the UK and US.[16]

Song (h) is New Age and song (k) is New Wave. Song (k) is simply titled "Bleak Midwinter."

a	1975	Julie Andrews	The Secret of Christmas
b	1998	Shawn Colvin	Holiday Songs and Lullabies
c	2003	The Moody Blues	December
d	2004	James Taylor	A Christmas Album
e	2006	Sarah McLauchlin	Wintersong
f	2007	Angelika Kirchschlager, Al-fred Eshwe & Tonkun-stlerochester Niederoster-reich	I Love...Classical Christmas
g	2008	Sarah Brightman	A Winter Symphony
h	2008	*2002*	*Christmas Dreams*
i	2010	Aled Jones	Christmas Gold
j	2010	Annie Lennox	A Christmas Cornucopia
k	2013	Erasure	Snow Globe
l	2016	GENTRI	Finding Christmas

It Came Upon a Midnight Clear

Lyrics: Poem by Minister Edmund Sears
Music: Richard Storrs Willis

Lyrics: 1849
Music: 1850

Francis J. Lapitino

Single (1917) – "Silent Night, Holy Night - Christmas Hymns – Selection," as part of a medley with other songs

The song is not about Christmas and the birth of Christ—which is not mentioned—but is a plea for peace after the Mexican-American War, which had just ended in 1848, one year before the poem the song is based on was written. The poem first appeared in the *Christian Register* on December 29, 1849. It is unknown what music the poem was first sung to, but just a year after the poem was written organist Richard Storrs Willis wrote the music it is now associated with. The tune, "Study No. 23," was rearranged to fit the lyrics by Willis himself, or by Uzziah Christopher Burnap.[17,18]

Song (g) is a medley with "Away in a Manger" and "The First Noel."

Songs (o) and (p) are New Age. Song (u) is a cappella.

A name you don't see often related to Christmas songs is Sam Phillips (s). I'm a big fan of her music and find her rendition characteristic of her other songs.

a	1947	Frank Sinatra	Christmas Songs by Sinatra
b	1950	*Ken Griffin at the Organ*	*Single – "B" Side of "Hark! The Herald Angels Sing"*
c	1952	*Leroy Anderson & Leroy Anderson and His Orchestra*	*A Leroy Anderson Christmas*
d	1954	*Percy Faith & His Orchestra*	*Music of Christmas*
e	1956	Burl Ives	Christmas Eve with Burl Ives
f	1956	Mario Lanza	Lanza Sings Christmas Carols
g	1966	Henry Mancini	A Merry Mancini Christmas
h	1967	Ella Fitzgerald	Ella Fitzgerald's Christmas
i	1967	*Morton Gould & The RCA Symphony Orchestra*	*Christmas Adagios*
j	1970	Jose Feliciano	Feliz Navidad
k	1972	The Singers Unlimited	Christmas Carols
l	1978	The Carpenters	Christmas Portrait
m	1982	Julie Andrews	Christmas with Julie Andrews

n	1992	The Manhattan Transfer	The Christmas Album
o	1999	*Krysna*	*Krysmas Joy*
p	2007	*Mannheim Steamroller*	*Christmas Song*
q	2008	*101 Strings*	*101 Strings Christmas - 30 Greatest Orchestral Holiday Favorites*
r	2014	Jackie Evancho, The City of Prague Philharmonic Orchestra, Sally Herbert, Richard Cottle & Shelly Poole	Someday at Christmas
s	2019	Sam Phillips	Cold Dark Nights
t	2020	Blackmore's Night	Winter Carols
u	2021	Pentatonix	Evergreen
v	2024	Sixpence None the Richer	The Dawn of Grace

Jesu, Joy of Man's Desiring (Baby Jesu Joy, Jesus Stays My Joy)

Lyrics: Martin Janus **Lyrics: 1661**
Music: J. S. Bach **Music: 1723**

Glasgow Orpheus Choir conducted by Sir Hugh Roberton Single (1948)

Martin Janus (AKA Martin Jahn) wrote a hymn in 1661 with a verse from the 16th stanza of that hymn called "*Jesu, meiner Seelen Wonne*" (English: "Jesus, My Soul's Wonder"). The verse was used in a cantata written by J. S. Bach in 1723 which he called "*Herz und Mund und Tat und Leben*" (English: "Heart and Mouth and Deeds and Life"). That cantata came to be known as "Jesu, Joy of Man's Desiring."

Song (a) is from Jigsaw's album "Letherslade Farm," named after the hideout of Britain's 1963 Great Train Robbery gang. Song (b), simply titled "Joy," became a hit with its Rock version of this song. Song (d) is performed by Andrew Lloyd Webber's brother. Song (f) is titled "Jesus Stays My Joy," and is an Instrumental with chorus, but no spoken words. Song (g) is titled "Herz in Mund und Tat und Leben," Bach's original title of this song. Song (h) is titled "Joy of Man's Desire" and is a medley with "Angels We Have Heard on High." It has a Rock Instrumental for "Joy of Man's Desire." Song (j) is mostly Instrumental but has some words in German. Song (l) is titled "Baby Jesu Joy."

a	1970	Jigsaw	Letherslade Farm
b	1971	Apollo 100	Joy (feat. Tom Parker}
c	1977	*Eugene Ormandy & The Philadelphia Orchestra*	*I Love...Classical Christmas*
d	1986	Julian Lloyd Webber	Encore! - Travels with My Cello Vol-

			ume 2
e	1992	Amy Grant	Home for Christmas
f	1995	*Cusco*	*A Choral Christmas*
g	1997	Adagio Trio	Stillpoint
h	1998	*Trans-Siberian Orchestra*	*The Christmas Attic*
i	2008	Sarah Brightman	A Winter Symphony
j	2013	Future of Forestry	Advent Christmas EP Volume 3
k	2017	*Herb Alpert*	*The Christmas Wish*
l	2019	*Caranua (feat. Chuck E. Myers)*	*A Celtic Christmas*

Jingle Bells

James Pierpont   1850

Banjoist Willie Lyle (1889) - No surviving copies
Edison Male Quartette (1898) - Oldest surviving copy

Both on Edison Cylinders, of the year of their performances

James Pierpont (1822-93) wrote this enormously popular Christmas song for a Thanksgiving program at his father's Sunday school. The song proved to be so popular the children were asked to sing the song again at Christmastime, and it has been tied to the latter holiday ever since. The song was copyrighted under the title "One Horse Open Sleigh" in 1857 while Pierpont was living in Savannah, Georgia, and its title was changed to "Jingle Bells, or the One Horse Open Sleigh" when the song was republished in 1859. Even though the song was published and copyrighted in Georgia, the composer's boyhood home of Medford, Massachusetts, insists it was actually written at the Simpson Tavern in Medford in 1850. They claim that the lyrics of the song tell of the sleigh rides held on Medford's Salem Street in the early 1800s. The city of Savannah counterclaims that Pierpont penned "Jingle Bells" while in Savannah, experiencing his first snowless winter, as an ode to his Massachusetts snowy upbringing.[19]

Kyna Hamill became interested in the "Jingle Bells" story while working as a volunteer with the Medford Historical Society & Museum. Hamill's research indicated that Pierpont, "a bit of a drinker, a bit of a wild guy," always needed money, so it didn't make sense that if "Jingle Bells" was written in 1850 and was well received, the starving writer would shelve it for seven years. It's also unclear when the people of Medford started sleigh racing on Salem Street. The earliest photographic evidence dates to the 1870s. There were a number of popular minstrel songs involving sleighs, such as "The Merry Sleigh Ride" and "Buckley's Sleighing Song," and Hamill is not surprised that "Jingle Bells" bears more than a passing resemblance to them. That's not to say "Jingle Bells" was plagiarized, says Hamill, but "Everything about the song is churned out and copied from other people and lines from other songs—there's nothing original about it. He's making money."[20]

"Jingle Bells" was the first song broadcast from space, by the crew of Gemini 6, on December 16, 1965.[21]

Song (h) is a medley with "God Rest Ye Merry, Gentlemen" and "Good King Wenceslas." Songs (m) and (o) are medleys with "Sleigh Ride."

Song (s) is a close remake of song (a).

Song (f) is a novelty song wherein dogs "sing" the song.

Songs (e) and (w) are jazz versions. Songs (u), (y) and (z) are New Age.

a	1943	Bing Crosby and The Andrews Sisters with Vic Schoen and His Orchestra	Single
b	1946	Frank Sinatra with The Ken Lane Singers	Single
c	1946	Perry Como with Russ Case, His Orchestra and Chorus	Perry Como Sings Merry Christmas Music
d	1953	Guy Lombardo & His Royal Canadians	Jingle Bells
e	1954	Urbie Green	A Cool Yuletide
f	1955	Don Charles & The Singing Dogs	Single
g	1958	Mitch Miller	Golden Treasury of Christmas Songs and Carols
h	1958	*101 Strings*	*The Glory of Christmas*
i	1959	Pat Boone	White Christmas
j	1959	Ray Conniff	Christmas Caroling
k	1963	Jim Reeves	Twelve Songs of Christmas
l	1964	Jo Stafford	Joyful Season
m	1965	Living Voices	The Little Drummer Boy
n	1966	Dean Martin	The Dean Martin Christmas Album
o	1966	Henry Mancini	A Very Mancini Christmas
p	1968	Burl Ives	Christmas Album
q	1970	Jose Feliciano	Feliz Navidad
r	1986	Johnny Mathis	Christmas Eve with Johnny Mathis
s	1990	Barry Manilow (with Expose)	Because It's Christmas
t	1994	Natalie Cole	Holly & Ivy
u	1995	*Mannheim Steamroller*	*Christmas in the Aire*
v	1998	Michael W. Smith	Christmastime
w	2005	Diana Krall	Christmas Songs (Bonus Track)

x	2006	Kimberley Locke	Christmas
y	2009	*Daniel Berthiaume*	*O Holy Night*
z	2015	Celtic Angels	New Age Christmas
aa	2022	*Boston Pops Orchestra & John Williams*	*Christmas Collection*
ab	2022	Joss Stone	Merry Christmas, Love
ac	2023	Adam Hawley	What Christmas Means to Me
ad	2023	Mark Tremonti	Mark Tremonti Christmas Classics New & Old

Jolly Old St. Nicholas

Poem: Emily Huntington Miller   **Lyrics (Poem): 1865**
Music: James R. Murray   **Music: 1874**

Possibly Ray Smith, with additional   Single (1949)
lyrics by songwriter Vaughn Horton

An American Christmas song apparently originating from the late 19th century. Some sources speculate that "Jolly Old St. Nicholas" was written by Benjamin Hanby, the songwriter of "Up on the Rooftop," a similar song, that he wrote in the 1860s.

Song (b) is a medley with "The Little Drummer Boy." Song (c) is a medley with "Up on the Housetop."

a	1951	Ames Brothers	Single
b	1962	Ray Conniff and The Ray Conniff Singers	We Wish You a Merry Christmas
c	1968	Vicky Carr	Firestone Presents Your Christmas Favorites Volume 7
d	1995	Andy Williams	We Need a Little Christmas
e	2003	Chicago	Christmas - What's It Gonna Be, Santa?
f	2009	Jim Brickman	Joy
g	2016	The Oxford Trinity Choir	Christmas Carols
h	2023	*Noble Music*	*Relaxing Christmas Instrumental Christmas Piano Music*

Joy to the World

Isaac Watts   **1719**
Orchestral arrangement: Lowell   **Orchestral arrangement: 1848**

Mason

Trinity Choir   Single (1911) – "B" side of "Come All
                                                                        Ye Faithful"

This is the most-published hymn in North America. It is based on a Christian inter-
pretation of Psalm 98 and Genesis 3. Watts didn't write this song to originally be a
Christmas carol, as the lyrics do not reflect Jesus' birth, but rather Christ's Second
Coming.[22]

Mason's tune is called "Antioch." The tune has some notes in common with Handel's "Messiah" (specifically the chorus "Lift up ye heads, o ye gates" and the ario-
so [vocal music less formal than an aria] "Comfort ye my people"). For this reason,
it has been described as "arranged from Handel." Nowadays, however, Handel's
scholars seem to agree that the resemblance is accidental. The most famous version
of the carol (and the fourth revision of the "Antioch" tune) was first published in
The National Psalmist (Boston, 1848) as "Joy to the World! The Lord Is Come."[23]

*Song (l) is different from song (k), and the former is included within a medley with
"For unto Us a Child Is Born." Song (m) is New Age. Song (y) is performed with
beautiful chimes. Song (t) is a cappella.*

a	1954	*Percy Faith & His Orchestra*	*Music of Christmas*
b	1954	*Mantovani*	*Christmas Carols*
c	1959	Pat Boone	White Christmas
d	1960	Nat King Cole	The Magic of Christmas
e	1962	*Robert Shaw & RCA Victor Symphony Orchestra*	*Carols for Christmas*
f	1962	*Eugene Ormandy & The Philadelphia Orchestra*	*The Glorious Sound of Christmas*
g	1963	Leonard Bernstein, New York Philharmonic & The Tabernacle Choir at Temple Square	I Love...Classical Christmas
h	1964	Jo Stafford	Joyful Season
i	1967	Ella Fitzgerald	Ella Fitzgerald's Christmas
j	1972	The Singers Unlimited	Christmas
k	1983	Amy Grant	Tennessee Christmas
l	1992	Amy Grant	Home for Christmas
m	1995	*Mannheim Steamroller*	*Christmas in the Aire*
n	2000	Judy Collins	Christmas with Judy Collins
o	2002	*Kenny G*	*The Classic Christmas Album*
p	2008	Casting Crowns	Peace on Earth
q	2008	*101 Strings*	*101 Strings Christmas - 30 Greatest Orchestral Holiday Favorites*

r	2008	Faith Hill	Joy to the World
s	2011	Ryan Molloy	Season's Greetings - A Jersey Boys Christmas
t	2015	Pentatonix	That's Christmas to Me
u	2016	Celtic Woman	The Best of Christmas
v	2020	For King and Country	A Drummer Boy Christmas
w	2022	*Boston Pops Orchestra & John Williams*	*Christmas Collection*
x	2022	*Lindsey Stirling*	*Snow Waltz*
y	2023	*Christmas Candles*	*Stress Relief Christmas Music*

Lo How a Rose E'er Blooming

Lyrics: Unknown
Music: Michael Praetorius

Lyrics: First printed in 1599
Music: 1609

English: Robert Shaw and His RCA Victor Chorale   *Christmas Hymns and Carols* (1946)

English translation of a German hymn called "*Es ist ein Ros entsprungen*" (literally, "A rose has sprung up"). The rose in the German text is a symbolic reference to the Virgin Mary.

One unusual performer below is Sting (f), who sings this song very well. Linda Ronstadt (g) is incredible, with her angelic voice.

a	1954	*Percy Faith & His Orchestra*	*Music of Christmas*
b	1967	The Johnny Mann Singers	We Wish You a Merry Christmas
c	1982	John Rutter and the Cambridge Singers and Orchestra	The Music of Christmas
d	1988	*Mannheim Steamroller*	*A Fresh Aire Christmas*
e	2000	Charlotte Church	Dream a Dream
f	2009	Sting	If on a Winter's Night ...
g	2020	Linda Ronstadt	A Merry Little Christmas

Love Came Down at Christmas

Poem: Christina Rossetti
Music (all different pieces): R O Morris, Harold Darke, Leo Sowerby, John Kelsall and John Rutter

Poem: 1885
Music: Many different pieces

Shawn Colvin   *Holiday Songs and Lullabies* (1998)

Love was born at Christmas. Love should be yours and mine and to God. It is a lovely love divine.

It is interesting that Shawn Colvin released this song before John Rutter's Cambridge Singers did.

a	2002	The Cambridge Singers	The John Rutter Christmas Album

March from The Nutcracker

Pyotr Ilyich Tchaikovsky   1892

Leopold Stokowski and The Phila-   Single (1935)
delphia Orchestra

The actual title of the piece is "March." The song appears early in the first act of the ballet. It's the third song in the act, just after the mini overture that kicks off the show and "Scene: The Christmas Tree" played during the lighting and decorating of the Christmas tree. The ballet is based on the book *The Nutcracker and the Mouse King* by E.T.A. Hoffmann, and an interpretation of Hoffman's story written by Alexandre Dumas (*The Three Musketeers*). The first performance of "The Nutcracker" took place in Russia in 1892. The San Francisco Ballet performed the first American production of "The Nutcracker" in 1944.[24]

Song (b) is jazz. Song (c) is performed with a brass ensemble and is just called "March." Song (d) is performed with synthesizers (think A Clockwork Orange*) and is called "Marche from the Nutcracker Suite."*

a	1950	*Andre Kostelanetz and His Orchestra*	*Nutcracker Suite - Music of Tchaikovsky*
b	1960	Duke Ellington & His Orchestra - Billy Strayhorn	The Nutcracker Suite - Ellington - Strayhorn - Tchaikovsky
c	1996	Dallas Brass	Dallas Brass Nutcracker
d	2003	Bells of the Sound	Ring We Now Noël
e	2012	*101 Strings*	*101 Strings Christmas - 30 Greatest Orchestral Holiday Favorites*

Now the Day Is Over

Lyrics: Sabine Baring-Gould   Lyrics: 1867
Music: Joseph Barnby   Music: 1868

Fred Waring and His Pennsylvanians	*Songs of Devotion* (1945)

There are alternate tunes[25] for this song:

- "Eudoxia" by Sabine Baring-Gould, 1868
- "Lyndhurst (Vail)" by Silas J. Vail (1818–1884)
- "St. Philip (Dykes)" by John B. Dykes, in *Church Hymns with Tunes*, 1874

a	1950	Jo Stafford and Gordon MacRae with Paul Weston and His Orchestra	Sunday Evening Songs
b	1957	Pat Boone	Hymns We Love
c	1958	Robert Shaw Chorale	A Mighty Fortress
d	1998	Shawn Colvin	Holiday Songs and Lullabies
e	1998	Michael Crawford	On Eagle's Wings

O Christmas Tree (German: O Tannenbaum)

Lyrics: Ernst Anschütz (1780-1861), based on a 16th century Silesian folk song by Melchior Franck (c. 1579-1639)
Music: August Zarnak (1777-1827), inspired by the same folk song

Modern lyrics: 1824
Music: 1819

Probably Alma Gluck–Paul Reimers (in German)	Single (1915)

Silesia is a historical region of Central Europe that lies mostly within modern Poland, with small parts in the Czech Republic and Germany. The song in its original form is rather sexist in nature. At the beginning of the song, which is intended as a man's love lament, the Christmas tree is invoked as a symbol of loyalty, which contrasts with the infidelity of the "girl" mentioned in the second verse, whose "false" and fickle nature is described in the two following verses using further images borrowed from nature. The 1824 lyrics by Anschütz transformed the love song into a Christmas song, retaining the first verse. It is probably the first song to establish a connection between the Christmas tree and Christmas. Until WWI, the love song was more frequently featured in popular songbooks than the Christmas song, a trend that was quickly reversed. After WWII, the song with Zarnak's text was only published sporadically, while the Christmas song only then experienced its widest distribution, which continues to the present day.[26]

The following songs are titled "O Christmas Tree": (c), (d), (h), (o), (p) and (q). The rest are titled "O Tannenbaum," except for (m), which is titled "Oh Tannenbaum."

Song (h) is a medley with "Deck the Halls," "The Wassail Song" & "Silent Night."

The following songs are sung in German: (f), (k), (m) and (n). Songs (i) and (l) are sung in German and English.

Songs (l) and (o) are New Age. Song (j) is jazz; Song (g) is performed beautifully with a large calliope with bells. ["Calliope" is from the ancient Greek word for "beautiful voice."] Song (p) is "medieval folk rock."

a	1954	*Mantovani and His Orchestra*	*Christmas Carols*
b	1954	*Percy Faith*	*The Essential Percy Faith - The Christmas Recordings*
c	1956	Mario Lanza	Lanza Sings Christmas Carols
d	1957	Fred Waring &The Pennsylvanians	Now Is the Caroling Season
e	1958	*101 Strings*	*The Glory of Christmas*
f	1960	Nat King Cole	The Magic of Christmas
g	1961	*Rita Ford's Music Boxes*	*A Music Box Christmas*
h	1963	*Living Strings*	*The Sound of Christmas*
i	1965	Ray Conniff and The Ray Conniff Singers	Christmas Caroling
j	1965	*Vince Guaraldi Trio*	*A Charlie Brown Christmas (Original 1965 TV Soundtrack)*
k	1983	Roger Whittaker	Weihnachten mit [Christmas with] Roger Whittaker
l	2001	Mannheim Steamroller (feat. Johnny Mathis)	Mannheim Steamroller – Christmas Celebration
m	2007	Die Sternensinger St. Nikolaus	Deutsche Weihnachten (Traditional German Christmas)
n	2008	Natalie Cole (feat. London Symphony Orchestra)	The Magic of Christmas
o	2009	*Daniel Berthiaume*	*O Holy Night*
p	2017	Blackmore's Night	Winter Carols
q	2021	Billy Idol	Happy Holiday

O Come, O Come, Emmanuel / AKA Veni Veni Emmanuel

English Translation: 1851
Music: 15th century

English Lyrics: John Mason Neale
Music: Unknown

Robert Shaw and His RCA Victor Chorale

Christmas Hymns and Carols (1946)

The text for "O Come, O Come, Emmanuel," in Latin *"Veni, veni, Emanuel,"* comes from a 7-verse poem that dates to possibly the 12th century, though the verses may be of 8th century origin.

Music, which was originally a processional melody for French Franciscan nuns, was added in the 15th century, but may also have 8th century origins.

It was used in a call and response fashion during the vespers, or evening, service. The original text created the reverse acrostic [a poem, word puzzle, or other composition in which certain letters in each line form a word or words] *"ero cras,"* which means "I shall be with you tomorrow" and is particularly appropriate for the advent season. A metrical version of five of the verses appeared in the 13th century, which was translated into English by J.M. Neale in 1851. Each of the five verses expounds upon one of the names for the Messiah.

It was published in *Mediaeval Hymns and Sequences* as "Draw Nigh, Draw Nigh, Emmanuel" and later altered by compilers to its current title.[27,28]

Songs (e) and (m) are New Age. Song (i) is "medieval folk rock." Song (p) is a cappella.

a	1957	Fred Waring &The Pennsylvanians	Now Is the Caroling Season
b	1957	The Mormon Tabernacle Choir	The Mormon Tabernacle Choir Sings Christmas Carols
c	1962	*The Philadelphia Orchestra - Eugene Ormandy, Conductor*	*The Glorious Sound of Christmas*
d	1966	Joan Baez	Noel (Bonus Track Version)
e	1988	*Mannheim Steamroller*	*A Fresh Aire Christmas*
f	1992	Neil Diamond	The Christmas Album
g	2000	Linda Ronstadt	A Merry Little Christmas
h	2001	Jaci Velasquez	Christmas
i	2002	Blackmore's Night	Winter Carols

j	2003	Whitney Houston	One Wish: The Holiday Album
k	2003	The von Trapp Children	Christmas with The von Trapp Children
l	2004	Aled Jones	The Christmas Album
m	2008	Enya	And Winter Came
n	2008	Sixpence None the Richer	The Dawn of Grace - A Collection of Original and Traditional Christmas Songs
o	2009	Tori Amos	Midwinter Graces
p	2012	Pentatonix	PTXmas
q	2012	Francesca Battistelli	Christmas
r	2020	For King and Country	A Drummer Boy Christmas
s	2022	*Lindsey Stirling*	*Snow Waltz*

O Holy Night (Cantique de Noel)

Lyrics: Placide Cappeau (1808-77), translated from French to English by John Sullivan Dwight (1813-1893) in 1855
Music: Adolphe Adam (1803-1856)

Lyrics: Based on a French poem written in 1843
Music: 1847

First recorded English version: Evan Williams

Single (1908) - as "Christmas Song"

This song did not sit well with church authorities. Soon after it was written, the 1848 Revolution broke out in France, and Adam worried some observers by calling "O Holy Night" a "religious Marseillaise," referring to the 1792 song adopted as the Gallic national anthem. Official publications on Catholic music began to fret about its popularity, calling its lyricist a socialist drunk. An unfounded rumor also circulated that Adolphe Adam was Jewish, a falsehood that is repeated to this day. In a more positive light, undocumented legends have persistently surrounded "O Holy Night," in terms of bringing hope in wartime settings. For example, it is claimed that trench-fighting during the Franco-Prussian War of 1870 (or alternately, during World War I) temporarily ceased while French troops sang the song to their opponents on Christmas Eve. A better documented instance of the nurturing power of "O Holy Night" was reported in *The Marine Corps Times* in December 2004. In Fallujah, Iraq, to convey a message of love from home, the Rev. Ron Camarda, a Catholic priest and Marine Reserve major, sang "O Holy Night" at the bedside of a dying American Marine.[29]

Song (ah) is a medley with "Ave Maria." Song (m), with classical guitar, is actually titled "Oh Holy Nite." Song (z) is New Age. Song (aa) is a cappella.

a	1958	Johnny Mathis	Merry Christmas
b	1958	*Mantovani*	*Christmas Carols*
c	1959	Pat Boone	White Christmas
d	1959	Perry Como with The Ray Charles Singers	Season's Greetings from Perry Como
e	1960	Nat King Cole	The Magic of Christmas
f	1963	Andy Williams	The Andy Williams Christmas Album
g	1963	Jackie Wilson	Merry Christmas from Jackie Wilson
h	1966	The Lettermen	For Christmas This Year
i	1967	Ella Fitzgerald	Ella Fitzgerald's Christmas
j	1968	Burl Ives	Christmas Album
k	1978	The Carpenters	Christmas Portrait
l	1981	Ann Murray	Ann Murray's Christmas Album
m	1990	*Ottmar Liebert*	*Poets & Angels - Music 4 the Holidays*
n	1992	Neil Diamond	The Christmas Album
o	1993	Harry Connick, Jr.	When My Heart Finds Christmas
p	1996	Glen Campbell	Home for the Holidays
q	1998	Celine Dion	These Are Special Times
r	1998	Vince Gill	A Christmas Collection
s	1999	Michael Crawford	A Christmas Album
t	1999	David Foster (feat. Michael Crawford)	The Christmas Album
u	2001	Josh Groban	Noel
v	2006	Celtic Woman	A Christmas Celebration
w	2007	Legacy Five	A Little Christmas
x	2008	*101 Strings*	*101 Strings Christmas - 30 Greatest Orchestral Holiday Favorites*
y	2008	Faith Hill	Joy to the World
z	*2009*	*Daniel Berthiaume*	*O Holy Night*
aa	2012	Pentatonix	PTXmas
ab	2013	Vittoro Grigolo, Jackie Evancho, William Hayward & The City of Prague Philharmonic Orchestra	I Love...Classical Christmas
ac	2016	Sarah McLauchlin	Wonderland
ad	2017	Casting Crowns	It's Finally Christmas
ae	2017	The Perrys	A Very Perry Christmas
af	2018	Sir Stephen Cleobury, Henry Websdale & The Choir of King's College, Cambridge	100 Years of Nine Lessons & Carols
ag	2019	Lea Michele	Christmas in the City
ah	2019	Idina Menzel	Christmas: A Season of Love

ai	2020	Carrie Underwood	My Gift
aj	2020	Leslie Odom, Jr.	The Christmas Album
ak	2021	Nat King Cole & Calum Scott	A Sentimental Christmas with Nat King Cole and Friends: Cole Classics Reimagined

O Little Town of Bethlehem (also Oh...) - "St. Louis" melody

Lyrics: Phillips Brooks   **1868**
Music: Louis Redner

Trinity Choir   Single (1916) – "B" side of "Angels
                                            from the Realms of Glory"

This song was inspired by a trip Brooks made to Bethlehem in 1865. He had spent a year's vacation traveling in Europe and the East. "After an early dinner, we took our horses and rode to Bethlehem," he wrote home during the Christmas week of 1865. "It was only about two hours when we came to the town, situated on an eastern ridge of a range of hills, surrounded by its terraced gardens. It is a good-looking town, better built than any other we have seen in Palestine...Before dark, we rode out of town to the field where they say the shepherds saw the star. It is a fenced piece of ground with a cave in it (all the Holy Places are caves here), in which, strangely enough, they put the shepherds. The story is absurd, but somewhere in those fields we rode through the shepherds must have been..."

Three years later he wrote the lyrics to this song. Redner, Brooks' organist, was approached by Brooks to write a song to go with his lyrics, and he wanted it right away. In Redner's own words: "As Christmas of 1868 approached, Mr. Brooks told me that he had written a simple little carol for the Christmas Sunday-school service, and he asked me to write the tune to it. The simple music was written in great haste and under great pressure. We were to practice it on the following Sunday. Mr. Brooks came to me on Friday, and said, 'Redner, have you ground out that music yet to "O Little Town of Bethlehem"?' I replied, 'No,' but that he should have it by Sunday. On the Saturday night previous my brain was all confused about the tune. I thought more about my Sunday-school lesson than I did about the music. But I was roused from sleep late in the night hearing an angel-strain whispering in my ear, and seizing a piece of music paper I jotted down the treble of the tune as we now have it, and on Sunday morning before going to church I filled in the harmony. Neither Mr. Brooks nor I ever thought the carol or the music to it would live beyond that Christmas of 1868." Strangely, a Reverand who had asked permission to print it in his Sunday-school hymn and tune book christened the music "Saint Louis." That name has stuck. Also curiously, in the United Kingdom, Canada, and Ireland the lyrics are played to the tune of "Forest Green," collected by Ralph Vaughan Williams and first published in 1906.[30]

Song (p) is a medley with "Little Drummer Boy." Song (q) is a medley with "Silent Night."

Song (r) is quite special, sampling Elvis Presley into a new song by Pentatonix, which usually performs a cappella.

a	1946	Perry Como	Perry Como Sings Merry Christmas Music
b	1946	*Robert Shaw and His RCA Victor Chorale*	*Christmas Hymns and Carols*
c	1948	Frank Sinatra	Christmas Songs by Sinatra
d	1952	*Leroy Anderson & Leroy Anderson and His Orchestra*	*A Leroy Anderson Christmas*
e	1958	*Mantovani*	*Christmas Carols*
f	1958	*101 Strings*	*The Glory of Christmas*
g	1959	Pat Boone	White Christmas
h	1960	Nat King Cole	The Magic of Christmas
i	1962	The Everly Brothers	Christmas with the Everly Brothers and the Boystown Choir
j	1967	Barbra Streisand	A Christmas Album
k	1967	Ella Fitzgerald	Ella Fitzgerald's Christmas
l	1992	*Andre Gagnon*	*Noel*
m	1998	Vince Gill	Breath of Heaven: A Christmas Collection
n	1998	Shawn Colvin	Holiday Songs and Lullabies
o	2006	Sarah McLauchlin	Wintersong
p	2010	Mariah Carey	Merry Christmas II You
q	2021	Nat King Cole	A Sentimental Christmas with Nat King Cole and Friends: Cole Classics Reimagined
r	2023	Pentatonix & Elvis Presley	The Greatest Christmas Hits

O Little Town of Bethlehem - "Forest Green" AKA "Ploughboy's Dream" melody

Lyrics: Phillips Brooks (1835-1893)
Music: Ralph Vaughan Williams (collected from a Mr. Garman)

Lyrics: 1868
Music: 1903

Julie Andrews

The Secret of Christmas (1975)

In the United Kingdom and the Commonwealth, and sometimes in the U.S. (especially in the Episcopal Church), the English hymn tune "Forest Green" is used instead of "St. Louis." "Forest Green" was adapted by Ralph Vaughan Williams from an English folk ballad called "The Ploughboy's Dream" which he had collected from a Mr. Garman of Forest Green, Surrey in 1903 and published in 1906.

a	2020	Blackmore's Night	Winter Carols
b	2022	Joss Stone	Merry Christmas, Love

Once in Royal David's City

Poem by Cecil Frances Alexander   **Lyrics: 1848**
Music by Henry Gauntlett   **Music: 1849**

Petula Clark   *A Christmas Carol* (1958)

Mrs. Cecil Frances Alexander was a country schoolmistress who wrote the words to help her pupils understand the mystery of the birth of Jesus and it was never intended to be kept only for Christmas. It was put together with Henry Gauntlett's simple tune "Irby."[31]

Song (e) is a "mashup" with "Away in a Manger."

a	1982	St. Winifred's School Choir	Christmas for Everyone
b	1991	The Chieftains with The Renaissance Singers	The Bells of Dublin
c	2008	Mary Chapin Carpenter	Come Darkness, Come Light - Twelve Songs of Christmas
d	2016	Celtic Woman	The Best of Christmas
e	2018	Eric Clapton	Happy Xmas

See, Amid the Winter('s) Snow AKA The Hymn for Christmas

Lyrics: Edward Caswall (1814-1878)   **Lyrics: 1858**
Music: Sir John Goss (1800-1880)   **Music: 1871**

Unknown   Unknown

Caswall wrote this song shortly after converting from the Church of England to the Roman Catholic Church.

a	1975	Julie Andrews	The Secret of Christmas
b	2010	Aled Jones	Christmas Gold
c	2010	Annie Lennox	A Christmas Cornucopia

Silent Night AKA Sleep in Heavenly Peace

Lyrics: Josef Mohr   **Lyrics: 1816**
Music: Franz Gruber   **Music: 1818**

Haydn Quartet   Recorded as "Silent Night, Hallowed
                                       Night" in 1908. Released as a Single
                                                                in 1909

"Silent Night" is the most recorded Christmas song, at 137,315 recordings as of late 2017.[32]

The traditional story about a broken organ at St. Nicholas Church in Oberndorf is fiction from a story published in the U.S. in the 1930s.

Europe was reeling in the aftermath of the Napoleonic Wars. Financial scarcity and insecurity abounded, further stoked by fires, floods and famine. But the conflict was, at least, finally over. In 1816, Josef Mohr, a Catholic priest assigned to a pilgrim church in Mariapfarr, Austria, which had just come under Austrian rule, wrote a poem called "*Stille Nacht*" to commemorate the coming of peace. Then, he put the poem aside.

Two years later, after a transfer to St. Nicholas Church in Oberndorf, Austria (near Salzburg), Mohr decided he wanted his poem set to music. On Dec. 24, 1818, he asked his friend and local schoolteacher Franz Gruber to compose a simple melody and guitar accompaniment. Because the guitar was not an instrument approved by the Church, the duo waited until the conclusion of Christmas Eve mass before debuting the song. Mohr sang tenor and strummed the guitar while Gruber sang bass, with the congregation coming in on the chorus.

In those days travelling musicians performed their songs at town markets. One of them was "Silent Night." In 1832, a group of musicians found themselves at a Christmas market in Leipzig, where the *Leipziger Tagblatt* newspaper wrote, "It was requested that the musicians perform the beautiful Christmas song 'Silent Night,' and they did." The following year Robert Friese, publisher of the *Neue Zeitschrift für Musik* (New Magazine for Music), published the song under the title *Ächthes Tyroler Volkslied* (Genuine Tyrolean Folk Song). Choirs began singing the tune, and eventually it was translated and spread around Europe.

In 1839 the Ludwig Rainer Choir, on tour in America, sang "Silent Night" for the first time in the U.S., in New York. The performance was given at the Alexander Hamilton Memorial in the Trinity Church cemetery at the end of Wall Street. The man who translated "*Stille Nacht*" into "Silent Night" was John Freeman Young. While assigned to New York's Trinity Church, he translated European hymns into English as a hobby.

By the 1850s, the carol was so popular and important that the court orchestra in Berlin wanted to trace its origins. The theory was that it may have been composed by Johann Haydn, the brother of well-known composer Joseph Haydn. Eventually, the inquiry made it back to Gruber, who wrote a brief history of the tune called "Authentic Origination of the Composition of the Christmas Carol 'Silent Night.'"[33,34,35]

Song (ab) is a medley with "O Come All Ye Faithful." Song (az) is a medley with "O Holy Night" and "O Little Town of Bethlehem." Song (av) is a medley with "The First Noel."

The following songs are titled "Stille Nacht": (r), (aw), (bc), and (cb). Some songs are titled "Silent Night, Holy Night."

The following songs are sung in German: (r), (ah), (aw), (bc), and (cb).

There are two entries for 101 Strings—(i) and (v). They are different renditions.

The following are New Age: (ao), (ar), (av), (bd), and (bq). Song (o) is performed with chimes, using what is called a "Symphonium." Song (bw) is "medieval folk rock."

Song (am) is a novelty song, with cats "singing" this song, like dogs "sang" "Jingle Bells" in a novelty rendition of that song.

Stevie Nick's (ai) version is outstanding.

Song (cf), a unique but great rendition, is actually titled "Silent Night (Rewrapped)." The same group (For King and Country) provided a totally different, more traditional version, in (by). For King and Country had the 2ⁿᵈ best-selling Christmas album of 2024 in Apple Music—their 2020 A Drummer Boy Christmas.[36]

a	1935	Bing Crosby with Victor Young and His Orchestra	Single
b	1942	Bing Crosby with John Scott Trotter and His Orchestra	Single
c	1942	Fred Waring and His Pennsylvanians	'Twas the Night Before Christmas
d	1946	Frank Sinatra with The Ken Lane Singers - Orchestra	Single

		under the direction of Axel Stordahl	
e	1946	Perry Como	Perry Como Sings Merry Christmas Music
f	1954	Percy Faith	Music of Christmas
g	1956	Burl Ives	Christmas Eve with Burl Ives
h	1957	Elvis Presley	Elvis' Christmas Album
i	1958	*101 Strings*	*The Glory of Christmas*
j	1958	Johnny Mathis	Merry Christmas
k	1958	*Mantovani*	*Christmas Carols*
l	1960	Nat King Cole	The Magic of Christmas
m	1960	Bobby Darin	The 25th Day of Christmas with Bobby Darin
n	1961	Mitch Miller	Holiday Sing Along with Mitch
o	1961	*Rita Ford's Music Boxes*	*A Music Box Christmas*
p	1962	The Everly Brothers	The Everly Brothers and the Boystown Choir
q	1962	Eugene Ormandy, Robert Page, Temple University Concert Choir & The Phila-delphia Orchestra	The Glorious Sound of Music
r	1963	Leonard Bernstein, New York Philharmonic & The Tabernacle Choir at Temple Square	I Love...Classical Christmas
s	1963	Andy Williams	The Andy Williams Christmas Album
t	1964	Al Martino	A Merry Christmas
u	1964	Jo Stafford	Joyful Season
v	1964	*101 Strings*	*101 Strings Christmas - 30 Greatest Orchestral Holiday Favorites*
w	1966	Dean Martin	The Dean Martin Christmas Album
x	1966	Joan Baez	Noel (Bonus Track Version)
y	1966	The Lettermen	For Christmas This Year
z	1966	Henry Mancini	A Merry Mancini Christmas
aa	1967	Ella Fitzgerald	Ella Fitzgerald's Christmas
ab	1968	David Rose	The David Rose Christmas Album
ac	1970	Jose Feliciano	Feliz Navidad
ad	1972	The Singers Unlimited	Christmas
ae	1975	The Salsoul Orchestra	Christmas Jollies
af	1978	The Carpenters	Christmas Portrait
ag	1982	Julie Andrews	Christmas with Julie Andrews
ah	1983	Roger Whittaker	*Weihnachten mit* (Christmas with) Roger Whittaker
ai	1987	Stevie Nicks	A Very Special Christmas

aj	1990	Sinead O'Connor	I Do Not Want What I Haven't Got
ak	1992	Neil Diamond	The Christmas Album
al	1992	The Manhattan Transfer	The Christmas Album
am	1994	Jingle Cats	Meowy Christmas
an	1994	Kenny G	Miracles - The Holiday Album
ao	1995	*Cusco*	*A Choral Christmas*
ap	1996	Glen Campbell	Home for the Holidays
aq	1999	Amy Grant	Christmas to Remember
ar	1999	*Krysna*	*Krysmas Joy*
as	2000	Linda Ronstadt	A Merry Little Christmas
at	2004	Vanessa Williams (feat. Cormac Breatnach)	Christmas with Vanessa Williams
au	2006	Sarah McLauchlin	Wintersong
av	2006	*PAH*	*Christmas for a New Age*
aw	2007	Die Sternensinger St. Niko-laus	*Deutsche Weinachten* (German Christmas)
ax	2007	Josh Groban	Noel
ay	2008	Sarah Brightman	A Winter Symphony
az	2008	Sixpence None the Richer	Christmas
ba	2008	Priscilla Ahn	The Hotel Café Presents...Winter Songs
bb	2008	Faith Hill	Joy to the World
bc	2009	Tori Amos	Midwinter Graces
bd	2009	*Daniel Berthiaume*	*O Holy Night*
be	2010	Annie Lennox	A Christmas Cornucopia
bf	2010	Norma Roberts Wilson	Listen to the Angels Sing
bg	2010	Pink Martini	Joy to the World
bh	2010	Paul Overstreet, Juice New-ton, Country Choir, Holly Dunn & Patty Loveless	Stars Come Out for Christmas - Special Edition II
bi	2011	Michael Bublé	Christmas
bj	2011	Richard Marx (duet with Sarah Watkins)	Christmas Spirit
bk	2012	Lady A	On This Winter's Night
bl	2013	Richard & Adam	The Christmas Album
bm	2013	Kelly Clarkson (feat. Reba McEntire & Trisha Year-wood)	Wrapped in Red
bn	2014	Idina Menzel	Holiday Wishes
bo	2014	Pentatonix	That's Christmas to Me
bp	2014	Michael W. Smith (feat. Lit-tle Big Town)	The Spirit of Christmas
bq	2015	Celtic Angels	New Age Christmas - Relaxing Christmas Classics

br	2017	Cheap Trick	Christmas Christmas
bs	2017	Elvis Presley & The Royal Philharmonic Orchestra	Christmas with Elvis and the Royal Philharmonic Orchestra
bt	2017	Lindsey Stirling	Warmer in the Winter
bu	2018	Christmas Duo	Christmas Jazz Music Collection 2018
bv	2019	Lea Michele	Christmas in the City
bw	2020	Blackmore's Night	Winter Carols
bx	2020	Carrie Underwood	My Gift
by	2020	For King and Country	A Drummer Boy Christmas
bz	2020	Francesca Battistelli	This Christmas
ca	2020	The Serenad3, Gloria Estefan & David Foster	Single
cb	2021	Art Garfunkel Jr.	*Wie Du: Hommage an meinen Vater* (Like You: Tribute to my father)
cc	2022	*Boston Pops Orchestra & John Williams*	*Christmas Collection*
cd	2022	Celtic Woman	Christmas Cards from Ireland
ce	2023	Christina Perri	Songs for Christmas
cf	2024	For King and Country	Single

Still, Still, Still

Music: From a traditional Salz-burg, Austria folk song, first printed by Maria Vinzenz Süss. Modern Lyrics: Georg Götsch

Music: 1819; first printing in 1865 English translation of lyrics: 1918

English: The Norman Luboff Choir

Songs of the World (1958)

Translates in English to "Hush, Hush, Hush." The words describe the peacefulness of the infant Jesus and his mother as the baby is sung to sleep.[37,38]

a	1988	*Mannheim Steamroller*	*A Fresh Aire Christmas*
b	2004	Aled Jones	The Christmas Album
c	2005	*Amy Camie*	*Christmas Love*
d	2012	*101 Strings*	*101 Strings Christmas - 30 Greatest Orchestral Holiday Favorites*
e	2022	*Alexis Ffrench*	*Single*

'Twas the Night Before Christmas

Poem: Clement Clarke Moore
Music: Ken Darby & Henry Living-
ston, Jr.

Poem: 1823
Music: 1942

Fred Waring and His Pennsylvanians

'Twas the Night Before Christmas
(1942)

The poem this song was based on, originally titled "A Visit" or "A Visit from St. Nicholas," was first published anonymously on Dec. 23, 1823, in a Troy, New York newspaper called *The Sentinel*. It wasn't until 1837 that Clement Clarke Moore accepted credit for writing "A Visit." He reportedly wanted to keep his authorship secret initially because he was a professor, and the piece wasn't considered a scholarly work at the time of its initial writing. Moore is said to have based his vision of Santa Claus on both St. Nicholas and a local Dutch handyman where he lived in New York. Legend has it that the handyman operated the sleigh that took Moore home.[39]

Art Carney (a) played Jackie Gleason's nutty sidekick in The Honeymooners *TV show in the 1950s. Interestingly, he played a drunken department store Santa who becomes the real Santa Claus in* The Twilight Zone *Christmas episode "The Night of the Meek" in 1960.*

a	1964	Art Carney	Santa and the Doodle-Li-Boop
b	1965	The Harry Simeone Chorale	O Bambino * The Little Drummer Boy
c	1965	Patti Page	Christmas with Patti Page
d	1988	Peter, Paul & Mary	A Holiday Celebration with The New York Choral Society

Up on the House Top (Ho Ho Ho) AKA Up on the Housetop

Benjamin Hanby

1864

Gene Autry with Carl Cotner's Orchestra

Single (1953) – "B" side of "Santa
Claus is Comin' to Town"

The title of this song was originally "Santa Claus." The year 1864 was a difficult one for young minister Benjamin Hanby. Because of his views on music in church services, the teaching of children, and his opposition to slavery, his pastoral experience had been very difficult. He resigned from his second church in that year and was struggling to make a living for his wife and two children by running a singing school and writing music for the John Church Music Publishing company. In his lifetime he would publish over 80 songs. The first version of the carol was performed by Rev. Hanby's students at a children's service on Christmas, 1864, and later at a Christmas dinner for poor children sponsored by the Society of Friends. Two additional stanzas were added by "Paulina" (probably Sophia Taylor Griswold) and more changes were made by editors in later years. "Up on the Housetop" may well have been the first American song of importance which elaborates on the theme of Santa Claus. It also is one of the first entirely secular Christmas songs composed in the United States.[40]

Song (f) is performed a cappella.

a	1962	Eddy Arnold	Christmas with Eddy Arnold
b	1962	Alvin, Simon & Theodore with David Seville	Christmas with The Chipmunks
c	1968	The Archies	The Archies Christmas Album
d	1983	Raffi	Raffi's Christmas Album
e	2007	Kimberley Locke	Christmas
f	2016	Pentatonix	A Pentatonix Christmas

We Three Kings (also "…Of Orient Are")

John Henry Hopkins   **1857**

Robert Shaw and His RCA Victor Chorale   *Christmas Hymns and Carols* (1946)

This is the first widely popular carol written by an American, John Henry Hopkins.[41] Son of John H. Hopkins, sometime Bishop of Vermont, Hopkins graduated from the University of Vermont, with a BA and MA. In New York City, he worked as a reporter, intending to prepare for a law career. Instead, he entered the General Theological Seminary, where he graduated in 1850. He then became the seminary's first music teacher (1855-57) and editor of the Church Journal (1853-68). Hopkins also served as a deacon (1850) and priest (1872), and as Rector of Trinity Church, Plattsburg, New York, and Christ Church in Williamsport, Pennsylvania.[42]

He wrote the song as part of a Christmas pageant for the General Theological Seminary in New York City.[43] The song celebrates the Biblical tradition of "Three Wise Men" presenting Baby Jesus with gifts of gold, frankincense and myrrh.

Song (c) is a medley with "O Come, All Ye Faithful" and "Joy to the World." Song (g) is a medley with "O Come, O Come, Emmanuel."

Song (j) sounds like it starts with the beginning of the theme of the 1960s TV Series Mission: Impossible. *The song is performed a cappella.*

Song (h) sounds a bit like "hillbilly" music. It is certainly different, but pleasant.

a	1961	The Mormon Tabernacle Choir	Christmas Carols Around the World
b	1964	The Beach Boys	The Beach Boys' Christmas Album
c	1966	Henry Mancini	A Merry Mancini Christmas
d	1967	Ella Fitzgerald	Ella Fitzgerald's Christmas
e	1970	Jose Feliciano	Feliz Navidad
f	1990	The Roches	We Three Kings
g	1992	Neil Diamond	The Christmas Album
h	1997	Nitty Gritty Dirt Band	The Christmas Album
i	1997	Roberta Flack	The Christmas Album
j	2006	Straight No Chaser	Christmas Cheers
k	2007	Olivia Newton-John	Christmas Wish
l	2010	Pink Martini	Joy to the World
m	2012	Celtic Woman	The Best of Christmas

While Shepherds Watched Their Flocks

Lyrics: Nahum Tate
Music: George Frederick Handel

Lyrics: First published in 1700
Music: "Christmas," 1728

Evelyn Griffiths and Master Charles Hawtrey

Single (1930)

Based on the Gospel According to Luke.[44] First Christmas hymn to be approved by the Church of England.[45]

Song (b) is a medley with "Pat-A-Pan."

a	1960	Bobby Darin	The 25th Day of Christmas with Bobby Darin
b	1962	Bing Crosby	I Wish You a Merry Christmas

2 Early 20ᵗʰ Century (1901-1950)

T he early 20th century was a formative period for Christmas music, producing many songs that have since become timeless classics. Phonographs and radio broadcasts helped popularize these songs, bringing them into homes during the holiday season. The advent of Hollywood musicals and Christmas-themed movies also introduced songs that became forever linked with the holiday.

It was also the time that most Christmas music became secular. Christmas itself was something to be celebrated, as opposed to Christmas being the celebration of the birth of Christ. The mythology of Christmas grew, beyond the immortal Santa Claus, whose origins went back to antiquity (i.e., St. Nicholas), further developed in the 19th century by Clement Clarke Moore's 1823 poem "A Visit from St. Nicholas" and Thomas Nast's images in the 1860s, as well as other material from other sources in that century. In the first half of the 20th century the mythology grew to include a reindeer with a glowing nose, a living snowman and a special drummer boy.

Before the 20th century, people were at the mercy of live bands to hear their Christmas favorites, or, if they could play piano, they could buy the sheet music and play the songs themselves. But now they could purchase recordings and play them. One of the earliest recordings of Christmas music was that of "Jingle Bells," written in 1857 and made available as a recording in 1889 on Edison wax cylinders. Already in the first decade of the century a number of traditional songs became available as recordings, including:

- "The First Noel," of unknown origin – **1902**
- "Hark! The Herald Angels Sing," lyrics from 1739 and music from 1840 - **1904**
- "O Holy Night," lyrics from 1843 and music from 1847 - **1908**
- "God Rest Ye Merry, Gentlemen," circa. 1650s - **1908**
- "Silent Night," lyrics from 1816 and music from 1818 - **1909**

This trend continued in the next decade, with "Joy to the World" in 1911, "O Christmas Tree" and "*Adeste Fideles*" in 1915, "O Little Town of Bethlehem (St. Louis Melody)" in 1916, and "It Came Upon a Midnight Clear" in 1917. The trend continued even further, for example Handel's "Hallelujah (Chorus)" and "Deck the Halls," both released in the 1920s (1926 and 1927, respectively). Some traditional songs took a long time to be released as recordings, but they all eventually did.

Songs written in the first decade of the 20th century include "Parade of the Wooden Soldiers" in 1905, released as a recording in 1922, and "The Twelve Days of

Christmas" in 1909, released as a recording by Fred Waring and His Pennsylvanians in 1947. In the second decade "Carol of the Bells" was written, in 1914, and released in 1923.

In the 1930s came the birth of Christmas songs written for recorded media. In 1934 two classics were recorded and released: "Santa Claus Is Comin' To Town", by Harry Reser and His Orchestra, and "Winter Wonderland," by Richard Himber and His Ritz-Carlton Orchestra, with vocal refrain by Joey Nash. In 1935, a song that had its origins in Tudor England, a half-millennia ago, now known as "(We) Wish You a Merry Christmas," was given the modern arrangement we know today and performed at a Christmas concert. The only difference from today's version is that it was sung "I Wish You..." It would not be recorded until 1951, by The Weavers.

In 1937 the first Christmas song from a movie was released. It was "I've Got My Love to Keep Me Warm," by Irving Berlin (his first Christmas song). It was written for the movie *On the Avenue*, where it was introduced by Dick Powell and Alice Faye.

The 1940s brought us many of the most enduring and commercially successful Christmas songs ever. During America's WWII years (1941-45) there was a need for lighthearted happy songs such as "White Christmas" (a bit maudlin, but in it were reminiscences of halcyon Christmases) as many sons fought the Axis Powers overseas in Europe and the Pacific. Some songs were sad and sentimental, but hopeful, like "I'll be Home for Christmas." "Have Yourself a Merry Little Christmas," dealing with separation from loved ones at Christmas, may have had nothing directly to do with WWII, but nonetheless people could relate to the separation, and it was hopeful too, the original lyrics including "we'll have to muddle through somehow" before reunification. During the WWII years "The Carol of the Drum" (later to renamed "The Little Drummer Boy") was released and not popular, as it was somewhat militaristic and not that happy or hopeful.

In 1940 Irving Berlin was asked to write songs for the upcoming movie musical *Holiday Inn*, starring Bing Crosby. The movie involved an implausible hotel that celebrated every holiday of the year. Berlin was OK with the generic "Happy Holiday" song he wrote, which would later become associated with Christmas songs even though it did not celebrate Christmas specifically. He was very happy with a love song he came up with for Valentine's Day, which he thought would be a hit. But he had a lot of difficulty writing the song for Christmas. He was not very familiar with the holiday, being an orthodox Jew from Imperial Russia. It also wasn't his favorite holiday; his infant son had died at Christmastime. But he succeeded in writing the song, "White Christmas." Bing liked it and sang it to the public on his NBC radio show, *The Kraft Music Hall*, on December 25, 1941. It was sung in the movie and released in 1942, with Bing Crosby, the Ken Darby Singers and John Scott Trotter and His Orchestra. It received the Oscar for best song of 1942. By the end of WWII Bing's recording had become the biggest-selling single of all time. It remains the best-selling Christmas single of all time.

In 1941 the first recording of "(The) Little Drummer Boy" was made, though at the time it was known as "The Carol of the Drum." It was made by The Trapp Family Singers, made famous by their portrayal (albeit an inaccurate one) in 1965's *The Sound of Music*. This song did not become a hit, however, until released by The Harry Simeone Chorale in 1965. As noted above, "The Carol of the Drum" was not very popular in the 40s. As families waited and prayed for their loved ones to return from war, they preferred songs like "I'll Be Home for Christmas" and "White Christmas" over this song. For almost 20 years, the song remained unknown.

In 1943, Bing released "I'll Be Home for Christmas." In that same year another Christmas classic was written: "Have Yourself a Merry Little Christmas." This was for the 1944 Judy Garland movie musical *Meet Me in St. Louis*. The soundtrack, including that song, was released in 1944. Since then, many have recorded that song.

In 1944 Donald Gardner and his wife were helping second graders in Smithtown [Long Island], NY compose a Christmas song. He asked them to complete the sentence, "All I want for Christmas is ..." and then began smiling as he heard most of them lisping wishes without the help of one or both front teeth. That night, in the space of 30 minutes, Gardner composed "All I Want for Christmas (Is My Two Front Teeth)," which was released four years later. Also in 1944, songwriter Frank Loesser came up with a ditty that he and his wife performed at parties, called "Baby, It's Cold Outside." He held on to this "private" tune until 1948, when he sold it MGM to be used in the romantic comedy film, *Neptune's Daughter*, wherein the first to sing it were Ricardo Montalban and Esther Williams.

In 1945 lyricist Robert Wells and musician (as well as singer) Mel Tormé wrote "The Christmas Song," on one sweltering day to keep cool. After rejections from publishers who thought they wouldn't make enough money from a seasonal song, they found Nat King Cole, very popular at the time, to gladly sing their tune. The first release of the song was in 1946 and was successful. But King, a perfectionist, re-recorded it in 1953, this time with arranger Nelson Riddle. He cut it again in 1960 with Riddle and released it in 1961; this is the version we hear every year. The same year this song was written, two other songwriters, Sammy Cahn and Jule Styne, had the same problem as Wells and Tormé: it was very hot, and they looked to writing a "cool" song to make them feel cooler. They came up with "Let It Snow," released that same year.

Famed singing cowboy Gene Autry sang his first Christmas song in 1947, "Here Comes Santa Claus (Right Down Santa Claus Lane)." In 1949, he had the opportunity to sing another Christmas song, "Rudolf the Red-Nosed Reindeer." The character of Rudolf did not come out of the blue; it had been created by Robert L. May in 1939 in a promotional give-away booklet for Montgomery Ward in Chicago, which operated a chain of department stores. That booklet sold over 6 million copies, so Rudolf was a low-risk character to write a song about. And who better to write a song about him than May's brother-in-law, Johnny Marks, who happened to be a songwriter? The song was a huge success, selling two million copies that year, becoming the best-selling song, just behind "White Christmas." This inspired songwriters Nelson and Rollins in 1949 to write a song about a new fictional Christmas-sy character—Frosty the Snowman. By the next year they pitched the song to Gene, who was anxious to follow up on the success of "Rudolf." Many recorded "Frosty the Snowman" the same year as Autry, 1950, including Jimmy Durante, Nat King Cole, and Guy Lombardo.

Another Christmas classic, "It's a Marshmallow World," was written in 1949 and released in 1950, with Bing Crosby providing his voice. Another song written in 1949 and sung by Bing (this time with the Andrews Sisters) was "Mele Kalikimaka," also released in 1950. Yet another classic written in 1949 was "Sleigh Ride," by Leroy Anderson. The song was released as an instrumental in 1949. The record company wanted a vocal version as well, which Mr. Anderson was not too keen about. But they did it anyway, and that version was released in 1950, with the popular Andrew Sisters providing the vocals. Anderson agreed it came out well.

Ah Bleak and Chill the Wintry Wind

Bates G. Burt & Alfred Burt   **1945**

The Singers Unlimited   *Christmas* (1972)

In 1922, Burt began composing annual carols, sending them as Christmas greeting cards to his parishioners in Marquette, and later Pontiac, Michigan.[46]

The Singers Unlimited was a four-part jazz vocal group formed by Gene Puerling in 1971. The group included Len Dresslar (the Jolly Green Giant in General Mills commercials), Bonnie Herman, and Don Shelton. They enjoyed singing carols by Burt.

Most performances use vocalizations instead of an orchestra of instruments. The following are beautiful examples of this, for me especially (d).

a	2005	Theo Blekmann	Scandinavian Yuletide Voices
b	2009	Exultate	All On a Christmas Morning
c	2010	Steve Meredith & Kathy Steadman	Christmas Cometh Caroling
d	2011	Justin A. Wilson	A Wilson & Company Christmas

All I Want for Christmas (Is My Two Front Teeth)

Donald Yetter Gardner   **1944**

Spike (Lindley Armstrong) Jones   Single (1948)
and His City Slickers

An early Christmas novelty song.

It was the beginning of the holiday season in 1944 when Gardner and his wife, Doris, were helping 22 second graders in Smithtown [Long Island], N.Y., compose a Christmas song. He asked them to complete the sentence, "All I want for Christmas is ..." and then began smiling as he heard 16 of them lisping wishes without the help of one or both front teeth. That night, in the space of 30 minutes, the 31-year-old music teacher composed the ditty that would bring him royalties until the end of his life.[47]

Song (a) below is different from the others, being a soft jazz version.

a	1949	Nat "King" Cole and His Trio with The Starlighters	Single (1949)

b	1962	Alvin & the Chipmunks	Chipmunks Christmas
c	1963	The Platters	Christmas with the Platters
d	1999	George Strait	Merry Christmas Wherever You Are
e	2016	Jimmy Buffet	Tis the SeaSon

Baby, It's Cold Outside

Frank Loesser   **1944**

Margaret Whiting & Johnny Mercer -   Single (1949)
Paul Weston's Orchestra

In 1944, Loesser wrote "Baby, It's Cold Outside" as a duet to sing with his wife. After performing it at a housewarming party, the couple became "instant parlor room stars" and began singing it at other entertainment industry parties. Loesser and his wife split up the song's dialogue, playing the male "wolf" and female "mouse," as the parts were dubbed in the original sheet music.

After four years of singing the tune together, Loesser surprised his wife when he sold "Baby, It's Cold Outside" to MGM in 1948 to be used in the romantic comedy film, *Neptune's Daughter*. Filmed partly in Florida and filled with polo and bathing suits, it hardly intimated the song's future holiday success. But the tune caught on, with two performances in the film—by Esther Williams and Ricardo Montalban and, in reversed roles, by Betty Garrett and Red Skelton—and picked up the Academy Award for Best Original Song in 1949.

According to his daughter, one reason her father sold the song was to get out from under its shadow. "If I don't let go of 'Baby' I'll begin to think I can never write another song as good as I think this one is," he told his disappointed wife.[48]

Since 2009 the political correctness of the song has been questioned, and in 2018, the airing of the song was canceled by a number of radio stations. However, the public has supported the original lyrics, and they continue to be played; in fact, the song has become more popular since the controversy. Nevertheless, in 2019, vocalists John Legend and Kelly Clarkson recorded the song with modified, "safer" lyrics, written by Legend and Natasha Rothwell. This recording created its own controversy.

All below are the non-PC versions, song (a) being the most popular.

a	1959	Dean Martin	Dino's Christmas
b	1988	Ann Murray (feat. Michael Bublé)	Ann Murray's Christmas Album
c	2006	James Taylor (feat. Natalie Cole)	James Taylor at Christmas
d	2014	Seth McFarlane (feat. Sara Bareilles)	Holiday for Swing!

e	2016	John Farnham & Olivia Newton-John	Friends for Christmas

The Bells of St. Mary's

A. Emmett Adams & Douglas Furber   1917

Mr. Herbert Payne (Ernest Pike)   Single (1919)

This song was revived in 1945, in the film of the same name, by Bing Crosby and Ingrid Bergman. Bing Crosby recorded the song in a single in 1945 called "Selections from The Bells of St. Mary's." The most-played version during the holidays is by Bob B. Soxx & the Blue Jeans, from the 1963 album *A Christmas Gift for You from Phil Spector*.

a	1945	Bing Crosby	Selections from The Bells of St. Mary's (Single, 1945)
b	1963	Bob. B. Soxx & The Blue Jeans	A Christmas Gift for You from Phil Spector

Blue Christmas

Billy Hayes and Jay W. Johnson   1948

Doye O'Dell   Single (1948)

Elvis Presley's version in 1957 is much more famous than the original. See (a) below.

a	1957	Elvis Presley	Elvis' Christmas Album
b	1968	Glen Campbell	That Christmas Feeling
c	1998	Vince Gill	Breath of Heaven: A Christmas Collection

Bright, Bright the Holly Berries (AKA This Is Christmas)

Wihla Hutson & Alfred Burt   1950

Fred Waring and the Pennsylvanians   *The Sounds of Christmas* (1959)

69

Alfred Burt wrote music for fifteen Christmas carols between 1942 and 1954.

a	1972	The Singers Unlimited	Christmas
b	2010	Steve Meredith & Kathy Steadman	Christmas Cometh Caroling
c	2014	The I-49 Brass	The Spirit of Christmas
d	2019	Ensamble Coral Invierno	Navidad Magica

Carol of the Bells

Mykola Leontovych   **1914**

Ukrainian National Chorus   Single (recorded in 1922, released in 1923), as "Shtchedryk"

Based on the Ukrainian New Year's song "*Shchedryk*" AKA "*Shtchedryk.*" English-language lyrics were written in 1936 by Peter Wilhousky, arranger for the NBC Symphony Orchestra. First single is "B" side to "Poor Hawthorne."

Songs (c) and (f) are New Age Versions. Song (g) is a cappella and (i) is an Instrumental with Violin and orchestral accompaniment. Song (d) is very popular and is played at the closing pinnacle of fireworks every night of the Christmas season at Epcot in Disney World, FL.

a	1954	*Percy Faith*	*The Essential Percy Faith*
b	1978	The Carpenters	Christmas Portrait
c	1993	Mannheim Steamroller	A Fresh Aire Christmas
d	1993	*David Foster*	*The Christmas Album*
e	1999	Natalie Cole (feat. London Symphony Orchestra)	The Magic of Christmas
f	2008	2002	Christmas Dreams
g	2012	Pentatonix	The Greatest Christmas Hits
h	2013	*Arthur Fiedler & Arthur Fiedler Chorus*	*I Love Classical Christmas*
i	2017	*Lindsey Stirling*	*Warmer in the Winter*
j	2022	Bad Wolves	(Single)

Christmas Candles

Leo Breen, Raymond Leveen, Wilbur Sampson   **1949**

The Andrews Sisters (with Guy   Single (1949)
Lombardo and His Royal Canadi-
ans)

A 1953 Guy Lombardo album simply labelled *Jingle Bells* includes this rendition of a song about family being together for Christmas dinner.

My father played that album, our only Christmas album at that time, every Christmas Eve, when we were told Santa had left us presents while we had eagerly awaited his arrival in my grandparents' apartment downstairs.

Christmas Dreaming (A Little Early This Year)

Irving Gordon & Lester Lee   **1947**

Frank Sinatra   Single (1947)

Short song about doing Christmas dreaming a little early this year because "your promise" must be the reason the happy season is here.

"Dreamy" song, with angelic voices in the background in (a) and a somewhat simpler version in (b), by "Laufey," who sounds like she's singing in the 1940s. Laufey's full name is Laufey Lin Bing Jónsdóttir, and hails from Iceland. She was only about 24 when she sang this song. Song (c) is a softer, jazz version that starts with notes from "Somewhere Over the Rainbow." As for Sinatra, who sang it first, it is as great as anything else he sings. Nice song.

a	1993	Harry Connick, Jr.	When My Heart Finds Christmas
b	2023	Laufey	A Very Laufey Holiday
c	2023	Stella Cole	Single

Christmas Island

Lyle Moraine   **1946**

The Andrews Sisters with Guy Lom-   Single (1946) bardo and His Royal Canadians

Anyone familiar with the Andrews Sisters and Guy Lombardo would identify them readily in this song. Sounds a bit older than it actually is—no large "Big Band" sound here. However, it is quite sweet.

The Christmas Song (Chestnuts...)

Mel Tormé & Robert Wells   **1945**

The Nat King Cole Trio with String   Single (1946)
Choir

According to James Tormé, Mel Tormé's son, the story behind the song goes like this: "In the summer of 1945, the year before the song's release, it was a very hot, sort of an oppressive summer... And my father went to the house of his then-writing partner, a guy called Bob Wells. And Wells was nowhere to be seen. But there was a spiral pad at the piano. There were four lines sort of scribbled down on it in pencil: chestnuts roasting on an open fire, Jack Frost nipping at your nose, yuletide carols being sung by a choir, and folks dressed up like Eskimos.

"And when Bob Wells eventually appeared he said, you know, Mel, I have tried everything to cool down. I've been in my pool. I had a cold drink. I've taken a cold shower. I'm nothing but hot. And I thought that maybe, you know, if I could just write down a few lines of wintery verse I could psychologically get an edge over this heat.

"So, my dad sort of looked at Bob, looked back down at the spiral pad, and then looked back at Wells and said, I think there's something here. And about 45 minutes later—no more than that—the song was born.

"The two of them...got kind of excited about it and drove it over to Van Heusen publishing, where those guys said to them, no. Nobody would ever want a song like this that's only really going to be popular one day of the year. So, they, a little bit dejected, took the song the same afternoon to the house of a guy called Nat [King] Cole.

"[They] played the song once for Nat and he said, play that again. And they played it one more time. And before they could get it done, he said, stop everything. That's my song."

They gave the song to Cole instead of doing it themselves because "Nat Cole was simply exploding at that particular moment in time. And so my dad and Bob Wells sort of...just put it in his hands and said, you know what? You take this. We want you to have this."[49]

[The "chestnuts roasting on an open fire" image was a memory from Wells' childhood in Boston, when there'd be vendors on street corners at Christmas, serving up paper cones full of roasted chestnuts.]

The very first recording was made on June 14, 1946, but not released until 1989. The first release, from a later recording, was on October 14, 1946.

Cole would record the holiday standard four more times in his career. In the first pressing of the King Cole Trio's 1946 version, he sang the last line of the bridge: "To see if *reindeers* really know how to fly." The song had already become a seasonal hit when Tormé and Wells pointed out the grammatical error.

"Nat, a true gentleman, and a dogged perfectionist, stewed over this mistake," Tormé recalled in his autobiography, "and sure enough, at the end of another recording session, with the same-sized orchestra at hand, he rerecorded our song, properly singing 'reindeer.' The second version is virtually identical to the first, but those early first pressings have become collectors' items."

In 1953, Cole recut the song with arranger Nelson Riddle, then again in 1960. This last version [released in 1961], with his voice at its smokiest, is the one that has become the definitive holiday standard. The opening line alone is one of the most recognizable moments in the huge canon of seasonal music.

It wasn't mentioned at the time, but Cole's version of "The Christmas Song" was the first holiday standard ever introduced by a black American. It opened the door for Lou Rawls, Ray Charles and many others to record their own takes on yuletide classics.[50]

As popular as the song became, however, it did not reach the Billboard Top 10 until January 7, 2023.

In 1963 Mel Tormé added a new verse at the beginning of the song, which he announced during *The Judy Garland Christmas Show*[51] that was recorded on December 6, 1963, and aired on December 22. It began, "All through the year, we waited..." At the end, he sang, with Judy, "Love and joy come to you, and all your loved ones too...," based on the "Here We Come A-Wassailing" song. [Tormé was a songwriter and arranger for *The Judy Garland Show*, which aired for only one season, 1963-64, on CBS; it could not keep up with the huge ratings *Bonanza* got in that time slot, on NBC.]

The following are all great in their own way. Song (ai) is New Age; Songs (f), (i) and (ae) are jazz; song (j) is old school Rock 'n Roll; (ag) and (aq) are a cappella. Some are gentle, like (af) and (bc). Some are more rousing, like (ap). The Carpenters (q) and Sara McLachlan (aw) sing Mel Tormé's new verse.

a	1957	Frank Sinatra	A Jolly Christmas from Frank Sinatra
b	1958	Johnny Mathis	Merry Christmas

c	1959	Perry Como with Mitchell Ayres and His Orchestra and The Ray Charles Singers	Season's Greetings from Perry Como
d	1960	*Fran Devol and His Rainbow Strings*	*The Old Sweet Songs of Christmas*
e	1961	Mitch Miller	Holiday Sing Along with Mitch
f	1961	*Ramsey Lewis Trio*	*Sound of Christmas*
g	1961	Nat King Cole	The Nat King Cole Story
h	1963	*Andre Kostelanetz and His Orchestra*	*Wonderland of Christmas*
i	1965	*Vince Guaraldi Trio*	*A Charlie Brown Christmas (Original 1965 TV Soundtrack)*
j	1965	*The Ventures*	*The Ventures' Christmas Album*
k	1966	The New Christy Minstrels	Columbia Christmas Collection ('63 - '66)
l	1966	*Percy Faith*	*The Essential Percy Faith*
m	1966	The Lettermen	For Christmas This Year
n	1967	Barbra Streisand	A Christmas Album
o	1968	Tony Bennett	Snowfall: The Tony Bennett Christmas Album
p	1970	Jose Feliciano	Felix Navidad
q	1978	The Carpenters	Christmas Portrait
r	1988	Diane Schuur	A GRP Christmas Collection
s	1992	The Manhattan Transfer & Tony Bennett	The Christmas Album
t	1992	Neil Diamond	The Christmas Album
u	1992	Mel Tormé	Christmas Songs
v	1993	Gloria Estefan	Christmas Through Your Eyes
w	1993	David Foster (feat. Celine Dion)	The Christmas Album
x	1994	Natalie Cole	Holly & Ivy
y	1998	Celine Dion	These Are Special Times
z	1999	Nat King Cole and Nat King Cole with Natalie Cole)	The Christmas Song (Expanded Edition)
aa	1999	*Kenny G*	*Miracles - The Holiday Album*
ab	2000	Christina Aguilera	My Kind of Christmas
ac	2000	Linda Ronstadt	A Merry Little Christmas
ad	2002	Lee Ann Womack	The Season for Romance
ae	2005	Diana Krall	Christmas Songs
af	2006	Celtic Woman	The Best of Christmas

ag	2006	The Swingle Singers	Unwrapped
ah	2006	James Taylor (feat. Toots Thielemans)	James Taylor At Christmas
ai	2007	Mannheim Steamroller (feat. Johnny Mathis)	Christmas Song
aj	2007	Mindy Smith	My Holiday
ak	2008	*101 Strings Orchestra*	*101 Strings Orchestra - 30 Greatest Orchestral Holiday Favorites*
al	2009	Lou Rawls	Merry Christmas from Lou Rawls
am	2010	Stephen Bishop	Stars Come Out for Christmas
an	2011	Scott Welland	The Most Wonderful Time of the Year
ao	2011	Michael Bublé	Christmas
ap	2012	Francesca Battistelli	Christmas
aq	2012	Pentatonix	PTXmas
ar	2012	Rod Stewart	Merry Christmas, Baby
as	2012	Paul McCartney	Holiday's Rule
at	2014	Idina Menzel	Holiday Wishes
au	2014	Jackie Evancho, The City of Prague Philharmonic Orchestra, et al	Someday at Christmas
av	2015	Patty Smyth	Come On December
aw	2016	Sarah McLachlan	Wonderland
ax	2017	*Herb Alpert*	*The Christmas Wish*
ay	2019	Bing Crosby & London Symphony Orchestra	Bing at Christmas
az	2019	Tony Bennett & The Royal Philharmonic Orchestra	Christmas with the Stars & The Royal Philharmonic Orchestra
ba	2022	Sarah Connor	Not So Silent Night
bb	2022	*Boston Pops Orchestra & John Williams*	*Christmas Collection*
bc	2023	Christina Perri	Songs for Christmas
bd	2023	Karla Bonoff	Silent Night

(Sweet Angie) The Christmas Tree Angel

M.K. Jerome & Jack Scholl   1950

The Andrews Sisters   Single (1950)

A sweet little angel comes down from the heavens on Christmas Eve to help Santa Claus dress up the tree. She colors the lights, sprinkles the snow, hangs up holly and mistletoe, and arranges the toys. Then, she returns to the top of the tree, where you can see her on Christmas morning.

Fantasia on Greensleeves

Ralph Greaves & Ralph Vaughan Williams   1934

Unknown   Unknown

Based on the English folk song "Greensleeves," arranged for strings and harp.

a	1983	Ralph Vaughan Williams - Leonard Slatkin & St. Louis Symphony Orchestra	Christmas Break - A Relaxing Classical Mix

Frosty the Snowman

Jack Rollins & Steve Nelson   1949

Gene Autry   Single (1950)

This song was hatched from the minds of songwriters Nelson and Rollins in 1949, impressed that two million copies had been sold of "Rudolf the Red-Nosed Reindeer" by Gene Autry. By the next year they pitched the song to Gene, who was anxious to follow up on the success of "Rudolf." Many recorded "Frosty" the same year as Autry, 1950, including Jimmy Durante, Nat King Cole, and Guy Lombardo.[52]

Both Gene Autry and Jimmy Durante (a) are usually associated with this song, the latter narrating the 1969 animated TV Special Frosty the Snowman. *Song (l) is an unusual different take on the song, basically New Wave. Song (p) is a cappella.*

a	1950	Jimmy Durante	A Holly Jolly Kids Christmas
b	1953	Guy Lombardo & His Royal Canadians	Jingle Bells
c	1953	Mitch Miller	Holiday Singalong with Mitch
d	1953	Arthur Godfrey	Christmas with Arthur Godfrey and All the Little Godfreys
e	1958	Ray Conniff	Christmas with Conniff
f	1962	Jan & Dean	Single. Available on: *Lost Christmas: Holiday Rarities* (1998)
g	1963	The Ronettes	A Christmas Gift for You from Ron Spector
h	1964	The Beach Boys	The Beach Boys' Christmas Album
i	1964	Brenda Lee	Merry Christmas from Brenda Lee
j	1979	Willie Nelson	Old Christmas Music
k	2003	Fiona Apple	Christmas Voices
l	2005	Cocteau Twins	Lullabies to Violaine, Vol. 2
m	2007	Kimberley Lock	Christmas
n	2008	*101 Strings Orchestra*	*101 Strings Orchestra - 30 Greatest Orchestral Holiday Favorites*
o	2021	Billy Idol	Happy Holidays
p	2021	Pentatonix (feat. Alessia Cara)	Evergreen
q	2023	Christina Perri	Songs for Christmas
r	2023	Seth McFarlane &. Liz Gillies	We Wish You the Merriest

Happy Holiday

Irving Berlin   1942

Bing Crosby with The Music Maids   Single (1942)
and Hal and John Scott Trotter and
His Orchestra

Sung in the beginning of the film *Holiday Inn* (1942), by Bing Crosby and Marjorie Reynolds (dubbed by Martha Mears). It is a song about all holidays, not just Christmas.

Andy Williams (a) started the tradition for many artists to include the song "It's the Holiday Season" within this song. Songs (c), (e) and (f) are examples of this. Song (d) is part of a medley with "White Christmas." Song (f) is a cappella.

a	1963	Andy Williams	The Andy Williams Christmas Album
b	1966	Percy Faith	Christmas Is...
c	1992	The Manhattan Transfer	The Christmas Album
d	2002	Barry Manilow	The Classic Christmas Album
e	2018	Martina McBride	It's the Holiday Season
f	2020	Pentatonix	We Need a Little Christmas
g	2023	Seth McFarlane &. Liz Gillies	We Wish You the Merriest

Have Yourself a Merry Little Christmas

Hugh Martin & Ralph Blane   1943

Judy Garland with Georgie Stoll and His Orchestra   *Meet Me in St. Louis Soundtrack* (1944)

Written in 1943 by Hugh Martin and Ralph Blane for the musical *Meet Me in St. Louis* (1944), this song nearly ended up discarded in the garbage bin. Martin, a Broadway composer, started working on a melody for the song but was struggling to find a bridge after completing the first 16 bars. "I found a little...tune that I liked, but couldn't make work, so I played with it for two or three days and then threw it in the wastebasket," he recalled in 1989. Fortunately, Blane, who had been working in the adjacent room, heard the tune and told him it was too interesting to discard.

The song comes during a scene when Garland's younger sister Tottie (played by Margaret O'Brien) is worried that Santa won't be able to find them if they move to New York. Garland's character sings "Have Yourself a Merry Little Christmas" to cheer her up. However, Garland complained that the lyrics were too sad to sing to a heartbroken seven-year-old. "The original version was so lugubrious that Judy Garland refused to sing it," admitted Martin. "She said, 'If I sing that, little Margaret O'Brien will cry, and they'll think I'm a monster.' So, I was young then and kind of arrogant, and I said, 'Well, I'm sorry you don't like it, Judy, but that's the way it is, and I don't really want to write a new lyric.' But Tom Drake, who played the boy next door, took me aside and said, 'Hugh, you've got to finish it. It's really a great song potentially, and I think you'll be sorry if you don't do it.' So, I went home, and I wrote the version that's in the movie."

In addition, the religious reference "if the Lord allows" was changed to "if the fates allow."

In 1957, Frank Sinatra (who had already recorded the song in 1948 with the original lyrics) approached Martin to record the song again, for his album *A Jolly Christmas from Frank Sinatra*. He requested a happier ending to the song. "The name of my album is *A Jolly Christmas*. Do you think you could jolly up that line for me?" Sinatra asked. Martin "tweaked" the song for Sinatra with a line about "hang a shining star upon the highest bough" instead of having to "muddle through somehow." [Interestingly, in Dean Martin's Dec. 21, 1967 Christmas Special, Sinatra sang the song with "muddle through."[53]]

Linda Ronstadt said she liked both the "muddle through" line and the bravado of the "hanging the shining star" replacement—so included both in her 2000 version.

As for Hugh Martin, who was 96 when he died in 2011, he remained convinced that "muddle through" was the most honest version. "It's just so kind of…down-to-earth," he said late in life.[54]

Johnny Mathis introduced a new verse to the song. In 1963 on his album *Sounds of Christmas*, he adds a *Christmas Carol*-esque introductory verse: "Christmas future is far away / Christmas past is past / Christmas present is here today / Bringing joy that will last." Some other artists followed suit.[55]

The songs below represent a lot of different kinds of music. Most are vocals with an orchestra, but there are many exceptions. Songs (s), (bb) and (bd) are smooth jazz; (d) and (ao) are soft Rock; (h) is doo-wop Rock; (aa) is New Age; (an) is a cappella; (ap) is Celtic and New Age; and (ax) is Violin with orchestral accompaniment.

As noted above, the original song had the "muddle through" lyric that Frank Sinatra had replaced with "highest bough." Most of the songs below use "highest bough," but the following use "muddle through": (i), (q), (y), (ab), (af), (ai), (ar), (at), (bd) and (be). Also, as noted above, Linda Ronstadt (r) uses both.

Additionally, as noted above, the original song had the lyric "if the Lord allows," which was changed to "if the fates allow." One rendition below uses the original lyric, that by Francesca Battistelli (ag).

Some renditions use the new verse introduced by Johnny Mathis. These are (g), (u), (p), and (y). Song (ba) has the music from the new verse but is not sung.

The original song as released by Judy Garland has what sounds like xylophone tones at the beginning, evidently because she is singing to a small child (though in the movie they are at the end). Some songs incorporate this at the beginning. In the list below, they are (ak), (ar), and (au).

As she is apt to do, Sarah McLachlan (z) changes the beat slightly from the original.

Even with the "highest bough" lyric, this is still a rather maudlin song. Three artists made it more upbeat than the others: Perry Como (e), Francesca Battistelli (ag), and Pentatonix (an).

| a | 1957 | Frank Sinatra | A Jolly Christmas from Frank Sinatra |
| b | 1965 | Eddie Fischer | Mary Christmas |

c	1966	The Lettermen	For Christmas This Year
d	1968	The Archies	The Archies Christmas Album
e	1968	Perry Como with the Ray Charles Singers	The Perry Como Christmas Album
f	1972	The Singers Unlimited	Christmas
g	1978	The Carpenters	Christmas Portrait
h	1990	Vince Vance and the Valiants	All I Want for Christmas Is You
i	1990	Mel Tormé	90s Holiday Hits
j	1992	Amy Grant	Home for Christmas
k	1992	*Andre Gagnon*	*Noel*
l	1992	The Manhattan Transfer	The Christmas Album
m	1994	*Kenny G*	*The Holiday Album*
n	1995	Roger Whittaker	The Christmas Song
o	1995	Luther Vandross	Christmas Voices
p	1996	Glen Campbell	Home for the Holidays
q	2000	Christina Aguilera	My Kind of Christmas
r	2000	Linda Ronstadt	A Merry Little Christmas
s	2002	Lee Ann Womack	The Season for Romance
t	2004	Vanessa Williams	Christmas with Vanessa Williams
u	2005	Bette Midler	Cool Yule
v	2005	Diana Krall	Christmas Songs
w	2005	Sarah Connor	Christmas in My Heart
x	2006	Celtic Woman	A Christmas Celebration
y	2006	James Taylor	James Taylor at Christmas
z	2006	Sarah McLachlan	Wintersong
aa	2007	Mannheim Steamroller (feat. Johnny Mathis)	Christmas Song
ab	2009	Scott Weiland	The Most Wonderful Time of the Year
ac	2010	Stephen Bishop	Stars Came Out for Christmas - Special Edition
ad	2011	Carole King	A Holiday Carole
ae	2011	Michael Bublé	Christmas
af	2012	Christina Perri	A Verry Merry Perri Christmas
ag	2012	Francesca Battistelli	Christmas
ah	2012	Rod Stewart	Merry Christmas, Baby
ai	2012	Tracey Thorn	Tinsel and Lights
aj	2012	Lady A	On This Winter's Night

ak	2013	Kelly Clarkson	Wrapped in Red
al	2014	Idina Menzel	Holiday Wishes
am	2014	Jackie Evancho, The City of Prague Philharmonic Orchestra, et al	Someday at Christmas
an	2014	Pentatonix	That's Christmas to Me
ao	2015	Patty Smyth	Come On December
ap	2015	Celtic Angels	New Age Christmas
aq	2016	John Farnham & Olivia Newton-John	Friends for Christmas
ar	2016	Kylie Minogue	Kylie Christmas
as	2018	Ingrid Michaelson	Ingrid Michaelson's Songs for the Season
at	2019	Bing Crosby & London Symphony Orchestra	Bing at Christmas
au	2019	Lea Michele	Christmas in the City
av	2019	Tony Bennett and the Royal Philharmonic Orchestra	Christmas with the Stars and the Royal Philharmonic Orchestra
aw	2020	Carrie Underwood	My Gift
ax	2022	*Daniel Hope & New Century Chamber Orchestra*	Single
ay	2022	Grace Gardner & Faith Zapata	Single
az	2022	Joss Stone	Merry Christmas, Love
ba	2022	Tasha Layton	This is Christmas
bb	2023	Giada Valenti & Royal Philharmonic Orchestra	Single
bb	2023	Mark Tremonti	Mark Tremonti Christmas Classics New and Old
bc	2023	Seth McFarlane &. Liz Gillies	We Wish You the Merriest
bd	2023	Norah Jones & Laufey	Single
be	2024	Stella Cole	Snow!

Here Comes Santa Claus (Right Down Santa Claus Lane)

Oakley Haldeman & Gene Autry   1947

Gene Autry

Single (1947) and *Rudolph the Red-Nosed Reindeer and Other Christmas Classics* (1947)

In the Summer of 1947, Country Music pioneer Art Satherley (1889-1986) suggested Gene record a new Christmas song he had discovered, "An Old Fashioned Tree." For its flipside, Gene remembered a song idea he'd gotten while participating in the annual Hollywood "Santa Claus Lane" parade the previous November. Astride his horse Champion Jr., ahead of St. Nick on his sleigh, he'd heard a child on the sidewalk shout, "Here comes Santa Claus!" Satherley took Gene's idea to Oakley Haldeman, the composer who operated Gene's music publishing division, and he came up with the melody. Cyrus Whitfield "Johnny" Bond (1915-1978), an American country music singer-songwriter, guitarist, composer and publisher, recorded a demo version of the song at his home studio, where Satherley, cocktail in hand, stood next to the microphone (as he usually did during recordings). The tingling of ice cubes was captured on the recording, inspiring the use of jingle bells on the August 28, 1947 Columbia session. After initial sales of two million following its December release, the song became a perennial top ten hit every Yuletide season for years to come. More importantly, it opened a whole new market for Gene—holiday discs aimed at children. Easter and Thanksgiving recordings would follow, as well as other Christmas hits.[56]

Song (e) is in a medley with "March of the Toys." Song (f) is jazz and (i) is a cappella. Song (g) is the most played rendition after the original and might even surpass the original.

a	1949	Doris Day	Doris Day - Personal Christmas Collection
b	1949	Bing Crosby & The Andrews Sisters	The Polar Express (Soundtrack from the Motion Picture)
c	1957	Elvis Presley	Traditional Christmas Music
d	1958	Ray Conniff	Christmas with Conniff
e	1960	*Frank DeVol and His Rainbow Strings*	*The Old Sweet Songs of Christmas*
f	1961	*Ramsey Lewis Trio*	*Sound of Christmas*
g	1963	Bob. B. Soxx & The Blue Jeans	A Christmas Gift for You from Phil Spector
h	1968	The Archies	The Archies Christmas Album

i	2018	Pentatonix	Christmas is Here!
j	2021	Billy Idol	Happy Holidays
k	2023	Seth McFarlane &. Liz Gillies	We Wish You the Merriest

The (or It's the) Holiday Season

Kay Thompson   1945

Kay Thompson / First recording by Andy Williams as part of a medley   *The Andy Williams Christmas Album* (1963)

Though Kay Thompson wrote and performed this song in 1945, it was not recorded until 1963, when Thompson presented it to Andy Williams, who sang it in a medley with "Happy Holiday," "Happy Holiday" occurring first in the medley. Since then, this medley has been popular with other singers. It is not sung by itself.

I Wonder as I Wander

John Jacob Niles   1933

Gladys Swarthout – Victor Orchestra, Jay Blackton Conductor   Single (1946)

While in Appalachian North Carolina, Niles attended a fundraising meeting held by evangelicals who had been ordered out of town by the police. According to Niles, a girl started to sing. "Her clothes were unbelievable dirty and ragged, and she, too, was unwashed. Her ash-blond hair hung down in long skeins…But, best of all, she was beautiful, and in her untutored way, she could sing. She smiled as she sang, smiled rather sadly, and sang only a single line of a song." The girl, named Annie Morgan, repeated the fragment seven times in exchange for a quarter per performance, and Niles left with "three lines of verse, a garbled fragment of melodic material—and a magnificent idea."[57]

A reverential and pleasant song, but sad. It's not the kind of thing you expect to hear on the radio or play at Christmastime. Song (c) is a cappella.

a	1949	Jo Stafford with Paul Weston and His Orchestra	(Single)
b	1952	Burl Ives	Folk Songs Dramatic and Humorous
c	1959	Fred Waring and The Pennsylvani-	The Sounds of Christmas

		ans	
d	1966	Joan Baez	Noël
e	1967	Barbra Streisand	A Christmas Album
f	1975	Julie Andrews	The Secret of Christmas
g	1996	Vanessa Williams	Star Bright
h	2000	Linda Ronstadt	A Merry Little Christmas

I'll Be Home for Christmas

Buck Ram, Walter Kent, & Kim Gannon   **1943**

Bing Crosby   Single (1943)

This song was written to honor soldiers overseas during WWII who longed to be home at Christmastime. The song is sung from the point of view of a soldier writing a letter to his family.

A lot of great artists chose to record this song. Most are standard styles of Christmas music. Song (q) is jazz and (ac) is Celtic New Age.

Some of the songs below begin with a spoken preamble that begins like this: "I'm dreaming tonight of a place I love…" These songs are (c), (h), (i), (o), (p), (r), (y), and (ai). Song (af) is an Instrumental that includes the preamble in instrumental form. Song (i) not only includes this but some bars of "Santa Claus Is Coming to Town," while (y) includes it with some bars of "Silent Night." Songs (b) and (ab) just start with bars from "Silent Night." (f) starts with some bars of "Deck the Halls."

a	1946	Perry Como (with Russ Case and His Orchestra)	Perry Como Sings Merry Christmas Music
b	1957	Frank Sinatra	A Jolly Christmas from Frank Sinatra
c	1958	Johnny Mathis	Merry Christmas
d	1959	Pat Boone	White Christmas
e	1964	The Beach Boys	The Beach Boys' Christmas Album
f	1966	Dean Martin	The Dean Martin Christmas Album
g	1966	The Lettermen	For Christmas This Year
h	1978	The Carpenters	Christmas Portrait
i	1992	Amy Grant	Home for Christmas
j	1992	Tony Bennett	Snowfall: The Tony Bennett Christmas Album (CD Re-issue)
k	1993	David Foster (feat. Roberta Flack & Peabo Bryson)	The Christmas Album

l	1996	Glen Campbell	Home for the Holidays
m	1999	*Kenny G*	*The Classic Christmas Album*
n	2000	Linda Ronstadt	A Merry Little Christmas
o	2001	Barbra Streisand	The Classic Christmas Album
p	2003	Whitney Houston	One Wish: The Holiday Album
q	2005	Diana Krall	Christmas Songs
r	2005	Bette Midler	Cool Yule
s	2006	Sarah McLachlan	Wintersong
t	1992	Tony Bennett	Snowfall: The Tony Bennett Christmas Album (CD Re-issue)
u	2011	*Andre Gagnon*	*Dans le silence de la nuit* (In the Silence of the Night)
v	2011	Deana Martin	White Christmas
w	2011	Michael Bublé	Christmas
x	2012	Kelly Clarkson	Kelly Clarkson -Greatest Hits - Chapter One
y	2012	Celtic Woman	The Best of Christmas
z	2012	Christina Perri	A Verry Merry Perri Christmas
aa	2012	Lady A	On This Winter's Night
ab	2013	Susan Boyle	Home for Christmas
ac	2015	Celtic Angels	New Age Christmas
ad	2017	Elvis Presley & The Royal Philharmonic Orchestra	Christmas with Elvis & The Royal Philharmonic Orchestra
af	2017	*Herb Alpert*	*The Christmas Wish*
ag	2018	Ingrid Michaelson & Will Chase	Ingrid Michaelson's Songs for the Season
ah	2019	Bing Crosby & The London Symphony Orchestra	Bing at Christmas
ai	2019	Idina Menzel (feat. Aaron Lohr)	Christmas: A Season of Love
aj	2019	Doris Day & Royal Philharmonic Orchestra	Christmas with the Stars and the Royal Philharmonic Orchestra

I've Got My Love to Keep Me Warm

Irving Berlin   **1937**

Ray Noble and His Orchestra - Vocal Refrain by Howard Barrie (Jan. 5, 1937)
Red Norvo and His Orchestra - Vocal Chorus Mildred Bailey (Jan. 8,

All Singles in 1937

1937)
Billie Holiday and Her Orchestra
(Jan.12, 1937)
Shep Fields and His Rippling
Rhythm Orchestra - Vocal Refrain by
Bob Goday (Jan. 18, 1937)
Alice Faye – Orchestra under direc-
tion of Cy Feuer (Jan. 24, 1937)
Glen Gray and The Casa Loma Or-
chestra - Vocal Chorus by Kenny
Sargent (Jan. 28, 1937)

Six singles were recorded and released in January 1937 alone.

Written by Irving Berlin for the 1937 movie *On the Avenue*, where it was introduced by Dick Powell & Alice Faye.

*Both Dean Martin (b) and his daughter Deana (f) sang this song. Dean's is proba-
bly the most popular, though Frank Sinatra's (c) version is very popular too.*

a	1956	Kay Starr	Kay Star Sings [Also on album *1950's Nostal-gia, Vol. 4* (2014)]
b	1959	Dean Martin	Dino's Christmas
c	1961	Frank Sinatra	Ring-A-Ding Ding! [Also on album *The Christ-mas Collection* (2004)]
d	1983	Amy Grant	Tennessee Christmas
e	2007	Kimberley Locke	Christmas
f	2011	Deana Martin	White Christmas

The Jolly Old Man in the Bright Red Suit

Sunny Skylar   **1949**

Vaughn Monroe And His Orchestra   Single (1949)
with The Moon Maids

Santa Claus is the jolly old man in the bright red suit and whiskers on his chin. He
brings toys to all children who have been good, and he knows who have misbe-
haved. This single was pressed on a 10" record colored green—for Christmas, a
common practice when this song was released and into the 1960s.

*No recordings except for the original of this song could be found, though the origi-
nal can be found in* 50s Christmas Classics—Vol 1.

Joyful, Joyful, We Adore Thee (The Hymn of Joy)

Henry Van Dyke   **1907**

Neues Symphonie-Orchester (German)   *IX. Symphonie (Ludwig van Beethoven)* (1923)

Vocal Version of the famous "Ode to Joy" melody of the final movement of Ludwig van Beethoven's final symphony, Symphony No. 9.

a	1989	Debby Boone	Be Thou My Vision - Great Hymns of Faith
b	1998	The Imperials	Songs of Christmas
c	2005	Carrie Underwood	My Gift

Jumpin' Jiminy Christmas

Stanley Cowan & Jidge Carroll   **1949**

Bob Eberly   Single (1949)

"B" side to "Here Comes Santa Claus (Right Down Santa Claus Lane)."

The original is not available, but (a) is an Instrumental.

a	1963	*Bert Kaempfert and His Orchestra*	*Christmas Wonderland*

Let It Snow (AKA Let It Snow, Let It Snow, Let it Snow OR Let It Snow! Let It Snow! Let It Snow!)

Sammy Cahn & Jule Styne   **1945**

Vaughn Monroe and His Orchestra - Vocal Refrain by Vaughn Monroe and The Norton Sisters   Single (1945)

On a hot summer day in Hollywood in 1945, the two authors of this song met with their publisher over the details of a contract. Styne suggested that if they wanted to stay cool, they should write a song about winter. Later, in a stifling hot room, Styne worked at a piano to write a melody that sounded "cool." Cahn looked out the window at the blistering hot sun and whispered, "let it snow." They exchanged memories of being snowed in, and Cahn came up with a mini movie about a man and woman trapped by a blizzard but warmed by a fire, and they were too much in love to say goodbye. Thus, the song was born.[58]

Song (h) is jazz; (w) is an Instrumental with violin and orchestral accompaniment. Song (g) is a medley with "Winter Wonderland." The most popular rendition is probably Dean Martin's 1959 version (b), which is different from his 1966 rendition (d).

Personally, I think Sarah McLachlan's version (t) is the best. It is a bit off-beat from the others, but her voice and rousing keyboards from Pierre Marchand (her producer since 1991) are phenomenal.

a	1949	Vaughan Monroe	I Am Vaughan Monroe
b	1959	Dean Martin	Dino's Christmas
c	1961	Mitch Miller	Holiday Sing Along with Mitch
d	1966	Dean Martin	The Dean Martin Christmas Album
e	1992	The Manhattan Transfer	The Christmas Album
f	1999	*Kenny G*	*The Classic Christmas Album*
g	2002	Lee Ann Womack	The Season for Romance
h	2005	Diana Krall & The Clayton-Hamilton Jazz Orchestra	Christmas Songs
i	2005	Carly Simon	(Single)
j	2006	Celtic Woman	The Best of Christmas
k	2008	Amy Sky	The Lights of December
l	2008	*101 Strings Orchestra*	*101 Strings Orchestra - 30 Greatest Orchestral Holiday Favorites*
m	2010	Stephen Bishop	Stars Came Out for Christmas - Special Edition II
n	2011	Deana Martin	White Christmas
o	2012	Lady A	On This Winter's Night
p	2012	Rod Stewart	Merry Christmas, Baby
q	2014	*Dave Koz (feat. Kenny G)*	*Dave Koz & Friends: The 25th of December*
r	2015	Human Nature (feat. Delta Goodrem)	The Christmas Album
s	2016	Kylie Minogue	Kylie Christmas
t	2016	Sarah McLachlan	Wonderland
u	2016	She & Him	Christmas Party
v	2016	John Farnham &	Friends for Christmas

		Olivia Newton-John	
w	2017	*Lindsey Stirling*	*Warmer in the Winter*
x	2018	Jesse J	This Christmas Day
y	2018	Ingrid Michaelson	Ingrid Michaelson's Songs for the Season
z	2019	Bing Crosby & London Symphony Orchestra	Bing at Christmas
aa	2019	Doris Day & Royal Philharmonic Orchestra	Christmas with the Stars and the Royal Philharmonic Orchestra
ab	2020	Francesca Battistelli	This Christmas
ac	2021	Michael Bublé	Christmas
ad	2022	Joss Stone	Merry Christmas, Love
ae	2023	Christina Perri	Songs for Christmas

The Little Boy that Santa Claus Forgot

James Leach, Michael Carr & Thomas Connor   **1937**

Ambrose and His Orchestra (Vocal Chorus by Vera Lynn)   Single (1937)

A little boy without a father sent a note to Santa for some soldiers and a drum. It broke his heart when he didn't get what he had asked for.

"B" side of "Moonlight on the Waterfall." Vera Lynn (1917-2020) is best known for her songs that supported the troops in WWII: "We'll Meet Again" and "(There'll Be Bluebirds Over) The White Cliffs of Dover," though she sang many songs in her incredibly long career. This song was released five times in 1937. Nat King Cole revived it in 1953 with his remarkable rendition.

a	1953	Nat "King" Cole with Orchestra conducted by Nelson Riddle	Single
b	1994	Natalie Cole	Holly & Ivy
c	2021	Nat King Cole	A Sentimental Christmas with Nat King Cole and Friends: Cole Classics Reimagined

(The) Little Christmas Tree

Mickey Rooney   **1950**

Nat King Cole with Orchestra con-   Single (1950)
ducted by Pete Rugolo

"B" side of "Frosty the Snowman." A little Christmas tree had no-one to buy it, until the singer of the song took it and cherished it. His boy will jump for joy when he sees it and he will show it to Santa. It will create peace on Earth. When he lights its star, the tree will be big enough for three.

(The) Little Drummer Boy (Carol of the Drum)

Katherine K. Davis   **1941**

First recording as "Carol of the   Trapp Family rendition: *Christmas*
Drum": The Trapp Family Singers   *with The Trapp Family Singers*
Second recording as "Carol of the   (1951)
Drum": The Jack Halloran Singers   Jack Halloran rendition: *Christmas Is*
First Recording as "The Little   *A-Comin'* (1957)
Drummer Boy": The Harry Simeone   Harry Simeone rendition: Single
Chorale   (1958)

The melody appears to be based on both Czech and Spanish compositions. Katherine Davis wrote lyrics in 1941 and named it "The Carol of the Drum."

Once released, "The Carol of the Drum" was not very popular. As families waited and prayed for their loved ones to return from war, they preferred songs like "I'll Be Home for Christmas" and "White Christmas" over Katherine's song. For almost 20 years, her song remained unknown, and she focused her efforts on other songs.

It wasn't until 1958 that "The Carol of the Drum" sprang into an instant hit. Harry Simeone, a famed orchestra and choir director of the time, came across the song. He was instantly inspired to blend voices to create a drum beat and he renamed the song "The Little Drummer Boy." The simple story of a poor child and his drum took over the nation. In the middle of rock-n-roll and doo-wop music, Katherine Davis's words became wildly successful.

By 1962, "The Little Drummer Boy" had been recorded more than a hundred times and on the nation's pop charts five times. By the end of that decade, only two other Christmas songs had generated more success—"White Christmas" and "Rudolph the Red-Nosed Reindeer."[59]

There is another song called "The Little Drummer Boy," written by Don Pelosi & Art Noel, that has 11 releases, all in 1938.

The Trapp Family is, of course, the same as that depicted in *The Sound of Music*.

The song was made into a stop-motion Christmas TV special in 1968.

Song (h) is a New Age version; (l) is a cappella; and (n) is an Instrumental with violin and orchestral accompaniment. The most famous version, heard on radios for many years, is (c).

a	1963	Andy Williams	The Andy Williams Christmas Album
b	1965	Burl Ives	Have a Holly Jolly Christmas
c	1965	Harry Simeone Chorale	The Little Drummer Boy
d	1966	Percy Faith	The Christmas Recordings
e	1972	Jose Feliciano	Feliz Navidad
f	1972	Eugene Ormandy & Robert Page	I Love Classical Christmas
g	1981	Joan Jett & The Blackhearts	I Love Rock 'N' Roll
h	1993	*Mannheim Steamroller*	*A Fresh Aire Christmas*
i	2006	Celtic Woman	The Best of Christmas
j	2008	*101 Strings Orchestra*	*101 Strings Orchestra - 30 Greatest Orchestral Holiday Favorites*
k	2011	Joseph Leo Bwarie	Seasons Greetings - A Jersey Boys Christmas
l	2013	Pentatonix	The Greatest Christmas Hits
m	2020	For King & Country	A Drummer Boy Christmas
n	2022	*Lindsay Stirling*	*Snow Waltz*

Little Jack Frost, Get Lost

Al Stillman & Seger Ellis   1948

Seger Ellis - With Dixie Dons and Orchestra   Single (1948)

Little Jack Frost get lost. You don't do a thing except make our feet cold and freeze up the ground. You turn off the heat in lover's lane.

a	1977	Bing Crosby (feat. Peggy Lee)	The Voice of Christmas - The Complete Decca Songbook

Looks Like a Cold, Cold Winter

Jack Fulton, Caesar Petrillo & Al Goering   **1950**

Bing Crosby   Single (1950)

"B" side of "A Marshmallow World."

Looks like a cold, cold winter, but it doesn't matter because we've got each other, and our hearts are aglow.

Ingrid Michaelson rejuvenated this old song in 2018, surpassing, in my opinion, the original. Her version actually "swings" more, recreating a "Big Band" sound of the 40s excellently.

a	1977	Bing Crosby & The Andrew Sisters	A Merry Christmas with Bing Crosby & The Andrew Sisters
b	2018	Ingrid Michaelson	Ingrid Michaelson's Songs for the Season
c	2020	B + K	Four Christmas Songs
d	2020	Gold Baby	Single

A Lovely Way to Spend Christmas

Harold Adamson & Jimmy McHugh   **1944**

Frank Sinatra   Single (as A Lovely Way to Spend an Evening) (1944)

Song is a re-branding of "A Lovely Way to Spend an Evening."

a	2008	Kristin Chenoweth, et al	A Lovely Way to Spend Christmas

(The) Man with the Bag (AKA Everyone's Waiting' for the Man with the Bag)

Dudley Brooks, Irving Taylor, & Hal Stanley   **1950**

Kay Starr with Orchestra conducted   Single (1950) by Frank DeVol

The "man with a bag" is of course Santa.

Song (b) is jazz, and an excellent rendition of this song. The most mellow of the songs below is (d), by She and Him. *"She and Him" are Zooey Deschanel (vocals, piano, ukulele) and M. Ward (guitar, production).*

a	2002	Lee Ann Womack	The Season for Romance
b	2005	Jane Monheit	The Season
c	2012	Black Prairie	Holidays Rule
d	2016	She & Him	Christmas Party
e	2018	Jessie J	This Christmas Day

(A) Marshmallow World (AKA It's a Marshmallow World)

Carl Sigman & Peter De Rose   1949

Bing Crosby with Lee Gordon Singers and Sonny Burke and His Orchestra   Single (1950)

The snow makes it seem like a marshmallow world.

Darlene Love's (a) and Dean Martin's (c) renditions are probably the most popular versions, though Francesca Battistelli's (e) energetic rendition is also very popular. Christina Perri's (i) rendition is adorable—she has such a gentle voice.

a	1963	Darlene Love	A Christmas Gift for You from Phil Spector
b	1964	Brenda Lee	A Rockin' Christmas with Brenda Lee
c	1966	Dean Martin	The Dean Martin Christmas Album
d	1977	Bing Crosby	Bing Crosby - The Voice of Christmas - The Complete Decca Christmas Songbook
e	2012	Francesca Battistelli	This Christmas
f	2016	She & Him	Christmas Party
g	2018	Ingrid Michaelson	Ingrid Michaelson's Songs for the Season
h	2022	Sasha Estefan-Coppola	Estefan Family Christmas
i	2023	Christina Perri	Songs for Christmas

Mele Kalikimaka

R. Alex Anderson   **1949**

Bing Crosby and Andrews Sisters   Single (1950)
with Vic Schoen and His Orchestra

"B" side of "Poppa Santa Claus." The author, from Hawaii, stated that "My stenographer at Vonn Hamm-Young told me that there was no Hawaiian Christmas song, and that was inspiration enough." At Cornell, he studied electrical and mechanical engineering and was a member of the Cornell University Glee Club. Despite lacking formal training as a composer, he wrote many songs as a Cornell student, and later on, after he served in WWI. In 1998 Anderson was inducted into the Hawaiian Music Hall of Fame. He died on May 29, 1995, a week short of his 101st birthday.[60]

Here the best rendition is the original, but Ingrid Michaelson's (a) rendition is also very good.

a	2018	Ingrid Michaelson, Allie Moss & Bess Rogers	Ingrid Michaelson's Songs for the Season

Merry Christmas

Fred Spielman & Janice Torre   **1949**

Judy Garland   Merry Christmas - M-G-M Stars
                                                                      (1952)

Sweet song wishing all to have a merry, merry Christmas with presents you want and friends near you. From the movie *In the Good Old Summertime* (1949).

a	2005	Bette Midler	Cool Yule

Nigh Bethlehem

Alfred Burt   **1947**

The Singers Unlimited   *Christmas* (1972)

Story of the first Christmas, with an oft-repeated refrain of "Noel, Noel, Noel." Alfred Burt (1920-54) was an American jazz musician who is best known for composing the music for fifteen Christmas carols between 1942 and 1954. Only one of the carols was performed in public outside his immediate family circle during his lifetime. He sent the carols with lyric and music as Christmas cards to friends and family.

Parade of the Wooden Soldiers

Ballard MacDonald & Leon Jessel   **1905**

International Novelty Orchestra (Nathaniel Shilkret)   Single (1922)

This sprightly march was originally written as a solo piano piece in 1897 by the German composer Leon Jessel, though it was then titled "Parade of the Tin Soldiers." In 1905, Jessel orchestrated the work, and it became a popular favorite worldwide. Sousa's band played it, and with a name change to "Parade of the Wooden Soldiers" it was subsequently used in vaudeville routines, Broadway shows, films, and cartoons, and was published in many different arrangements.

Since 1933, the Radio City Music Hall Rockettes have marched to this tune in their Christmas Spectacular. The renowned American composer and pops orchestrator Morton Gould worked as staff pianist at Radio City Music Hall at that time, and later made his own colorful orchestral arrangement, heard in this concert. With that Christmas connection, and the charming fantasy-like quality of the music, "Parade of the Wooden Soldiers" has become a beloved children's Christmas tradition.[61]

Note that this is a different song than "March of the Toys," which appeared in the 1934 film *Babes in Toyland*, more popularly known as *March of the Wooden Soldiers*. That song is from an operetta the film is based on, of the same name, *Babes in Toyland*.

For a traditional, Instrumental version see (a). For an early 60s rock version that you usually hear on the radio at Christmastime, see (b).

a	1959	*Boston Pops Orchestra - Arthur Fiedler, Conductor*	*Pops Christmas Party*
b	1963	The Crystals	A Christmas Gift for You from Phil Spector

Ring, Christmas Bells

Minna Louise Hohman   **1944**

As "Carol of the Bells": Hugo Winterhalter's Orchestra and Chorus (1953)
Examples of song as "Ring, Christmas Bells" are by Frank DeVol and His Rainbow Strings (1960) and Ray Conniff (1962)

As "Carol of the Bells": *Christmas Magic* (1953)
As "Ring, Christmas Bells": *The Old Sweet Songs of Christmas* (Devol, 1960) and *We Wish You a Merry Christmas* (Conniff, 1962)

English-language variant of "Carol of the Bells" featuring nativity-based lyrics. Most renditions with chorus of "Carol of the Bells" heard in the US are really "Ring, Christmas Bells," as they contain the nativity-based lyrics. Instrumentals of both songs are the same.

Rocking AKA Rocking Carol AKA Rocking Little Jesus AKA Little Jesus, Sweetly Sleep

Percy Dearmer, translated into English from a traditional Czech carol　　　　**1928**

Petula Clark　　　　*A Christmas Carol* (1958)

Based on the traditional Czech carol *Hajej, nyne*, this is basically a lullaby to Jesus sung while rocking his cradle. There are some alternative copyrighted words by Christopher Massey.[62]

a	1982	Julie Andrews	Christmas with Julie Andrews
b	1989	Olivia Newton-John	Warm and Tender
c	1998	Shawn Colvin	Holiday Songs and Lullabies
d	2010	Aled Jones	Christmas Gold

Rudolph the Red-Nosed Reindeer

Johnny Marks　　　　**1949**

Gene Autry and The Pinafores with Orchestral Accompaniment　　　　Single (1949)

Ten years before this song was penned, in 1939, the character of Rudolf was created by Robert L. May. May was a copyrighter for Montgomery Ward in Chicago, which operated a chain of department stores. His superiors asked for a Christmas story that they could give away to shoppers as a promotional gimmick. Montgomery Ward had, in the past, purchased coloring books that they gave away at Christmastime. They wanted to give away a booklet of their own.

May drew in part on the story of "The Ugly Duckling" and his own background of being bullied because he had been shy and small. He came up with a character that would be ostracized by his own kind because of a physical abnormality—a glowing red nose. He wrote the story of Rudolf in verse and tried it out on his daughter Barbara. She was thrilled with the story, but, because of the red nose, his boss was concerned that the character would be associated with drunkards, certainly not suitable for a Christmas story. May came up with the idea to have a friend in the art department sketch some deer at a zoo—adding to them glowing red noses. That appeased his boss, and the story was approved. Montgomery Ward distributed 2.4 million copies of the booklet in 1939, and though WWII's paper shortages curtailed printing for the next several years, a total of 6 million copies were sold by 1946.

Since May had created the story when employed by Montgomery Ward, he received no royalties. Unfortunately, May's wife had died, and he was deeply in debt with medical bills. He persuaded the corporate president of Montgomery Ward, Sewell Avery, to turn the copyright over to him in January 1947.

"Rudolf" was printed commercially that year and shown in theaters as a short cartoon in 1948. May's sister Margaret's husband, Johnny Marks, a songwriter and radio producer, wrote the song and got famous singing cowboy Gene Autry to record it in 1949. It sold two million copies that year, becoming the best-selling song, just behind "White Christmas." In 1964, a stop-motion animated Rudolf would appear in a Christmas special created by Rankin-Bass with songs by Marks.

There are differences between the song and the original story. In the story, Rudolf was not a reindeer at the North Pole with Santa. Santa "discovered" him as he delivered presents to his house. Worried by thickening fog, he asked Rudolf to lead his team.[63] As they say, the rest "went down in history."

Song (d) is early 60s Rock 'n Roll, (h) is New Age, and (m) is a cappella.

a	1953	Guy Lombardo & His Royal Canadians	Jingle Bells
b	1959	Dean Martin	Dino's Christmas
c	1961	Mitch Miller	Holiday Sing Along with Mitch
d	1963	The Crystals	A Christmas Gift for You from Phil Spector
e	1964	Burl Ives	Rudolph the Red-Nosed Reindeer (Original 1964 TV Soundtrack)
f	1965	Burl Ives	Have a Holly Jolly Christmas
g	1988	*Arthur Fiedler & Boston Pops Orchestra*	*I Love Classical Christmas*

h	1995	*Mannheim Steam-roller*	*Christmas in the Aire*
i	2004	Don Mclean	Stars Came Out for Christmas - Special Edition I
j	2008	*101 Strings Orchestra*	*101 Strings Orchestra - 30 Greatest Orchestral Holiday Favorites*
k	2018	Jessie J	This Christmas Day
l	2020	Francesca Battistelli	This Christmas
m	2020	Pentatonix	We Need a Little Christmas
n	2023	Christina Perri	Songs for Christmas

Santa Claus Is Comin' To Town

J. Fred Coots & Haven Gillespie   **1933**

Harry Reser and His Orchestra   Single (1934)

The song was written in October 1933 by Haven Gillespie and J. Fred Coots, reportedly on a New York subway car while traveling to a music publisher's office. Gillespie, known for his children songwriting talent and charged with Coots to come up with a children's tune, jotted the melody and the lyrics down on an envelope before reaching the publisher's office. They were frustrated, however, at their inability to get it recorded and sold. Record labels thought the appeal too narrow to be successful.

Fortunately, Eddie Cantor, a well-known comedian in the 1930s, decided to sing the song for his radio audience in 1934. Cantor sang it live in a performance that was never recorded. The song proved a hit, and it was recorded later by Tom Stacks in a memorable arrangement by Harry Reser and his Orchestra.

The song became the big hit of Christmas 1934—radio audiences went wild for the song and requests for sheet music were off the charts. What followed from Cantor's radio show would eventually make a millionaire of Haven Gillespie.

A "swinging" version of the song by Perry Como in the mid-1940s was popular and kept it at the forefront of Christmas celebration into the 1950s. Through the 1950s and 1960s the song kept coming back. It was recorded, it seemed, by nearly everyone. Elvis, Frank Sinatra, Dean Martin, Johnny Mathis, Andy Williams, Sammy Davis Jr and scores of others took it on and made it their own. It never fell from the Christmas spotlight.[64]

In 1975, Bruce Springsteen was on tour for his breakthrough third album, *Born to Run.* After selling out a string of showcase concerts at Manhattan's buzziest venue, The Bottom Line, a concert was arranged for Long Island at C. W. Post College (currently, the C. W. Post Campus of Long Island University) in Brookville on December 12, 1975. Specifically, the concert would take place in the building that preceded the current Tilles Center for the Performing Arts. The venue was called the Concert Hall, nicknamed the Dome because of the circular-shaped ceiling.

It was sold out.

People waited on line starting at 1 PM for an 8 PM show, even though a massive snowstorm had hit Long Island with the temperature dropping to 12 degrees. "Santa Claus Is Comin' to Town" came as the second song of the encore and took the crowd by surprise. Springsteen's rendition was based on the arrangement producer Phil Spector had the Crystals record on his 1963 holiday album, *A Christmas Gift for You from Phil Spector.*

Fortunately, it was recorded. The song was initially released to FM radio stations in 1976 and instantly went into heavy rotation every holiday season. But it wasn't sold in stores at first; it could only be heard on the radio. In 1981, "Santa Claus Is Comin' to Town" ended up on the Christmas compilation, *In Harmony 2*, and was released as a single. In 1985, the song was rereleased as the B-side to Springsteen's hit, "My Hometown."[65]

Many interpretations of this classic are below. Songs (j) and (x) are jazz. Song (ae) is Celtic New Age. Song (k) is very popular during the holiday season, utilizing Phil Spector's "Wall of Sound," as are all the songs in his album A Christmas Gift for You from Phil Spector.

a	1943	Bing Crosby & The Andrews Sisters with Vic Schoen and His Orchestra	Single
b	1946	Perry Como and The Satisfiers with Russ Case and His Orchestra	Perry Como Sings Merry Christmas Music
c	1948	Frank Sinatra	Christmas Songs by Sinatra
d	1950	Eddy Arnold	Single ("B" Side of "White Christmas")
e	1953	Guy Lombardo & His Royal Canadians	Jingle Bells
f	1959	Ray Conniff	Christmas with Conniff
g	1959	Perry Como with Mitchell Ayres and His Orchestra and The Ray Charles Singers	Season's Greetings from Perry Como
h	1961	Alvin & The Chipmunks	Chipmunks Christmas

i	1961	Mitch Miller	Holiday Sing Along with Mitch
j	1961	*Ramsey Lewis Trio*	*Sound of Christmas*
k	1963	The Crystals	A Christmas Gift for You from Phil Spector
l	1964	The Beach Boys	The Beach Boys' Christmas Album
m	1964	Jo Stafford	Joyful Season
n	1964	Brenda Lee	A Rockin' Christmas with Brenda Lee
o	1965	Burl Ives	Have a Holly Jolly Christmas
p	1968	The Archies	The Archies Christmas Album
q	1968	Tony Bennett	Snowfall: The Tony Bennett Christmas Album
r	1970	Jackson 5	Jackson 5 Christmas Album
s	1970	Jose Feliciano	Feliz Navidad
t	1978	The Carpenters	Christmas Portrait
u	1981	Bruce Springsteen	Single
v	1992	Neil Diamond	The Christmas Album
w	1992	The Manhattan Transfer	The Christmas Album
x	2005	Diana Krall	Christmas Songs
y	2008	Faith Hill	Joy to the World
z	2011	Michael Bublé	Christmas
aa	2012	Colbie Caillat	Christmas in the Sand
ab	2012	Celtic Woman	The Best of Christmas
ac	2012	Rod Stewart	Merry Christmas, Baby
ad	2012	Richard Marx (Duet with Sara Nemetz)	Christmas Spirit
ae	2015	Celtic Angels	New Age Christmas
af	2016	John Farnham & Olivia Newton-John	Friends for Christmas
ag	2016	Kylie Minogue (feat. Frank Sinatra)	Kylie Christmas
ah	2018	Jessie J	This Christmas Day
ai	2018	Martina McBride	It's the Holiday Season
aj	2019	Delta Spirit	A Dualtone Christmas

Silver Bells

Ray Evans (lyrics) & Jay Livingston (music)   1950

Bing Crosby & Carol Richards   Single (1950)

Though the song was initially written for the movie *The Lemon Drop Kid*, and filmed in that movie during the summer of 1950, Crosby & Richards' version, recorded later that summer, was the first version heard by the public as the film wasn't released until spring of 1951. In the movie, it is sung by Bob Hope and Marilyn Maxwell, in an expertly choreographed scene[66] that has them sing it as they walk through a very busy street, with passersby hustling all around them and some singing along. Jay Livingston stated the following in *American Songwriter Magazine*, July–August 1988: "We wrote a song called 'Tinkle Bell,' about the tinkly bells you hear at Christmas from the Santa Clauses and the Salvation Army people. We said, 'This is it, this will work for the picture,' so I took it home and played it for my wife. She said, 'You wrote a song called "Tinkle Bell"? Don't you know that word has a bathroom connotation?' So I went back to Ray [Evans] the next day and told him we had to throw the song out, and we did."

Songwriters Ray Evans & Jay Livingston were a very successful team. Ray Evans & Jay Livingston's credits include writing "Buttons and Bows" (1947), which won them their first Oscar; "Mona Lisa" (1950), which sold a million records for Nat King Cole, and won the pair a second Best Song Oscar; and the song "Que Sera, Sera (Whatever Will Be, Will Be)," featured in the movie *The Man Who Knew Too Much* (1956), which won them a third Oscar. They also wrote popular TV themes for shows including *Bonanza* and *Mister Ed*, the latter of which Livingston sang.

It is difficult to make this song other than pleasant and beautiful. The following are all that way, with one exception: (aa). William Shatner was a great starship captain but his "singing" leaves much to be desired. The song is worth it to listen, though, for its outrageousness and Shatner being partnered with Ian Anderson of Procol Harum.

All the Instrumentals below are beautiful. There are two New Age renditions, (o) and (q). Even though I am a great Mannheim Steamroller (q) fan, in my opinion David Arkenstone (o) provides a prettier New Age version. I was surprised to find (x), (ad) and (ae) with versions of this song, as I never associated 80s New Wave sensations (Belinda Carlisle was in the Go-Go's in the 80s) singing this song or any Christmas song, for that matter. Speaking of celebrities of song from around that period, Rod Stewart provides us with (w).

Song (d) is sung in a medley with "Jingle Bells" and song (j) is sung in a medley with "Little Christmas Tree Waltz."

Song (r) has a preamble that starts with "Christmas makes you feel emotional…" that comes from the song that it is performed in The Lemon Drop Kid, *though in the movie it is performed in the middle of the song. This preamble is not performed in the original release, before the movie. A beautiful instrumental version of this preamble is performed in (s).*

My personal favorite, and a favorite of many radio stations is (i)—by The Supremes. Simply beautiful.

a	1958	Ray Conniff	Christmas with Conniff

b	1958	Johnny Mathis (with Percy Faith)	The Essential Percy Faith - The Christmas Recordings
c	1959	Pat Boone	White Christmas
d	1960	*Frank DeVol and His Rainbow Strings*	*The Old Sweet Songs of Christmas*
e	1961	Mitch Miller	Holiday Sing Along with Mitch
f	1964	Brenda Lee	Merry Christmas from Brenda Lee
g	1964	Jo Stafford	Joyful Season
h	1965	Burl Ives	Have a Holly Jolly Christmas
i	1965	The Supremes	Merry Christmas
j	1965	Living Voices	The Little Drummer Boy
k	1966	Dean Martin	The Dean Martin Christmas Album
l	1966	The New Christy Minstrels	Columbia Christmas Collection ('63-'66)
m	1968	Perry Como with The Ray Charles Singers	The Perry Como Christmas Album
n	1994	*Kenny G*	*The Holiday Album*
o	1995	*David Arkenstone*	*The Best of Narada Christmas*
p	1998	Vince Gill	Breath of Heaven: A Christmas Collection
q	2001	*Mannheim Steam-roller*	*Christmas Extraordinaire*
r	2002	America	Holiday Harmony
s	2008	*101 Strings Or-chestra*	*The Classic Christmas Songs*
t	2011	Michael Bublé (feat. Naturally 7)	Christmas
u	2012	Colbie Caillat	Christmas in the Sand
v	2012	Lady A	On This Winter's Night
w	2012	Rod Stewart	Merry Christmas, Baby
x	2013	Erasure	Snow Globe
y	2016	Sarah McLachlan	Wonderland
z	2017	Elvis Presley & The Royal Philharmon-ic Orchestra	Christmas with Elvis & The Royal Philharmon-ic Orchestra
aa	2018	William Shatner (feat. Ian Ander-son)	Shatner Claus
ab	2019	Lea Michelle	Christmas in the City
ac	2019	Marc Martel, Amy Grant & Michael W. Smith	Single
ad	2021	Billy Idol	Happy Holidays

ae	2022	Belinda Carlisle	Single
af	2022	*Boston Pops Orchestra -& John Williams*	*Christmas Collection*

Sleigh Ride (AKA Sleighride)

Instrumental: Leroy Anderson
Lyrics: Mitchell Parish

Instrumental: 1949
With Lyrics: 1950

Instrumental: Boston Pops Orchestra (Arthur Fielder conducting)
Vocal: The Andrew Sisters

Instrumental: Single (1949)
Vocal: Single (1950)

In Leroy Anderson's own words: "'Sleigh Ride' was one of the first things I wrote when I got out of the Army and moved up here to Woodbury, Connecticut. Actually, I first came here in 1946; you may remember there was a housing shortage then, and my mother-in-law was living up here, had a cottage that was vacant, so since we had no other place to go, we packed our 14-month old daughter, plus the upright piano, and came on up here to Woodbury, and during that first summer that we were here, I started 'Fiddle-Faddle.' I didn't finish that until the following winter, and 'Sleigh Ride' and 'Serenata.' And 'Sleigh Ride,' I remember, was just an idea because, it was just a pictorial thing, it wasn't necessarily Christmas music, and it was written during the heat wave.

"I had felt that the original theme of 'Sleigh Ride' was not strong enough to start the number but would make a good middle section. I finally worked out a satisfactory main theme, introduction and coda and finished the orchestra score on February 10, 1948. 'Sleigh Ride' was first performed on May 4, 1948, in Symphony Hall, Boston as an extra at a Pops concert conducted by Arthur Fiedler."

Mills Music suggested to Leroy that a lyricist be hired to write lyrics for "Sleigh Ride." The publisher thought that lyrics would help to make the piece more popular. Mitchell Parish had written the lyrics for "Stardust" and other songs. He had a reputation for being able to write very good lyrics for an existing composition. Normally a lyricist would collaborate with the composer and often would choose the title. Not in this case. Leroy was impressed with Mitchell Parish and was satisfied that the lyrics that Parish had written were good.

ASCAP, the American Society of Composers, Authors and Publishers, named "Sleigh Ride" the most popular piece of Christmas music in the USA in 2009, 2010, 2011, 2012, 2015 and again in 2021. Leroy Anderson's original recording of "Sleigh Ride" was the version most often played in 2010 based on performance data tracked by the airplay monitoring service, *Mediaguide*, from over 2,500 radio stations nationwide. "Sleigh Ride" was aired 174,758 times in 2010, making it the most-played holiday song on radio for the second year in a row. "Sleigh Ride" was played

118,918 times during the same period in 2009. Also, over 8,000 individual record-ings of "Sleigh Ride" have been made worldwide in all styles of music since 1948.[67]

Leroy Anderson (1908-1975) was the composer of many other pieces. From the author's book, *Life in the 60s: The True Story* (2019), pg. 65: "In NYC, Eyewitness News premiered on ABC in 1968. Its opening theme song was a very busy instru-mental from the 1967 movie *Cool Hand Luke* by Lalo Shifrin and its closing theme song was the beautiful, sleepy instrumental 'Forgotten Dreams' (1954), by Leroy Anderson, who also wrote 'The Syncopated Clock' (1945), used for 25 years as the intro to The Late Show, and the great Christmas classic 'Sleigh Ride' (1948)."

Another famous song of his was "The Typewriter" (1950), which features an actual typewriter as a percussion instrument. Jerry Lewis performs this song on a typewrit-er in his movie *Who's Minding the Store* (1963).

I love the many Instrumentals of this song, particularly the one performed by its creator, Leroy Anderson. That's not to say I dislike the vocal ones. Song (g) is very popular as it is from the famous Phil Spector album. Songs (q) and (r) are jazz, while (x) is a cappella.

a	1952	*Leroy Anderson*	*A Leroy Anderson Christmas*
b	1958	Johnny Mathis (with Percy Faith)	The Essential Percy Faith - The Christmas Recordings
c	1959	*Arthur Fiedler & Boston Pops Or-chestra*	*Pops Christmas Party*
d	1961	Mitch Miller	Holiday Sing Along with Mitch
e	1961	*Ramsey Lewis Trio*	*Sound of Christmas*
f	1963	*Bert Kaempfert*	*Christmas Wonderland*
g	1963	The Ronettes	A Christmas Gift for You from Phil Spector
h	1965	*The Ventures*	*The Ventures' Christmas Album*
i	1968	The Archies	The Archies Christmas Album
j	1975	The Salsoul Or-chestra	Christmas Jollies
k	1978	The Carpenters	Christmas Portrait
l	1993	Harry Connick, Jr.	When My Heart Finds Christmas
m	1994	Neil Diamond	A Cherry Cherry Christmas
n	1999	*Kenny G*	*The Classic Christmas Album*
o	1999	Natalie Cole (feat. London Symphony Orchestra)	The Magic of Christmas
p	2002	America	Holiday Harmony
q	2005	Diana Krall & The Clayton-Hamilton Jazz Orchestra	Christmas Songs

r	2005	Jane Monheit	The Season
s	2007	Juice Newton	The Gift of Christmas
t	2008	*101 Strings Orchestra*	*The Classic Christmas Songs*
u	2011	Carole King	A Holiday Carole
v	2012	Fun.	Holidays Rule
w	2013	Human Nature (feat. Jessica Mauboy)	The Christmas Album
x	2014	Pentatonix	That's Christmas to Me
y	2019	Bing Crosby & London Symphony Orchestra	Bing at Christmas
z	2019	Celtic Woman	The Magic of Christmas
aa	2019	Idina Menzel	Christmas: A Season of Love
ab	2020	Francesca Battistelli	This Christmas
ac	2022	Lindsay Stirling	Snow Waltz
ad	2023	Christina Perri	Songs for Christmas
ae	2023	Seth McFarlane &. Liz Gillies	We Wish You the Merriest

Snowfall

Claude Thornhill (Music). Lyrics added later by Ruth Thornhill   **1941**

Instrumental: Claude Thornhill and His Orchestra
Vocal: The Ray Charles Singers

Instrumental: Single (1941)
Vocal: *Winter Wonderland* (1956)

Beautiful, but simple song, lyrically, about snowfall.

a	1992	The Manhattan Transfer	The Christmas Album

Snowy White Snow and Jingle Bells

Dennis Berger, Harold Irving, Johnny Sheridan, Ralph Ruvin & Billy Reid   **1949**

Dorothy Squires with Orchestra conducted by Billy Reid

Single (1949)

Nice upbeat, innocent song.

a	1950	Toni Harper	50s Christmas Classics

Some Children See Him

Whila Hutson (Lyrics) and Alfred
Burt (music)

Lyrics: 1949
Music: 1951

"Tennessee" Ernie Ford

The Star Carol - "Tennessee" Ernie
Ford Sings His Christmas Favorites
(1958)

Whila Hutson, a close friend of Alfred Burt's family, provided lyrics for carols that Alfred would write the music for, after his father Bates—who had previously written lyrics—passed away. In 1949, she rode in a car with Alfred's wife Anne and their daughter Diane. According to Diane, Whila noticed that Anne "even saw Jesus as a little child would see him." Whila "realized that if she were a child in Africa, she would see the world much differently...an African child would see Jesus as a black man. Then she realized a Chinese child would see the Son of God with almond eyes, while an Indian child would see Jesus with dark hair and brown skin. As she never had before, Wihla grasped the concept of God's being a universal spirit...Wihla eased the car to the side of the road." All the lyrics were written on that roadside but were not set to music by Alfred until 1951.[68]

Sweet song, as an Instrumental or Vocal.

Sixpence None the Richer (b) is best known for their hits "Kiss Me" (1998) and "There She Goes" (1999).

a	2001	*Mannheim Steam-roller*	*Christmas Extraordinaire*
b	2008	Sixpence None the Richer	The Dawn of Grace

There Is No Christmas Like a Home Christmas

Carl Sigman & Mickey Addy

1950

Perry Como with Orchestra and
Chorus conducted by Mitchell Ayres

Single (1950)

Not to be confused with Perry Como's much more successful song "(There's No Place Like) Home for the Holidays" released just four years later, Perry Como pretty much "owns" this song. There are only three other known vocal versions (including one that is part of a medley) and two Instrumentals.[69]

Toyland

Victor Herbert & Glen Mac-Donough   **1903**

Corinne Morgan with The Haydn Quartet   Single (1904)

First performed live in the operetta *Babes in Toyland* (1903). The operetta's critics spoke of "wondrous stagecraft, the elaborate scenery and astonishing special effects, splendid costumes, beautiful girls, and above all, that superlative score by Herbert which far outshone the songs for 'The Wizard of Oz,' the hugely popular extravaganza that immediately preceded and inspired 'Babes' at Columbus Circle's Majestic Theatre." Though a smash hit in New York and on tour, it didn't quite financially surpass "Oz" because, it has been suggested, of its "impossibly complicated" story.[70]

This was made into a vehicle for Laurel and Hardy, with major differences, in 1934, and is often advertised as *March of the Wooden Soldiers*.

Anyone who has been a regular watcher of Bonanza, Little House on the Prairie *or* Highway to Heaven *will instantly recognize David Rose's (b) music in this song. Interestingly, he also wrote the bawdy song known as "The Stripper."*

a	1963	*Living Strings*	*The Sound of Christmas*
b	1968	*David Rose*	*The David Rose Christmas Album*
c	1986	Johnny Mathis	Christmas Eve with Johnny Mathis

The Twelve Days of Christmas

Frederic Austin   **1909**

Fred Waring and His Pennsylvanians   Single (1947) - "B" side of "White Christmas"

The 12 days of Christmas is the period in Christian theology that marks the span between the birth of Christ and the coming of the Magi, the three wise men. It begins on December 25 (Christmas) and runs through January 6 (the Epiphany, sometimes also called Three Kings' Day). The earliest known version first appeared in a 1780 children's book called *Mirth With-out Mischief.* Some historians think the song could be French in origin, but most agree it was designed as a "memory and forfeits" game, in which singers tested their recall of the lyrics and had to award their opponents a "forfeit"—a kiss or a favor of some kind—if they made a mistake. The lyrics varied over time, but the lyrics and music we know today come from an English composer named Frederic Austin, in 1909. A popular theory is that the lyrics to "The 12 Days of Christmas" are coded references to Christianity; it incorrectly posits that the song was written to help Christians learn and pass on the tenets of their faith while avoiding persecution.[71]

If ever there was a list of "must-have" songs for Christmas, this would be near the top. Sure, it's repetitive and the "gifts" make no sense, but it is an icon of Christmas. You would think that a non-vocal version of this song would make no sense, but (g) did it. There are simple sung versions (but nonetheless good): (a), (b), (d), (e) and (h), but also classy versions, like (c) and (f).

a	1961	Mitch Miller	Holiday Sing Along with Mitch
b	1962	Ray Conniff	We Wish You a Merry Christmas
c	1963	The Tabernacle Choir of Temple Square, New York Philharmonic & Leonard Bernstein	I Love Classical Christmas
d	1964	Burl Ives	The Very Best of Burl Ives Christmas
e	1979	John Denver & The Muppets	A Christmas Together
f	1999	Natalie Cole (feat. London Symphony Orchestra)	The Magic of Christmas
g	2002	*101 Strings Orchestra*	*101 Strings Orchestra - 30 Greatest Orchestral Holiday Favorites*
h	2019	Bing Crosby & The Andrew Sisters	Bing at Christmas

(We) Wish You a Merry Christmas

Arthur Sydney Warrell (1935 arrangement)

1935 (first documented arrangement of song as known today)

The Weavers

Single (Sept. 1951) - "B" side of "One for the Little Bitty Baby" *We Wish You a Merry Christmas* (Nov. 1951)

Traditional English West Country tune, possibly from Somerset. May have originated in Tudor times (1485 to 1603). Older records of songs like it are nothing like the one known today. Warrell was appointed Lecturer in Music at Bristol University in 1909, played the organ at numerous churches, conducted the Bristol Royal Orpheus Glee Society and in later years made a number of broadcasts on the BBC Radio. He first performed it at a Christmas concert at the University Great Hall on Friday December 6, 1935, though in this first version it was "I" wish you a merry Christmas, not "we."[72]

There are a number of different kinds of music here: (a) is jazz; (b) is children's; (d) is early Rock 'n Roll; (g) is Celtic New Age; (i) is Celtic; and (k) is a cappella.

a	1960	*The Kingston Trio*	*The Last Month of the Year*
b	1961	Alvin & The Chipmunks	Chipmunks Christmas
c	1962	The Everly Brothers	Christmas with the Everly Brothers and the Boystown Choir
d	1965	*The Ventures*	*The Ventures' Christmas Album*
e	1972	Eugene Ormandy, The Philadelphia Orchestra, The Philadelphia Orchestra Chorus & Robert Page	I Love Classical Christmas
f	1981	Tanglewood Festival Chorus, Boston Pops Orchestra & John Williams	Christmas Collection
g	2006	Enya	Amarantine (Christmas Edition)
h	2008	*101 Strings Orchestra*	*101 Strings Orchestra - 30 Greatest Orchestral Holiday Favorites*
i	2012	Celtic Woman	The Best of Christmas
j	2013	The Galway Christmas Singers	Family Christmas: Favorite Carols and Holiday Songs
k	2021	Pentatonix	Evergreen

Welsh Carol (Awake Were They Only)

Caradog Roberts   1928

First release unknown. There is a 2000 version by Linda Ronstadt

Appears in *A Merry Little Christmas* (2000)

Traditional Welsh carol.

What Are You Doing New Year's Eve?

Frank Loesser   **1947**

Margaret Whiting with Frank DeVol   Single (1947)
and His Orchestra

Lovers meet at Christmastime, and one daringly asks, "What are you doing New Year's Eve?" Loesser also wrote "Baby, It's Cold Outside."

Song (b) is jazz.

a	2002	Lee Ann Womack	The Season for Romance
b	2005	Diana Krall & The Clayton-Hamilton Jazz Orchestra	Christmas Songs
c	2018	Ingrid Michaelson	Ingrid Michaelson's Songs for the Season

When Santa Claus Gets Your Letter

Johnny Marks   **1950**

Gene Autry   Single (1950)

When Santa Claus gets your letter to ask for Christmas toys, he'll take a look in his good book he keeps for girls and boys. "B" side of "Frosty the Snowman." Johnny Marks wrote "Rudolf the Red-Nosed Reindeer."

Mr. Green Jeans & Captain Kangaroo (a) were the stars of The Captain Kangaroo Show, *which graced the TV airwaves for 29 years, 1955 to 1984. "Captain Kangaroo" was Bob Keeshan, who had also done a stint in* Howdy Doody, *as Clarabelle the Clown. Mr. Green Jeans was Hugh Brannum, vocalist, arranger, and composer, who had worked with Fred Waring & The Pennsylvanians, noted here in a number of Christmas song renditions. Bob Keeshan was as nice in true life as on TV, according to an associate of mine, who was adopted by a friend of Keeshan's, and visited their house often.*

a	1963	Mr. Green Jeans & Captain Kangaroo	Ultimate Christmas

White Christmas

Irving Berlin   **1940**

Bing Crosby with Ken Darby Singers   Single (1942)
and John Scott Trotter and His Or-
chestra

"White Christmas" was written in 1940 by Irving Berlin (1888-1989) for the 1942 movie *Holiday Inn* starring Bing Crosby and Fred Astaire. Berlin, an Eastern European immigrant by the real name of Israel Beilin, couldn't read or write music, yet composed continually, using his "musical secretary," Helmy Kresa, to pen the songs he wrote on the piano. Berlin had to write a song about each of the major holidays of the year. He did not have trouble with a song for Valentine's Day, "Be Careful, It's My Heart," and it was expected to be the hit song from the movie. Berlin, however, with an orthodox Jewish upbringing, found that writing a song about Christmas was the most challenging. He also wasn't fond of the day; his infant son had died in 1928 at Christmastime. Nonetheless, he was a very hard worker and pounded out the song. He introduced "White Christmas" to Kresa on January 8, 1940, proclaiming heartily, "I want you to take down a song I wrote over the weekend. Not only is it the best song I ever wrote, but it's also the best song anybody ever wrote." When Bing first heard Berlin audition "White Christmas" in 1941 he assured Irving that he had created a winner.

Bing Crosby introduced "White Christmas" to the public on his NBC radio show, the Kraft Music Hall, December 25, 1941. Apparently, no recording of this broadcast survived WWII. He then recorded the song for Decca on May 29, 1942, with the John Scott Trotter Orchestra. *Holiday Inn* was released in August 1942. It received the Oscar for best song of 1942.

By the end of WWII Bing's recording had become the biggest-selling single of all time. It hit the charts on Oct. 3, 1942, and rose to #1 on Oct. 31, where it stayed for an amazing 11 weeks. In the following years it hit the top 30 pop charts another 16 times, even topping the charts again in 1945 and Jan. 1947. The song remains Bing's best-selling recording, and the best-selling Christmas single of all-time. It is the world's most frequently recorded song. It has been recorded in Dutch, Yiddish, Japanese and even Swahili.

Bing's single of "White Christmas" sold more than 30 million copies worldwide and was recognized as the best-selling single in any music category for more than 50 years until 1998 when Elton John's tribute to Princess Diana, "Candle in the Wind," overtook it in a matter of months. Bing's recording of "White Christmas" has sold additional millions of copies as part of numerous albums, including his best-selling album *Merry Christmas*, which was released in 1949.

The most familiar version of "White Christmas" is not the one Crosby recorded in 1942, however. Bing was called back to the Decca studios on March 19, 1947, to re-record "White Christmas" because of damage to the 1942 master due to its frequent use.[73]

The success of the song led eventually to a movie based on the song. The movie *White Christmas* was released in 1954 and became the leading box-office draw of 1954.

Song (k) is a medley with "We Wish You a Merry Christmas."

As probably everyone would agree, this is Bing Crosby's song. Many have sung it, and sung it well, but no one exactly as Bing. When my mother emigrated from Austria in 1946, this was her favorite song.

As noted above, the song was written for Bing to sing in the 1942 musical Holiday Inn. *In that same year it was recorded for a single, with the Ken Darby Singers and John Scott Trotter and His Orchestra backing him up. Also as mentioned above, he re-recorded the song in 1947, trying to match his 1942 recording exactly as possible; this is the rendition we hear every year. In 1954, he sang it again, in the musical* White Christmas. *This rendition, which he sang with Danny Kaye, Peggy Lee and Trudy Stevens, was released that same year (c). In 2019, samples of his voice were included in a song that also features the a cappella band Pentatonix and orchestration from the London Symphony Orchestra. That rendition (br) is incredibly beautiful. Fortunately, there is a video[74] of that rendition, which is one of the most moving Christmas videos I have ever experienced.*

The original song included a spoken prelude that starts, "The sun is shining, the grass is green, the orange and palm trees sway..." in reference to the writer being in the non-Winter-like city of LA. Most artists skip this part, but a number of them include this prelude. Songs below that include it as a prelude are (t), (ab), (ao), (as), and (at); (n) uses it in the middle of the song. Celtic Woman (ay) uses opening bars from "Somewhere Over the Rainbow" as a prelude. Bobby Vinton (r) used the opening bars of "O Holy Night" as a prelude.

Frank Sinatra released his rendition in 1957 (d). That same year, he sang it with Bing on an episode of The Frank Sinatra Show, *aired on ABC in color (a rarity prior to 1966) on December 20, 1957[75]. This rendition was not released until 2004 (av).*

The Drifters (b) gave the song a more modern (at the time) beat in 1954. Some artists incorporated that beat: (bd), (bu), and, to a lesser extent, (bj).

There are two Rock versions below: (au) and (bo). The Moody Blues (au) ease more into it, starting with a traditional version; this is an excellent rendition.

Christina Perri has two versions: by herself (bx) and with Ingrid Michaelson (bp).

There is plenty more to be said of the great renditions below. But the best thing to do is to find them and listen. I enjoyed them all (except for (bq)—that's for laughs).

a	1953	Guy Lombardo & His Royal Canadians	Jingle Bells
b	1954	The Drifters	Single
c	1954	Bing Crosby, Danny Kaye, Peggy Lee and Trudy Stevens	Selections from Irving Berlin's White Christmas
d	1957	Frank Sinatra	A Jolly Christmas from Frank Sinatra
e	1957	Fred Waring & The Pennsylvanians	Now is the Caroling Season
f	1958	Johnny Mathis	Merry Christmas
g	1958	*Mantovani*	*Christmas Carols*
h	1959	Dean Martin	Dino's Christmas
i	1959	Pat Boone	White Christmas
j	1959	Perry Como with Mitchell Ayres and His Orchestra and The Ray Charles Singers	Season's Greetings from Perry Como
k	1960	*Frank DeVol and His Rainbow Strings*	*The Old Sweet Songs of Christmas*
l	1961	Mitch Miller	Holiday Sing Along with Mitch
m	1963	Andy Williams	The Andy Williams Christmas Album
n	1963	Darlene Love	A Christmas Gift for You from Phil Spector
o	1963	*Living Strings*	*The Sound of Christmas*
p	1964	The Beach Boys	The Beach Boys' Christmas Album
q	1964	Jo Stafford	Joyful Season
r	1964	Bobby Vinton	Kissin' Christmas: The Bobby Vinton Christmas Album
s	1965	Burl Ives	Have a Holly Jolly Christmas
t	1965	Eddie Fischer	Mary Christmas
u	1965	Peggy Lee	Happy Holiday
v	1965	The Supremes	Merry Christmas
w	1965	*The Ventures*	*The Ventures' Christmas Album*
x	1966	Dean Martin	The Dean Martin Christmas Album
y	1966	The Lettermen	For Christmas This Year
z	1966	The New Christy Minstrels	Columbia Christmas Collection ('63-'66)
aa	1966	Percy Faith	Christmas Is...
ab	1967	Barbra Streisand	A Christmas Album

ac	1967	*Os Santos*	*Natal Jovem*
ad	1968	Tony Bennett	Snowfall: The Tony Bennett Christmas Album
ae	1970	Jose Feliciano	Feliz Navidad
af	1981	Kenny Rogers	Christmas
ag	1983	Amy Grant	Tennessee Christmas
ah	1987	Air Supply	The Christmas Album
ai	1988	*Arthur Fiedler, Boston Pops Orchestra & Alfred Krips*	*I Love Classical Christmas*
aj	1992	Michael Bolton	Christmas Hits
ak	1993	David Foster (feat. Wynonna, BeBe Winans, CeCe Winans, Johnny Mathis, Natalie Cole, Michael Crawford, Vanessa Williams, Peabo Bryson, Roberta Flack, Tom Jones, Celine Dion & Tammy Wynette)	The Christmas Album
al	1994	*Kenny G*	*The Holiday Album*
am	1995	Roger Whittaker	The Christmas Song
an	1997	Louis Armstrong	Ella & Louis Christmas
ao	2000	Linda Ronstadt	Merry Little Christmas
ap	2001	*Mannheim Steamroller*	*Christmas Extraordinaire*
aq	2002	America	Holiday Harmony
ar	2002	Bright Eyes	A Christmas Album
as	2002	Lee Ann Womack	The Season for Romance
at	2003	Bette Midler	Cool Yule
au	2003	The Moody Blues	December
av	2004	Frank Sinatra with Bing Crosby	Frank Sinatra - The Christmas Collection
aw	2005	Diana Krall	Christmas Songs
ax	2005	(Unknown)	*A Most Excellent New Age Christmas*
ay	2006	Celtic Woman	A Christmas Celebration
az	2007	Josh Groban	Noel
ba	2008	*101 Strings Orchestra*	*101 Strings Orchestra - 30 Greatest Orchestral Holiday Favorites*

bb	2011	Scott Weiland	The Most Wonderful Time of the Year
bc	2011	Deana Martin (duet with Andy Williams)	White Christmas
bd	2011	Michael Bublé (Duet with Shania Twain)	Christmas
be	2013	Kelly Clarkson	Wrapped in Red
bf	2014	Idina Menzel	Holiday Wishes
bg	2014	Michael W. Smith (feat. Lady Antebellum)	The Spirit of Christmas
bh	2015	*Hamburg Radio Dance Orchestra*	*Family Christmas: Favorite Carols and Holiday Songs*
bi	2015	Celtic Angels	New Age Christmas - Relaxing Christmas Classics
bj	2016	John Farnham & Olivia Newton-John	Friends for Christmas
bk	2016	Sarah McLachlan	Wonderland
bl	2016	Pentatonix (feat. The Manhattan Transfer)	A Pentatonix Christmas
bm	2017	Elvis Presley & The Royal Philharmonic Orchestra	Christmas with Elvis & The Royal Philharmonic Orchestra
bn	2017	Sleeping At Last	Christmas Collection, Vol. 1
bo	2018	Eric Clapton	Happy Xmas
bp	2018	Ingrid Michaelson (feat. Christina Perri)	Ingrid Michaelson's Songs for the Season
bq	2018	William Shatner (feat. Judy Collins)	Shatner Claus
br	2019	Bing Crosby, Pentatonix & London Symphony Orchestra	Bing at Christmas
bs	2019	Lea Michelle (feat. Darren Criss)	Christmas in the City
bt	2019	Dean Martin & Royal Philharmonic Orchestra	Christmas with the Stars and the Royal Philharmonic Orchestra
bu	2020	Meghan Trainor (feat. Seth	A Very Trainor Christmas

		MacFarlane)	
bv	2021	Norah Jones	I Dream of Christmas
bw	2022	Josh Stone	Merry Christmas, Love
bx	2023	Christina Perri	Songs for Christmas

(I Love the) Winter Weather

Ted Shapiro   **1941**

Benny Goodman and His Orchestra   Single (1941)
- Vocal Chorus by Peggy Lee and
Art London

I love the winter weather because I've got my love to keep me warm.

Songs (a) and (c) are medleys with "I've Got My Love to Keep Me Warm," which is the perfect complementary song for this one. Song (c) is jazz.

a	1968	Tony Bennett	Snowfall: The Tony Bennett Christmas Album
b	2004	Vanessa Williams	Christmas with Vanessa Williams
c	2005	Jane Monheit	The Season

Winter Wonderland

Felix Bernard & Dick Smith   **1934**

Richard Himber and His Ritz-Carlton   Single (1934) - "B" side of "Were
Orchestra - Vocal Refrain by Joey   You Foolin'?"
Nash

Dick Smith, who wrote the lyrics to this song, was on a fast track as a professional songwriter when he contacted tuberculosis in 1931. Undaunted by his illness, he wrote the song while in a Sanitarium in 1934. He died the next year, one day short of his 34th birthday. Smith, who had graduated from Honesdale High School in Pennsylvania in 1920, showed a talent for writing songs and poetry from his boyhood days in school. He was born and raised at 922 Church Street, across from Honesdale's Central Park. His late sister Marjorie W. Smith claimed her brother was inspired by the beauty of the freshly fallen snow in the park. Like Dick Smith, Felix Bernard, who wrote the music, died young. He was 47 when he died in Los Angeles, California, on October 20, 1944.[76]

Guy Lombardo And His Royal Canadians took this song to the #2 spot on the Billboard charts the same year it was first recorded. 1946 recordings by the Andrews

Sisters and Perry Como established the song as a Yuletide favorite. According to the American Society of Composers, Authors and Publishers (ASCAP), in 2007 the 1987 Eurythmics version of this song topped the list of the most performed holiday songs for the previous five years.[77]

Song (h) is a medley with "Skater's Waltz." (l) is a medley with "Jingle Bells" and "Snow Bells." (q) is a medley with "Silver Bells." (s) is a medley with "Sleigh Ride." (am) is a medley with "Don't Worry, Be Happy." (au) is a medley with "Christmas / Baby Please Come Home."

There are a variety of different kinds of music here. (j) and (ab) are jazz. (k) is Rock 'n Roll. (t) and (aa) are New Wave. (y) is New Age; (am) is a cappella. (as) is farce.

a	1946	Perry Como and The Satisfiers with Russ Case and His Orchestra	Perry Como Sings Merry Christmas Music
b	1953	Guy Lombardo & His Royal Canadi-ans	Jingle Bells
c	1953	Rosemary Clooney with Paul Weston & His Orchestra	Single. Also, on *Christmas - 16 Most Requested Songs*
d	1958	Johnny Mathis (with Percy Faith)	The Essential Percy Faith - The Christmas Recordings
e	1959	Dean Martin	Dino's Christmas
f	1959	*Arthur Fiedler & Boston Pops Orchestra*	*I Love Classical Christmas*
g	1959	Perry Como with Mitchell Ayres and His Orchestra	Season's Greetings from Perry Como
h	1960	*Frank DeVol and His Rainbow Strings*	*The Old Sweet Songs of Christmas*
i	1961	Mitch Miller	Holiday Sing Along with Mitch
j	1961	*Ramsey Lewis Trio*	*Sound of Christmas*
k	1963	Darlene Love	A Christmas Gift for You from Phil Spector
l	1963	*Living Strings*	*The Sound of Christmas*
m	1964	Jo Stafford	Joyful Season
n	1965	Burl Ives	Have a Holly Jolly Christmas
o	1965	*The Ventures*	*The Ventures' Christmas Album*
p	1966	Dean Martin	The Dean Martin Christmas Album
q	1966	Henry Mancini	A Merry Mancini Christmas
r	1968	Tony Bennett	Snowfall: The Tony Bennett Christmas Album

s	1984	Dolly Parton	Once Upon a Christmas
t	1987	Eurythmics	A Very Special Christmas
u	1994	*Kenny G*	*The Holiday Album*
v	1994	Neil Diamond	A Cherry Cherry Christmas
w	1995	Roger Whittaker	The Christmas Song
x	1998	Vince Gill	Breath of Heaven: A Christmas Collection
y	2001	*Mannheim Steamroller*	*Christmas Extraordinaire*
z	2002	America	Holiday Harmony
aa	2005	Cocteau Twins	Lullabies to Violaine, Vol. 2
ab	2005	Diana Krall & The Clayton-Hamilton Jazz Orchestra	Christmas Songs
ac	2008	Faith Hill	Joy to the World
ad	2008	Kate Havnevik	The Hotel Café Presents...Winter Songs
ae	2008	*101 Strings Orchestra*	*101 Strings Orchestra - 30 Greatest Orchestral Holiday Favorites*
af	2011	Michael Bublé	Christmas
ag	2011	Scott Weiland	The Most Wonderful Time of the Year
ah	2011	Rick Faugno	Seasons Greetings - A Jersey Boys Christmas
ai	2012	Celtic Woman	The Best of Christmas
aj	2012	Colbie Caillat	Christmas in the Sand
ak	2012	Michael Bublé (feat. Rod Stewart)	Christmas
al	2013	Leona Lewis	Christmas, with Love
am	2014	Pentatonix (feat. Tory Kelly)	Pentatonix -The Greatest Christmas Hits
an	2016	Kylie Minogue	Kylie Christmas
ao	2016	Sarah McLachlan	Wonderland
ap	2017	*Herb Alpert*	*The Christmas Wish*
aq	2018	Ingrid Michaelson, Allie Moss & Hannah Winkler	Ingrid Michaelson's Songs for the Season
ar	2018	Martina McBride	It's the Holiday Season
as	2018	William Shatner (feat. Todd Rundgren & Artimus Pyle)	Shatner Claus
at	2019	Bing Crosby & London Symphony Orchestra	Bing at Christmas
au	2019	Idina Menzel	Christmas: A Season of Love
av	2021	Billy Idol	Happy Holidays
aw	2022	Josh Stone	Merry Christmas, Love

ax	2023	Laufey	A Very Laufey Holiday
ay	2023	Seth McFarlane &. Liz Gillies	We Wish You the Merriest

---

You're All I Want for Christmas

Glen Moore & Segar Ellis   1948

Frankie Laine and Carl Fischer's Orchestra

Single (1948) - "B" Side of "Tara Talara Tala"

The tune "Algiers Strut" is an old New Orleans jazz standard, most associated with Kid Thomas and his Algiers Stompers. In 1948, jazz musicians Glen Travis Moore and Seger Ellis put lyrics to the tune, re-titled it "You're All I Want for Christmas."[78]

A sweet, sentimental song.

a	1962	Frankie Avalon	Frankie Avalon's Christmas Album
b	1964	Al Martino	A Merry Christmas

3 Latter 20th Century (1951-2000)

The latter half of the 20th century saw a diverse and rich array of Christmas music emerge, blending traditional holiday themes with contemporary styles like rock, pop, soul, and jazz. Christmas music reflected the attitudes of the time wherein they were composed. There was massive change in this period, from the conservative 50s to the rebellious 60s and massive cultural change in the ensuing years.

In the seemingly innocent period 1951-1959, crooners from the first half of the century continued singing traditional hits with new singers following their example. Singing Cowboy Gene Autry, "riding" (pun intended) on his fortunate successes with Christmas tunes "Rudolf the Red-Nosed Reindeer" in 1949 and "Frosty the Snowman" in 1950, would release another Christmas song, "He'll Be Coming Down the Chimney (Like He Always Did Before)" in 1951. That same year, Bing Crosby released his rendition of "It's Beginning to Look a Lot Like Christmas," after Perry Como had released it earlier in the year. In 1954, Bing starred in the movie *White Christmas* and joined Danny Kaye, Peggy Lee and Trudy Stevens singing in the album released that same year called *Selections from Irving Berlin's White Christmas*. In 1956 Bing sang "I Heard the Bells on Christmas Day," based on the 19th century Henry Wadsworth Longfellow poem of the same name, with music by Johnny ("Rudolf the Red-Nosed Reindeer") Marks.

In 1954, Perry Como first sang his signature Christmas hit "(There's No Place Like) Home for the Holidays." In 1956, Harry Belafonte sang his big Christmas hit (and very beautifully) "Mary's (Little) Boy Child."

Frank Sinatra had a big hit with the beautiful song "(The) Christmas Waltz" in 1954. He included it in his fabulous 1957 Christmas album *A Jolly Christmas from Frank Sinatra*, which also included hits such as "Mistletoe and Holly" and his new rendition of "Have Yourself a Merry Little Christmas," the latter song already having been released by him in 1948, but for his *Jolly* album he wanted it to have a happier ending. He had the co-author of the song, Hugh Martin, change the lyric "we'll have to muddle through somehow" to "hang a shining star upon the highest bough." Most later singers (and there have been many) sing it "His" way.

Dean Martin released his Christmas album of the period, *Dino's Christmas*, in 1959. He did not sing any original songs, though some of them have become deeply associated with him: "Baby It's Cold Outside" (original from 1949), "I've Got My Love to Keep Me Warm" (original from 1937), and "Let It Snow" (original from 1945). He also provided memorable renditions of "Rudolf the Red-Nosed Reindeer," "White Christmas," and "Winter Wonderland."

Johnny Mathis released his first Christmas album in his period, his 1958 *Merry Christmas*. He would release (so far) six more Christmas albums in his career—two in the 60s, one in the 80s and three in the 21st century.

Elvis Presley, a powerhouse of hits in this period, released *Elvis' Christmas Album* in 1957. It included Christmas standards released before by other artists. One of them, not so well-known, was "Blue Christmas," originally performed by Doye O'Dell in a 1948 release. Elvis' version blew that rendition away, and his became a big hit, popular to this day. *Elvis' Christmas Album* is the best-selling Christmas album of all time, having sold more than 20 million copies worldwide.

There was a cornucopia of "Novelty Songs" in this period, performed by juveniles or cartoon characters. The hits included: "I Saw Mommy Kissing Santa Claus" by Jimmy Boyd, age 13, in 1952, for a short time banned by the Catholic Archdiocese of Boston; "I Want a Hippopotamus for Christmas" by Gayla Peevey, age 10, in 1953; "Nuthin' for Christmas" by Barry Gordon, age 6, in 1955; and "The Chipmunk Song (Christmas Don't Be Late)" by "Alvin and the Chipmunks" in 1958.

But also in this period "cooler" artists like Bobby Helms ("Jingle Bell Rock" – 1957), Chuck Berry ("Run Run Rudolf" – 1958) and Brenda Lee ("Rockin' Around the Christmas Tree" – 1958) belted out tunes that were different from before, introducing Rock 'n Roll to the Christmas lexicon. Other songs that strayed from the "innocence" and tradition of this period were the sultry "Santa Baby" by Eartha Kitt in 1953 and the Jazzy "Cool Yule" by Louis Armstrong & The Commanders that same year.

In the early 60s there was a breakthrough when the album *A Christmas Gift for You from Philles Records* (later renamed *A Christmas Gift for You from Phil Spector*) was released. This album provided brand-new interpretations of Christmas classics utilizing Spector's famous "wall of sound" and the doo-wop style of the period. The artists for these songs were people of color, now readily accepted by the masses into their living rooms (at least, their sounds were). This fantastic album has endured into present-day, its songs remaining standards after all these years.

Of course, more traditional Christmas songs were released in the 60s. Sinatra included his version of "I've Got My Love to Keep Me Warm" in his generic *Ring-A-Ding Ding!* album in 1961. In 1968 he released a Christmas album that included his whole family, called *The Sinatra Family Wish You a Merry Christmas*. Dean Martin released a Christmas album in 1966, appropriately called *The Dean Martin Christmas Album*, of Christmas standards, including a new rendition of "Let it Snow," different from his recording in 1959, and a rendition of "It's a Marshmallow World," first released by Bing Crosby in 1950. The latter would become more popular than Bing's version, and is heard frequently to this this day, along with the version from the *A Christmas Gift for You from Phil Spector* album. Bing Crosby and Frank Sinatra got together, with Fred Waring & His Pennsylvanians, in 1964 to bring us "We Wish You the Merriest," a song written by Les Brown in 1961.

A slew of Christmas animated holiday TV specials gave us both new releases of old classics and new music. It started with *Rudolf the Red-Nosed Reindeer* in 1964, all the songs of which were written and composed by "Rudolf" composer Johnny Marks, including the Burl Ives classic "Have a Holly Jolly Christmas." Then, in 1965, with a lot of anticipation from children at the time (including me), famed comic strip character Charlie Brown got his own animated TV special, *A Charlie Brown Christmas*. Jazz pianist Vince Guaraldi was tapped to write the score for this one. He was considered an odd choice to score this classic, and the use of jazz was questioned. But the jazz score worked perfectly, and the rest is history. This album was the top-selling album in 2024 on Apple Music, almost 60 years after its release. In 1966, Dr. Seuss' *How the Grinch Stole Christmas!* premiered, with a rousing soundtrack and a popular song released, "Welcome Christmas." Finally, in 1969, *Frosty the Snowman* graced our airwaves, and Jimmy Durante once again became associated with the song, which he had originally released in 1950, right after Gene Autry first did.

Broadway also gave us Christmas songs in the 60s. The lesser known "Be a Santa" from the play *Subways Are for Sleeping* (1961-1962), released in 1962, gave us tap-dancing Santa's. But more recognizable, and popular to this day, was "We Need a Little Christmas," from *Mame*. It was released by The New Christy Minstrels in 1966, but Percy Faith's version of the same year became the more enduring version. Percy Faith also provided us that year with the lovely "Christmas Is…"

In 1960 Lou Monte gave us the novelty song "Dominick the Donkey." Two great songs were introduced in 1963: "Pretty Paper," written by Willie Nelson and sung by Roy Orbison, and "It's the Most Wonderful Time of the Year," by Andy Williams. In 1964 we got "That Holiday Feeling" from Steve Lawrence & Eydie Gorme. Also in 1964, The Beach Boys graced us with their classic *The Beach Boys' Christmas Album*, with traditional songs and new ones, like "Little St. Nick," "The Man with All the Toys," and "Santa's Beard," which continue to be popular today. In 1966 Elvis took an obscure song from 1965 called "If Every Day Was Like Christmas" by Bobby West and made it a hit, popular to this day.

The 60s to the early 70s were a time of political statement and anti-war sentiment, and two songs stand out in this area: "Do You Hear What I Hear?" in 1962, a plea for a peaceful resolution to the Cuban Missile Crisis, and the Lennons' plea for peace in the Vietnam conflict in "Happy Xmas (War Is Over)" in 1971. There were other songs, albeit with less-specific goals, that were anti-war: "Someday at Christmas" by Stevie Wonder in 1966, which expresses hope that someday men will no longer play with bombs like toys, and the light-hearted "Snoopy's Christmas" by The Royal Guardsmen in 1967, which has the Red Baron putting his aggression with Snoopy on hold for Christmas, as real-life troops did during an unofficial Christmas armistice in WWI.

The 70s gave us its share of classics, beginning in 1970 with three new Christmas hits that have endured to today. In "Merry Christmas, Darling" the Carpenters performed a song first written in the 1940s and made it into a hit utilizing Richard Carpenter's musical talents and Karen Carpenter's unique vocal talents. In "Feliz Navidad," Jose Feliciano gifted us with one of the most happy, festive Christmas tunes ever, ironically written when he was feeling lonely, separated from his family at Christmas. 1970 also gave us the good-natured hit by The Jackson 5, "Give Love on Christmas Day."

The 70s continued giving us new Christmas songs, using new 70s sounds. In 1971 Donny Hathaway gave us the brassy "This Christmas." In 1973 a group called Wizzard released the enormously happy tune "I Wish It Could Be Christmas Every Day," written by Roy Wood, a founding member of Electric Light Orchestra. Also in 1973, Elton John released his signature Christmas song, "Step into Christmas." Gilbert O' Sullivan, a hitmaker in the 70s, released his pretty "Christmas Song" in 1974.

In 1975, we were fortunate that Emerson, Lake & Palmer keyboardist Keith Emerson had encouraged each member of the band to come up with solo material, as Greg Lake came up with one of the classiest Christmas songs ever, "I Believe in Father Christmas." Also in that year, singer Dana provided us with the sad but pretty "It's Gonna Be a Cold, Cold Christmas."

The late 70s were, of course, dominated by disco. The Salsoul Orchestra entered the Christmas song game, releasing songs with a disco beat, but fortunately a subdued one. The most famous was 1976's "Merry Christmas All," a pretty song that most of us would remember but not by its title.

In 1977 Bing Crosby taped his annual Christmas TV special, this one called *Bing Crosby's Merrie Olde Christmas*, filmed in England. Upon the insistence of his children, he booked David Bowie as his musical guest. Though they were an unlikely pairing, after some silly banter they sang "Peace on Earth–Little Drummer Boy," which had Bing sing mostly "Drummer Boy" while Bowie sang the short but beautiful new song "Peace on Earth," with both singing "Peace" at the end. Bing prematurely said, "It's a pretty thing, isn't it?" after the song, and in some releases of it that quip was kept in. Bing never saw the special, at least not when broadcast; he died shortly before that.

In 1978 the Eagles took the 1960 Charles Brown song "Please Come Home for Christmas" and made it a hit. In 1979, Paul McCartney graced us with the quirky but endearing "Wonderful Christmas Time." In that same year, the silly but popular novelty song "Grandma Got Run Over by a Reindeer" was released by "Elmo & Patsy," a veterinarian and his ex-wife.

The 80s showcased a variety of hits. One important year was 1984. The Pretenders released "2000 Miles." George Michael and Wham! released their Christmas hit, "Last Christmas." Bob Geldof and Midge Ure wrote a song called "Do They Know It's Christmas?" to raise money for the 1983–1985 famine in Ethiopia. It was performed by a supergroup assembled by Geldof and Ure consisting of popular British and Irish musical acts that they called Band Aid and consisted of 37 vocalists. It raised more than $24 million (over $78 million in 2024 dollars).

In 1985 Ray Charles gave us the lovely "The Spirit of Christmas," questioning why that spirit could not last all year round. In 1986 Chris Rea released "Driving Home for Christmas," the lyrics of which he wrote while actually being driven home at Christmas by his wife. That song has a sort of fairy-tale backstory: they had run out of money, and he was flipping through what small amount he had as he headed home, but when arriving home found a huge check in the mail, for his hit "Fool If You Think It's Over." In 1987 a Christmas song was released that actually was titled as a "Fairytale"—"Fairytale of New York," by The Pogues. This song wasn't usual Christmas fare, being about a visitor from Ireland being thrown into an NYC drunk tank at Christmas, but it was refreshing and entertaining. In 1989, another unique Christmas song was released—"(My) Grown-Up Christmas List," sung by Natalie Cole. The song called not for Santa and presents, but resolutions to the world's problems.

In the 80s two major Christmas motion pictures were released—*Santa Claus: The Movie* (1985) and *National Lampoon's Christmas Vacation* (1989). The former faded quickly into obscurity, but the latter was a hit, and is regular viewing even today. Its theme, sung by Mavis Staples, is a wonderful Christmas tune.

A new form of music was introduced to Christmas fare in the 80s: Rap. The first Christmas Rap song was performed by a group of white girls called The Waitresses, in a 1981 song appropriately called "Christmas Wrapping." The first popular Christmas Rap song performed by African Americans was "Christmas in Hollis," by Run DMC in 1987.

Another form of music, unique in itself (but may be considered New Age) was introduced in the 80s by Mannheim Steamroller, a synth band that gave us a brand-new sound to Christmas classics, like "Deck the Halls" in 1984.

The 90s started out well. "Christmas All Over Again" was released by Tom Petty and the Heartbreakers in 1992. Amy Grant released her second Christmas album, *Home for Christmas*, that same year, following up on the success of 1983's *A Christmas Album* (with a third album to be released in 1999, *A Christmas to Remember*). In 1993, Gloria Estefan, formerly of The Miami Sound Machine, released her *Christmas Through Your Eyes* Album, which included the title song and "Love on Layaway."

But in 1994, there arrived an explosive single and album by Mariah Carey: "All I Want for Christmas Is You" and *Merry Christmas*, respectively. The single was an immediate success, reaching number six on the Billboard Hot Adult Contemporary chart in the United States and number two in the United Kingdom and Japan. The album was also very successful. These successes gave impetus to others that releasing Christmas songs and albums was "cool."

In 1995 different sounds were released on Christmas albums. Mannheim Steamroller released its unique sounds on their *Christmas in the Aire* album. That same year explosive hard rock debuted in the Christmas album *Dead Winter Dead* by the group Savatage, which included the song "Christmas Eve Sarajevo 12/24." In the following year Savatage changed their name to The Trans-Siberian Orchestra, re-releasing their 1995 album as *Christmas Eve and Other Stories* in 1996. This album would be followed by two more albums in 1998, *The Ghosts of Christmas Eve* and *The Christmas Attic*.

There were two Christmas movies of note in the late 20th century, *Home Alone* (1990) and *Dr. Seuss' How the Grinch Stole Christmas* (2000). The former included the beautiful song "Somewhere in My Memory," while the latter included the popular "Where Are You Christmas? / Christmas, Why Can't I Find You," sung by Faith Hill.

As in earlier times, there were novelty songs. Most were created by Bob Rivers (AKA Bob Rivers & Twisted Radio), collected in two albums: *Twisted Christmas Boxed Set* (1993) and *Chipmunks Roasting on an Open Fire* (2000).

During the last year of the century, 2000, a number of other important releases were made. "My Only Wish (This Year)" was a single released by Britney Spears. The album *My Kind of Christmas* was released by Christina Aguilera. Finally, the famous—or infamous, depending on your taste—single "Christmas Shoes" by Newsong was released.

After December Slips Away

Bonnie Keen & Lowell Alexander   **1995**

First Call (Mel Tunney, Marty   *Beyond December* (1995)
McCall, and Bonnie Keen)

Song about the melancholy following the Christmas season.

All Alone on Christmas

Steven Van Zandt   **1992**

Darlene Love   *Home Alone 2: Lost in New York
Original Soundtrack Album* (1992)

Song about being alone on Christmas, from the 1992 movie *Home Alone 2: Lost in New York*, written by a member of Bruce Springsteen's E Street Band, who was also a mobster on *The Sopranos*. Performer Darlene Love is best known for the Phil Spector-produced "Christmas (Baby Please Come Home)."

All Because

BeBe and CeCe Winans   **1993**

BeBe and CeCe Winans   *First Christmas* (1993)

Song about all the great things that have resulted from the birth of Christ. The artists are members of the Winans family, a family of gospel music artists from Detroit, Michigan.

All I Want for Christmas

William Anderson   **1985**

Ray Charles   *The Spirit of Christmas* (1985)

A catchy, happy tune by the great Ray Charles wherein he describes what he wants for Christmas, which turns out to be the simple things, like friendship, snow, children and presents.

All I Want for Christmas

Ronnie Rodgers   1995

Toby Keith   *Christmas to Christmas* (1995)

Toby Keith lists things that his sweetheart can buy him for Christmas but all he wants is "a new year with you."

All I Want for Christmas Is You

Andy Stone & Troy Powers   1990

Vince Vance & The Valiants   *All I Want for Christmas Is You* (1990)

The title says it all. The singer doesn't want anything for Christmas but "you." Both renditions are done in late 50s / early 60s style.

a	2021	Kelly Clarkson	(Single)

All I Want for Christmas Is You

Mariah Carey & Walter Afanasieff   1994

Mariah Carey   *Merry Christmas* (1994)

This song has sold 16 million copies worldwide, making it one of the best-selling digital singles of all time. As of 2023, the Associated Press estimates the song's royalty earnings at $100 million. From the New York Post article[79] "8 Things You Didn't Know About 'All I Want for Christmas Is You'":

1. Carey didn't even want to record a Christmas album. At the time, Christmas albums were considered to be for older artists who had been put out to pasture. Carey was 24.
2. The song was written in 15 minutes.
3. The video features a secret cameo, her husband, Tommy Mattola.
4. No actual musicians play on the song. Although the song sounds like a full band played it, Afanasieff put the song together on his computer. The only things added were the vocals of Carey and her backing singers.
5. Carey made Christmas happen early for the recording. The vocals were recorded in the dog days of August in New York, but that didn't stop Car-

ey from getting into the yuletide spirit. "We had Christmas trees and lights brought into the studio to get us in the mood," laughed Afanasieff. "There was even talk of bringing in some snow at one point, but we didn't go with that, thank God!"

6. It's a smash-hit ringtone. In 2009, it became the first holiday ringtone to be certified double platinum for more than two million sales.
7. Goats love the song. In 2010, a British goat farmer discovered that his animals produce more milk when Carey's Christmas classic is played on a loop—in contrast to "The Chipmunk Song (Christmas Don't Be Late)" by Alvin and the Chipmunks, which reportedly brought milk production to a screeching halt.
8. Carey and the song's co-writer are no longer in contact. Afanasieff hasn't heard from Carey since they worked together on 1997's *Butterfly* album, after which she decided to explore a more R&B-influenced direction.

A lawsuit was filed against singer/songwriter Mariah Carey and co-writer Walter Afanasieff for their song by Andy Stone of Vince Vance and the Valiants, claiming her had written a song of the same name in 1989, which was true. However, the two songs were not musically related at all, so Stone's copyright infringement argument hinged on the use of the title. The lawsuit was dropped.[80]

All the songs below are very different from the original. Song (a) is a mellow version by a Country band. Song (b) is Celtic New Age. Song (c) is an Instrumental version, with violin played by Lindsey Stirling, an incredible violinist with an enormous following on YouTube. Song (d) slows the song down, beautifully I might add. (d) has a lovely video[81].

a	2012	Lady A	On This Winter's Night
b	2015	Celtic Angels	New Age Christmas
c	*2017*	*Lindsey Stirling*	*Warmer in the Winter*
d	2018	Ingrid Michaelson & Leslie Odom, Jr.	Ingrid Michaelson's Songs for the Season

All Is Well

Michael W. Smith & Wayne Kirk-patrick   **1989**

Michael W. Smith   *Christmas* (1989)

"All is well" because Christ has been born.

a	1999	Michael Crawford	A Christmas Album
b	2005	Michael W. Smith (feat. Carrie Underwood)	The Spirit of Christmas

c	2020	Carrie Underwood	My Gift

Ave Maria

Vladimir Vavilov   1970

Vladimir Vavilov   *Lutnevaa Muzyka XVI-XVII Vekov*
                                                              (1970)

No relation to the classic "Ave Maria," this is a musical hoax generally misattributed to Baroque composer Giulio Caccini. Vavilov himself published and recorded it on the Melodiya label with the ascription to "Anonymous" in 1970[82]. It is a real song, and a beautiful one at that.

Song (b) is an Instrumental New Age version.

a	2014	Jackie Evancho	Awakening
b	2015	*Acoon Hibino*	*Kokoroto Wo Totoneru - Lovefrequency 528 Hz*

A Baby Just Like You

John Denver & Joe Henry   1975

John Denver   *Rocky Mountain Christmas* (1975)

John Denver wrote this song at the request of Frank Sinatra on the occasion of the birth of his first grandchild, Nancy Sinatra's daughter Angela. When Denver recorded the song, he substituted the name with his then-infant son, Zachary. It appears in the television special *John Denver & The Muppets: A Christmas Together* (1979). Frank Sinatra recorded the song as well.

a	1975	Frank Sinatra	Single

Barnyard Christmas

Jack Stearn   1958

Spike Jones and His City Slickers,   Single (1958)
with The Bell Sisters

Silly but cute song about Christmas in a barnyard, intended for children.

Be a Santa

Betty Comden, Adolph Green, &   **1961**
Jule Styne

Sydney Chaplin and Chorus   Single (1962)
Subways Are for Sleeping (1961;
Instrumental version, by Percy Faith)

From the Broadway Play, *Subways Are for Sleeping* (1961-1962). Sydney Chaplin was comedic actor Charlie Chaplin's son. Jule Styne was co-author of "Let It Snow." This is a catchy, happy tune about all the "Santa's" in NYC at Christmastime.

The musical was inspired by the experiences of Edmund G. Love, who had become homeless in the early 50s and had to sleep in subway trains. He documented this, along with his experiences with other people doing the same, in a 1958 book. With proceeds from the book, he ate dinner, in alphabetical order, at every restaurant listed in the Manhattan yellow pages directory.

Both the original and (c) have tap-dancing sounds, as in the play the Santa's were tap-dancing.

a	1965	Living Voices	The Little Drummer Boy
b	1994	Michelle Nicastro & Guy Haines	A Broadway Christmas
c	2012	Sandy Bainum	This Christmas
d	2016	Mitch Miller	Christmas Sing-Along with Mitch (CD with Bonus Tracks)

Bel Astre

Raymond Davelot & Abbe Pelle-   **1992**
grin

Andre Gagnon   *Noel* (1992)

"Bel astre" is a French phrase that translates to "dandy" in English. This song is an amazingly beautiful orchestral piece associated with Christmas, though there is no obvious connection.

The Bell that Couldn't Jingle

Burt Bacharach & Larry Kusik   1962

Paul Evans - Orchestra arranged   Single (1962)
and conducted by Burt Bacharach

A cute song about a bell that can't jingle, until Santa arrives and has Jack Frost fix it. It appears to be the only Christmas song known to be penned by prolific songwriter Burt Bacharach.

a	2024	Ben Folds	Sleigher

Bells Are Ringing

Mary Chapin Carpenter   1980

Mary Chapin Carpenter   *Christmastime in the City* (1980)

Somber song about peace coming to us from an infant Jesus, despite the fact that we may possess nothing.

Bells of Christmas

Nelson Riddle & Don Costa   1968

Frank Sinatra & the Sinatra Family   *The Sinatra Family Wish You a Merry Christmas* (1968)

The song "Greensleeves" (AKA "What Child Is This?") with different lyrics, about bells ringing out to the world, sending messages of love.

Blame It on the Mistletoe

Toby Keith   1995

Toby Keith   *Christmas to Christmas* (1995)

A song about finding love after a simple kiss under the mistletoe.

The Blessed Dawn of Christmas

Harry Connick, Jr.   **1993**

Harry Connick, Jr.   *When My Heart Finds Christmas*
(1993)

A pretty, reverent song about the blessedness of Christmas Day and the birth of Jesus. The album was the best-selling holiday album in the U.S. in 1993, and one of the most popular for at least three decades.

The Blessings

Teddy Gentry, Randy Ow-   **1996**
en, Ronnie Rogers, & Greg Fowler

Alabama   *Christmas Vol. II* (1996)

A man offers thanks to God for all the blessings in life he has received.

Breath of Heaven (Mary's Song)

Amy Grant   **1992**

Amy Grant   *Home for Christmas* (1992)

Soliloquy of Mary, the Mother of God, expressing her concerns to "The Breath of Heaven" of having the honor of carrying Jesus in her bosom.

a	1998	Vince Gill	Breath of Heaven: A Christmas Collection

Can't Wait 'til Christmas Day

"Vince Vance" (AKA Andy Stone)   **1989**

Vince Vance and The Valiants   *All I Want for Christmas Is You*
(1989)

Children singing how they "can't wait 'til Christmas Day."

Candlelight Candle

John Rutter   **1984**

The Cambridge Singers   *Christmas Night: Carols of the Nativity* (1987)

Beautiful song celebrating the birth of Christ.

a	1999	Michael Crawford	A Christmas Album

Captain Santa Claus (and his Reindeer Space Patrol)

James Ross Boothe & Joe Beal   **1957**

Bobby Helms   Single (1957)

Santa's sleigh breaks down and his helpers build a rocket ship. "B" side of "Jingle Bell Rock."

Carol for Another Christmas

Henry Mancini   **1966**

Henry Mancini and His Orchestra   *A Merry Mancini Christmas* (1966)

A very pretty Instrumental by one of the greatest film composers, Henry Mancini (1924-94). Mancini won four Academy Awards, a Golden Globe, and twenty Grammy Awards. His works include the theme and soundtrack for the *Peter Gunn* TV series as well as the music for *The Pink Panther* film series and "Moon River" from *Breakfast at Tiffany's*.

Caroling, Caroling

Wihla Hutson & Alfred Burt   **1954**

Fred Waring & The Pennsylvanians   *The Sounds of Christmas* (1959)

This well-known Christmas song was originally written to accompany a Christmas card. Alfred Burt composed the music for fifteen Christmas carols between 1942 and 1954. He died in 1954.

Song (b) is a medley with "The First Nöel," "Hark! The Herald Angels Sing" & "Silent Night." Song (d) is a medley with "Happy Holiday." The most popular version is probably Nat King Cole's (a), though (b) and (d) are also quite popular.

a	1960	Nat King Cole	The Magic of Christmas
b	1968	Perry Como with The Ray Charles Singers	The Perry Como Christmas Album
c	1972	The Singers Unlimited	Christmas
d	1986	Johnny Mathis	Christmas Eve with Johnny Mathis
e	1992	The Manhattan Transfer	The Christmas Album
f	2019	Idina Menzel	Christmas: A Season of Love

Celebrate Me Home

Bob James and Kenny Loggins   1977

Kenny Loggins   *Celebrate Me Home* (1977)

This popular song at Christmastime is on Loggins' debut album.

Children's Christmas Song

Harvey Fuqua & Isabelle Freeman   1965

The Supremes   *Merry Christmas* (1965)

This gentle, happy song for children that includes children singing is pleasing for all to listen to.

The Chimney Song

Brian Silva & Dennis Amero   1987

Bob Rivers   *Twisted Christmas* (1988)

This spooky novelty song tells of Santa Claus getting stuck in a chimney…and remaining there as time goes by, rotting away!

The Chipmunk Song (Christmas Don't Be Late)

Ross Bagdasarian (under the stage name of David Seville)   **1958**

Ross Bagdasarian (with "Alvin and the Chipmunks")   *Let's All Sing with The Chipmunks* (1958)

This popular song won three Grammy Awards in 1958, for Best Comedy Performance, Best Children's Recording, and Best Engineered Record (non-classical); it was also nominated for Record of the Year. It reached No. 1 on the Billboard Hot 100 Pop Singles chart, the only Christmas record to reach No. 1 until Mariah Carey's "All I Want for Christmas Is You" did so 61 years later in 2019. It eventually sold 12 million copies.

Chipmunks Roasting on an Open Fire

Bob Rivers, Joe Bryant, & Spike O'Neill   **2000**

Bob Rivers   *Chipmunks Roasting on an Open Fire* (2000)

Novelty song spoofing "The Christmas Song" AKA "Chestnuts Roasting on an Open Fire" by using the same tune but with lyrics detailing chipmunks roasting instead of chestnuts. Spoof also of Alvin and the Chipmunks, who sang "The Chipmunk Song (Christmas Don't Be Late)" back in 1958.

Christ Is Born

Monsignor (later Cardinal) Domenico Bartolucci; English Lyrics by Ray Charles   **1968 (first English recording)**

Perry Como   *The Perry Como Christmas Album* (1968)

Ray Charles and the Ray Charles singers had gone to see Father Bartolucci in his apartment, where they found that the Father had a big Ampex tape machine and a box of tapes. He brought out a tape of this gorgeous piece that he had written and played it for the singers; the words were in Latin.[83]

Christmas

Jackie DeShannon, Jimmy Holiday, & Randy Myers   **1969**

Jackie DeShannon   Single (1969)

"B" side of "Do You Know How Christmas Trees Are Grown." Artist best known for hits "What the World Needs Now Is Love" (1965) and "Put a Little Love in Your Heart" (1969). This song celebrates good things about Christmas.

Christmas (Baby Please Come Home)

Ellie Greenwich, Jeff Barry, & Phil Spector   **1963**

Darlene Love   *A Christmas Gift for You from Phil Spector* (1963)

Originally named *A Christmas Gift for You from Philles Records*, the above album was voted no. 142 on Rolling Stone magazine's list of the 500 greatest albums of all time in 2003 and the greatest Christmas album of all time in 2019.

As can be seen below, Darlene Love, the original artist for this song, joined Cher in singing it 60 years later (f). (d) is a Celtic New Age version.

a	1987	U2	I Believe in Father Christmas
b	1994	Mariah Carey	Merry Christmas
c	2013	Leona Lewis	Christmas, With Love
d	2015	Celtic Angels	New Age Christmas
e	2019	Robbie Williams (feat. Bryan Adams)	The Christmas Present
f	2023	Cher (with Darlene Love)	Christmas

A Christmas All Alone

Daniel Jannsen & Walter Keske   **1966**

The Lettermen   *For Christmas This Year* (1966)

In this pretty but sad tune, the Lettermen lament over being separated from a love at Christmastime, a time that people spend in joy, and having to wait until June to be together again, this time as man and wife.

Christmas All Over Again

Tom Petty   1992

Tom Petty & The Heartbreakers   *A Very Special Christmas Volume 2*
(1992)

Jeff Lynne of ELO oversaw the production of this song and played three different instruments (including the bass and bells). He also sang background vocals, and you can hear Jeff Lynne at the end of the song when Tom recites his Christmas list. When Tom says, "Chuck Berry songbook," Jeff Lynne responds, "I'll have one of them." Petty wrote the song on a ukelele. George Harrison had visited him and given him a ukelele and spent a whole afternoon teaching him the chords.[84]

a	2020	The Goo Goo Dolls	New Christmas Music

Christmas and Love

Lassaye Holmes   1970

Charley Pride   *Christmas in My Hometown* (1970)

Before becoming a singer, Charley was a player in Negro league baseball. He was the first Black superstar of Country Music. This song tells of a poor man, who has a wife and three kids, but almost no material things; however, he is satisfied with the peace and goodwill that Jesus brings at Christmas.

Christmas and You

C. W. Kehner & R. Faith   1962

Frankie Avalon   *Frankie Avalon's Christmas Album*
(1962)

Heartthrob Frankie Avalon reminisces about a Love he met at Christmas that he will not forget and will dream about.

Christmas Angel

Bobby Vinton & Jack Lloyd   1964

Bobby Vinton   *Kissin' Christmas: The Bobby Vinton
                                        Christmas Album* (1964)

A girl Bobby meets at Christmastime brings him joy, as an angel would.

Christmas Auld Lang Syne

Francis Military & Manny Kurtz   1960

Bobby Darin   *The 25th Day of December with
                                        Bobby Darin* (1960)

This song is to the tune of "Auld Lang Syne," but with different lyrics that describe a Christmas "back home."

The Christmas Blues

Sammy Cahn & David Jack Holt   1953

Dean Martin   *Single* (1953)
                                        Christmas with Dean Martin (1959)

Dean is sad at Christmastime because he has no-one. Sammy Cahn is co-author of "Let It Snow! Let It Snow! Let It Snow!" He was nominated for 31 Academy Awards, five Golden Globe Awards, an Emmy Award, and a Grammy Award.

Christmas Can't Be Far Away

Felice and Diadorius Boudleaux Bryant   1954

Eddy Arnold   *Eddy Arnold and His Guitar* (1954)

Everyone is nice, so "Christmas can't be far away." This husband-wife songwriting team wrote such great hits as "All I Have to Do Is Dream," "Bye, Bye, Love," "Love Hurts" and "Wake Up, Little Susie."

a	1965	Burl Ives	Have a Holly Jolly Christmas

Christmas Can't Be Very Far Away

Wayne Jackson & Roger Cook   **1999**

Amy Grant   *Christmas to Remember* (1999)

Snow, cold weather, snowballs, mall Santa's and Christmas lights all mean "Christmas can't be very far away."

Christmas Card

Robert Gurian & Jimmy Krondes   **1963/1964**

The New Christy Minstrels   *Christmas with the New Christy Minstrels: Complete!* (1963/1964)

The singers see all the wonderful things of Christmas in a Christmas card.

Christmas Chopsticks ('Twas the Night Before Christmas)

Frederick Heider   **1951**

Mindy Carson With Hugo Winterhalter's Orchestra and Chorus   Single (1951)

Combines a simple waltz for piano ("Chopsticks") with "A Visit from St. Nicholas," a poem first published anonymously under the title "Account of a Visit from St. Nicholas" in 1823 and later attributed to Clement Clarke Moore (1779-1863), who claimed authorship in 1837.

Guy Lombardo (a) was known as "Mr. New Year's Eve" for performing with his "Royal Canadians" every New Year's Eve in New York City from 1929 to 1976, live on radio first and then switching to live TV in 1956. In 1959 they changed their venue from the Roosevelt Hotel to the prestigious Waldorf Astoria. He was an icon in Long Island, NY, living in the village of Freeport on the south shore for years, and was buried in East Farmingdale, Long Island. A long stretch of road in Freeport, adjacent to a canal and lined with bars and restaurants, was named Guy Lombardo Avenue, a name it retains today. Interestingly, he participated in hydroplane racing.

Guy Lombardo and his band performed at the New York World's Fair 1964-1965. One of the biggest thrills for my parents was dancing to his music when we visited the Fair. I was bored silly.

a	1953	Guy Lombardo and His Royal Canadians	Jingle Bells

Christmas Day

Brian Wilson   1964

The Beach Boys   *The Beach Boys' Christmas Album*
(1964)

Gentle song about the joys of Christmas.

a	2011	She & Him	A Very She & Him Christmas

Christmas Eve

Allyn Ferguson & Sidney Shaw   1961

Johnny Mathis & The Percy Faith   2003 CD Bonus Track of *Merry*
Orchestra   *Christmas* (1958)

Walking in the snow on Christmas Eve with the one you love.

Christmas Eve

Sheldon Harnick & Jerry Bock   1963

Yvette Lawrence   *A Broadway Christmas* (1994)

The song is from the Broadway show *She Loves Me*, which premiered in 1963. This song, however, was cut prior to opening. The song is about "the wondrous night of Christmas Eve."

Christmas Eve

Music by Gerard Andre Biesel and lyrics by Ray Charles   **1968**

Perry Como   *The Perry Como Christmas Album* (1968)

Christmas Eve is a time for kids to sleep and await presents but the biggest present is "peace on Earth to all men."

Christmas Eve

Maria Christensen & Curt Frasca   **1998**

Celine Dion   *These Are Special Times* (1998)

Christmas Eve with that special someone.

Christmas Eve Sarajevo 12/24

Paul O'Neill, Jon Oliva & Robert Kinkel   **1995**

Savatage (later members of The Trans-Siberian Orchestra)   *Dead Winter Dead* (1995) [as Savatage]
Christmas Eve and Other Stories (1996) [as The Trans-Siberian Orchestra]

This is a Rock instrumental medley of "God Rest Ye Merry, Gentlemen" and "*Shchedryk*," a Ukrainian New Year's song that "Carol of the Bells" was based on. It was first released on the Savatage album *Dead Winter Dead* in 1995. It was re-released by the Trans-Siberian Orchestra, a side project of several Savatage members, on their 1996 debut album *Christmas Eve and Other Stories*.

Christmas Everyday

Peter McCann   **1981**

Kenny Rogers   *Christmas* (1981)

We remember Christmas day but because of Jesus' birth it is really Christmas every day.

The Christmas Feeling

Mel Tormé   **1992**

Mel Tormé   *Christmas Songs* (1992)

A few bars of "The Christmas Song," which Mel co-wrote, precede this song about how the wonderful things of Christmas give you a special Christmas feeling that you wish you had all year. Mel Tormé was known as "the velvet fog" for his characteristic low, gentle voice.

A Christmas Festival

F. Mendelssohn, F. Gruger, G. Handel, J. Wade, C. Wesley, I. Watts & J. Mohr   **1959**

Arthur Fiedler and the Boston Pops Orchestra   *Pops Christmas Party* (1959)

A wonderful Instrumental medley of many classic Christmas songs.

Christmas Heart

Connie Pearce & Arnold Miller   **1961**

June Christy   *This Time of Year* (1961)

June Christy shares a song from "a really Christmas heart" wherein she lists what she would give people in times of need, like "a peaceful country stream."

Born Shirley Luster, Christy's *This Time of Year* is her only Christmas album, consisting entirely of original songs, composed by the husband-and-wife songwriting team of Connie Pearce and Arnold Miller. Reviewer Nick Dedina stated that "with the unjustly neglected *This Time of Year* Christy decided to address the fact that every single Christmas album seems to feature the same few seasonal songs. *This Time of Year* is that rarest of things—a winter concept album of all new material that can be listened to even when the holidays are over."[85]

A reviewer at *Records.Christmas* listed this album in the top section of a list of 100 Christmas records of all time (on par with Phil Spector and Ella Fitzgerald), stating:

"I have no hesitation naming June Christy's *This Time of Year* the greatest Christmas album of all time. The massive ambition of writing ten lyrical and melodic masterpieces is matched by fantastic arrangements and beautiful performances from all concerned. This is the full range of grown-up Christmas experience condensed into one truly singular package."[86]

Christmas Holiday

Peter De Angelis & Robert Marcucci   **1962**

Frankie Avalon   *Frankie Avalon's Christmas Album* (1962)

Frankie's Love has gone, and "white snow looks so very blue."

Christmas in the Air

Pachelbel, Paul O'Neill, Jon Oliva, & Robert Kinkell   **1998**

Trans-Siberian Orchestra   *The Christmas Attic* (1998)

Rock song about "Christmas in the air," where there is "goodwill everywhere."

Christmas in Dixie

Randy Owen, Jeff Cook, Teddy Gentry & Mark Herndon   **1982**

Alabama   *The Classic Christmas Album* (1982)

Lovely song about not only Christmas in Dixie, but all around the United States.

Christmas in Herald Square

J. Vintaloro & T. Tamburello   **1998**

Tony Bennet   *The Classic Christmas Album* (1998)

Tony Bennet lovingly describes Christmas' sights, sounds and smells in Herald Square, NYC.

Christmas in Hollis

D.M.C., Jam Master Jay, Run   1987

Run DMC   *A Very Special Christmas* (1987)

This album included songs by various artists. Hollis is the neighborhood in Queens, NYC that the members of Run DMC grew up in. This is an early Christmas Rap song, but not the first (see "Christmas Wrapping").

Christmas in Love

C. Sambataro, Jock Bartley & John Sambataro   1980

Firefall   Single (1980)

The title says it all.

Firefall was a soft-rock band that produced several hits, the top of which was "You Are the Woman" (1976); they also did very well with "Just Remember I Love You" (1977).

Personal note: my ex-wife presented this single to me on our first Christmas together (1983). It was a single-sided 7" record pressed on vinyl embedded on paper. In the 60s children's records were sometimes made that way, usually as an insert in a book.

Christmas in My Heart

Douglas Fraser, Julia Fraser & Rosalyn Winters   1985

Ray Charles   *The Spirit of Christmas* (1985)

Lovely song from Ray Charles, describing all the good things about Christmas.

Christmas in New York

Lou Christie & Herbert Twyla   1974

Lou Christie (feat. The Crayons)   Single (1974)

Yes, it's all about Christmas in NYC, and all its wondrous sights.

Christie (Luigi Alfredo Giovanni Sacco) used a falsetto voice patterned after Frankie Valli, in hits such as "Lightning Strikes" (1966), "Rhapsody in The Rain" (1966) and "I'm Gonna Make You Mine" (1969).

Two more songs about Christmas in NYC and with the same title were released in the 21st century, so far. See Chapter 4.

Christmas Is(…)

Percy Faith & Spence Maxwell   1966

Percy Faith and His Orchestra   *Christmas Is… (1966)*

Christmas is…just about everything. A beautiful Christmas classic.

Vanessa Williams (a) approached this song entirely differently than Percy Faith, providing a jazzy version.

a	2004	Vanessa Williams	Christmas with Vanessa Williams

Christmas is a Birthday

Dick Manning & Gregory Paul Deutsch   1964

Burl Ives   *Have a Holly Jolly Christmas* (Recorded 1964; Released 1965)

Joyful song reminding us that Christmas is a birthday—of Jesus.

Christmas is Coming

Vince Guaraldi   1965

Vince Guaraldi   *A Charlie Brown Christmas Soundtrack* (1965)

Guaraldi was contacted by television producer Lee Mendelson to compose music for a documentary on the comic strip "Peanuts" and its creator, Charles M. Schulz.

Although the special went unaired, these selections were released in 1964 as *Jazz Impressions of a Boy Named Charlie Brown*. Coca-Cola commissioned a Christmas special based on Peanuts in 1965 and Guaraldi returned to score the special.

A Charlie Brown Christmas was conceived in April 1965, outlined in a single day, and produced in just 6 months. It wasn't seen by network executives until one week before it was scheduled to air—and they didn't like it. They thought it was "flat and disjointed, confusing in some spots." They were convinced it would be a failure.[87]

Christmas is for Everyone

Richard Loring & Dorothy Wayne   1986

Johnny Mathis (with the International   *Christmas Eve with Johnny Mathis*
Children's Choir)   (1986)

Christmas is for everyone, young and old. Pretty song. Sung in a medley with "Where Can I Find Christmas."

Christmas is Here Again

Roger Whittaker   1978

Roger Whittaker   *Christmas with Roger Whittaker*
                                                                                (1978)

Whittaker joyfully sings about Christmas being here again, with all that comes with it, but "all that I want is to know that you love me." Whittaker (1936-2023) was a Kenyan-born British singer-songwriter and musician who found much success in Germany in the 70s and 80s, even though he didn't know German; he sang his songs phonetically.

Christmas is the Season

Paul Westin, Larry Keith & Alan   1964
Bergman

Jo Stafford   *Joyful Season* (1964)

The artist gleefully sings about Christmas bells, and that Christmas is the season of bells.

Jo Stafford (1917-2008) had a career that spanned five decades, from the late 1930s to the early 1980s. She was the lead singer of the Pied Pipers, whom bandleader Tommy Dorsey hired in 1939 to perform vocals with his orchestra. From 1940 to 1942, the group often performed with Dorsey's new male singer, Frank Sinatra.

Christmas is the Time to Say "I Love You"

Billy Squier   **1981**

Billy Squier   Single (1981)

B-side of single "My Kinda Lover." Billy Squier, rock sensation of the early 80s, sang this song about the "laughter and the cheer" of Christmas.

Christmas Just Ain't Christmas Without You

Troy Powers   **1989**

Vince Vance and The Valiants   *All I Want for Christmas Is You*
                                                            (1989)

This song complements the Valiants' Christmas song "All I want for Christmas Is You," which is the title of the album that has both songs in it. The title of this song is exactly what it's about.

"Vince Vance" is just a character portrayed by Andy Stone (born Andy Franichevich Jr.), the only permanent member of the group. The remainder of the Valiants are rotating musicians.

Christmas Like a Lullaby

John Denver   **1990**

John Denver   *Christmas Like a Lullaby* (1990)

Christmas is "like a lullaby" for baby Jesus. Denver sings of being in Australia at Christmas, and that Christmas for him is back home in Colorado.

The Christmas List

Peggy Lee   **1965**

Peggy Lee   *Happy Holiday* (1965)

Peggy wonders what she needs to get for Christmas, to be ready for the Holiday, along with children who join her in song.

A Christmas Love Song

Alan Bergman, Marilyn Bergman,   **1991**
& Johnny Mandel

Blossom Dearie and Mike Renzi   *Christmas Spice So Very Nice - Vol-*
                                                            ume XVI (1991)

All the artist wants is "you"; that is the gift that made their dreams come true.

John Alfred Mandel (1925-2020) was an American composer and arranger of popular songs, film music and jazz. The musicians he worked with include Count Basie, Frank Sinatra, Peggy Lee, Barbra Streisand, and Tony Bennett. He won five Grammy Awards, from 17 nominations. One of his most recognizable songs is "Suicide Is Painless," the theme song for the movie and TV series *M*A*S*H*.

a	1992	The Manhattan Transfer	The Christmas Album

Christmas Lullaby

Mannheim Steamroller   **1995**

Mannheim Steamroller   *Christmas in the Aire* (1995)

The 1995 version is a New Age Instrumental. Mannheim Steamroller released the song again in 2007 with lyrics, that Olivia Newton-John sings *(a)*. A mother sings a lullaby to her little one, after Christmas is over, wishing that it dreams of Christmas.

I had the pleasure of meeting Olivia Newton-John, in addition to seeing her in concerts. A friend was assigned to photograph her one night, and I tagged along as an "assistant." It was a fundraising event for public television on Long Island. She was sad and withdrawn that evening; something during that time was bothering her. But when she posed for the photos and appeared on the TV camera, she was the kind, happy and nice Olivia that was a part of her public persona.

a	2007	Mannheim Steamroller (feat. Olivia Newton-John)	Christmas Song

Christmas Magic

Betey M. Zavell & Samantha Ridge   **1962**

Frankie Avalon   *Frankie Avalon's Christmas Album*
(1962)

Sweet, pretty song with angelic chorus about Christmas being more than just a tree but instead being about love, with magic that comes year-round.

Christmas Memories

Alan Bergman, Marilyn Bergman,   **1975**
& Don Costa

Frank Sinatra   Single (1975)

"B" side of "A Baby Just Like You." The Christmas memories include what most what expect: singing carols, walking in snow, baking cookies, Christmas morning, etc. A very warm, sentimental song.

Barbara Streisand (a) recorded this song as "Christmas Mem'ries."

a	2001	Barbra Streisand	The Classic Christmas Album
b	2016	She & Him	Christmas Party

Christmas Memories

Randy Albright, John Greenbaum   **1985**
& Becky Hobbs

Alabama   *Christmas* (1985)

The group *Alabama*'s Christmas memories: a snow-covered road, leading to the house the songwriter was raised, with a lit Christmas tree and fireplace. The songwriter laments about how things have changed, like the passing of his father, but that more good times are ahead.

Christmas Must Be Tonight

Robbie Robertson   **1977**

The Band   *Islands* (1977)

Song about the story of the first Christmas.

a	2015	Train	Train - Christmas in Tahoe

Christmas Passing Through

Suzzy Roche   **1990**

The Roches   *We Three Kings* (1990)

Simple song about Christmastime, with references to the birth of Christ, and proclaiming peace on Earth.

Christmas Serenade

Nicola Paone   **1952**

Nicola Paone and His Gang   Single (1952)

"B" side of "New Year Song." Short children's song wishing a Merry Christmas "to one and all" many times. A young girl talks of things occurring at Christmas.

Christmas Song

Gilbert O' Sullivan   **1974**

Gilbert O' Sullivan   Single (1974)

Very nice song about not wishing for a white Christmas, but peace in the world. Joined by a choir of children.

Born Raymond O'Sullivan, this artist achieved his most significant success during the early 1970s with hits such as "Alone Again (Naturally)," "Clair" [about babysitting] and "Get Down" [about his dog].

The Christmas Spirit

Teddy Gentry, Randy Owen, &   **1996**
Ronnie Rogers

Alabama   *Christmas Vol. II* (1996)

The Christmas Spirit is in the air like the day Christ was born, which they describe.

Christmas Time

Janice Gugliuzza, Ronald Dista-   **1976**
sio, & Vincent Montana Jr.

Salsoul Orchestra   *Christmas Jollies* (1976)

A description of Christmastime, done in a 70s disco, somewhat Latin beat.

Christmas Time

Bryan Adams & Jim Vallance   **1985**

Bryan Adams   Single (1985)

Well-known song celebrating solidarity at Christmastime.

Christmas Time

Edward Cole & Ray Charles   **1985**

Ray Charles   *The Spirit of Christmas* (1985)

Christmastime is "really more than giving"; it's more about receiving God's message of peace and love, and our spreading of that.

Christmas Time

The BoDeans   **1989**

BoDeans   Single (1989)

Christmastime images and celebrations, done in New Wave Rock.

Christmas Time Is Here (AKA Christmastime…)

Vince Guaraldi   **1965**

Vince Guaraldi

A Charlie Brown Christmas Sound-
track (1965)
- Instrumental
- Vocal

Classic tune from the 1965 TV Christmas special, *A Charlie Brown Christmas*, with both Vocal and Instrumental versions on the album.

Songs (c), (h) and (i) are soft jazz versions. Since Vince Guaraldi was a jazz musi-cian, the song can be considered jazz either way, but the aforementioned versions have more of a distinctly soft jazz sound.

a	1998	Kenny Loggins	December
b	1998	Shawn Colvin	Holiday Songs and Lullabies
c	2005	Diana Krall	Christmas Songs
d	2006	Sarah McLachlan	Wintersong
e	2008	Tony Bennett featuring The Count Basie Big Band	A Swingin' Christmas
f	2018	Ingrid Michaelson	Ingrid Michaelson's Songs for the Season
g	2019	Idina Menzel	Christmas: A Season of Love
h	2021	Norah Jones	I Dream of Christmas
i	2022	Alicia Keys	Santa Baby
j	2022	Gloria Estefan	Estefan Family Christmas
k	2024	Laufey	A Very Laufey Holiday

Christmas to Christmas

Ron Hellard & Alan Rhody   **1985**

Lee Greenwood

Christmas to Christmas (1985)

The singer will spend "Christmas to Christmas" with his Love, "but love is always in season."

a	1995	Toby Keith	Christmas to Christmas

A Christmas to Remember

Amy Grant, Chris Eaton & Beverly Darnall   **1989**

Amy Grant   *A Christmas to Remember* (1989)

It's going to be "a Christmas to remember"—waking up to "a world of white," lighting up the fire and playing some Nat King Cole.

Christmas Shoes

Eddie Carswell and Leonard Ahl-strom   **2000**

NewSong   *Sheltering Tree* (2000) - Bonus Track

Based on an urban legend about a boy who lacks the money to buy a pair of new shoes for his dying mother. The song's narrator supplies the extra money so the boy's mother can wear the shoes, "if Mama meets Jesus tonight." A book and a TV movie both based on the song came out in 2002. It peaked at No. 31 on the Billboard Hot Country Songs chart, spent one week at No. 1 on the Adult Contemporary chart, reached No. 42 on the Hot 100 chart and is certified as a gold record (more than 500,000 copies). However, some consider it overplayed and nauseating. They consider it to be one of the worst (or *the* worst) Christmas songs of all time. According to Jennifer Rutherford, a California collector of more than 600 "terrible" holiday songs, "Christmas Shoes" is intended to be touching and liked. However, "in most people it provokes a divine rage, gasps of horror...like finding syrupy angel statues in a country store. You're supposed to find it cute and enjoyable, but all you feel is nausea."[88]

Christmas Through Your Eyes

Gloria Estefan & Diane Warren   **1993**

Gloria Estefan   *Christmas Through Your Eyes* (1993)

She wants to see Christmas through the eyes of a child again, thinking the world was hers and the world was kind.

The Christmas Tree

David Rose   **1968**

David Rose   *The David Rose Christmas Album*
                                                        (1968)

Pretty, happy Christmas Instrumental.

Christmas Tree

Harry Simeone   **1965**

Harry Simeone Chorale   *The Little Drummer Boy* (1965)

An ode to a Christmas tree.

Christmas Vacation

Barry Mann & Cynthia Weil   **1989**

Mavis Staples   *National Lampoon's Christmas Va-
                                        cation Soundtrack* (1989)

Wonderful theme song to the 1989 classic Christmas comedy movie *National Lampoon's Christmas Vacation.*

I looked for a long time for the original song for digital download, but it was not available, assumedly because of rights issues with the movie. Fortunately, I found the version below, which comes quite close to the original.

a	2010	Dominik Hauser & Katie Campbell	A Christmas Carol: Christmas at the Cinema

(The) Christmas Waltz

Sammy Cahn & Jule Styne   **1954**

Frank Sinatra   Single (1954)

Beautiful classic Christmas song, by the same songwriting duo that gave us "Let It Snow! Let It Snow! Let It Snow!" This song was on the "B" side of the "White Christmas" Single.

On July 16, 1957, Frank Sinatra re-recorded this song with the Jimmy Joyce Singers and Orchestra for his A Jolly Christmas from Frank Sinatra *album (a). [He re-recorded it again on August 12, 1968, for* The Sinatra Family Wish You a Merry Christmas *album.] I personally think his recordings of this gem are the best, but all the renditions listed below are excellent. Peggy Lee's (c) rendition begins with some bars from "The First Noel." The Carpenters (e) version is very popular, getting probably more airtime than the other renditions. (h) and (l) have impressive orchestral accompaniments. (l) is special in that it has at the beginning the same initial bars of the song that only Frank Sinatra had. (i) is a jazz version. Laufey's (o) rendition stands out as her voice sounds like it came from the 1940s. Christina Perry (p) is unique in that it includes the "Merry Christmas, Merry Christmas, may your every dream come true" prelude that Sinatra's backup singers sing; Perri is also notable as she has such a sweet, gentle voice.*

a	1957	Frank Sinatra	A Jolly Christmas from Frank Sinatra
b	1963	*Living Strings*	*The Sound of Christmas*
c	1965	Peggy Lee	Happy Holiday
d	1966	The Lettermen	For Christmas This Year
e	1978	The Carpenters	Christmas Portrait
f	1986	Johnny Mathis	Christmas Eve with Johnny Mathis
g	1998	Michael W. Smith	Christmastime
h	1999	Natalie Cole (feat. London Symphony Orchestra)	The Magic of Christmas
i	2005	Jane Monheit	The Season
j	2008	Kristin Chenowith, et al	A Lovely Way to Spend Christmas
k	2011	She & Him	A Very She & Him Christmas
l	2014	Jackie Evancho, The City of Prague Philharmonic Orchestra, Sally Herbert, Richard Cottle & Shelly Poole	Someday at Christmas
m	2016	*Louise Goulet*	*Christmas Christmas: Magical Holiday Favorites*
n	2017	Sleeping at Last	Christmas Collection, Vol. 1
o	2022	Laufey	A Very Laufey Holiday
p	2023	Christina Perri	Songs for Christmas

Christmas Will Be Just Another Lonely Day

Lee Jackson & Patti Seymour   1964

Brenda Lee   *Merry Christmas from Brenda Lee*
                                                                    (1964)

"Christmas will just be another lonely day" without "you," but Santa Claus will surely bring "you" back. Relatively upbeat song involving romantic separation.

A Christmas Wish

Bobby Goldsboro   1968

Bobby Goldsboro   *Single* (1968)

"B" side of "Look Around You (It's Christmas Time)." Another romantic separation song at Christmastime, but Bobby, though miserable, wishes the best Christmas for his separated lover. Sweet, if sad, song.

(The) Christmas Wish

D. A. Whitman   1979

Kermit the Frog with the Muppets   *John Denver and the Muppets: A Christmas Together* (1979)

From the 1979 Christmas TV Special *John Denver and the Muppets: A Christmas Together*. You don't have to believe in Christmas, but if you believe in love that would be enough to celebrate with me. Truth binds us together, and there will be peace on Earth all year. *Very nice sentiments expressed from a puppet frog.*

A Christmas World

Pat Garvey & Victoria Garvey   1963

The New Christy Minstrels   *Merry Christmas!* (1963)

Spring and summer have come to an end, and a Christmas world is young again.

Christmas Wrapping

Chris Butler   1981

The Waitresses   *A Christmas Record* (1981)

The album has songs by various artists. The "Wrapping" In "Christmas Wrapping" has another meaning: "Rapping," which this song does. Recorded in 1981, this is a very early Rap song, certainly the first Christmas one, this one 6 years prior to "Christmas in Hollis" (1987) by Run DMC.

a	2016	Kylie Minogue	Kylie Christmas

Christmastime

Sol Selegna   1967

Stevie Wonder   *A Christmas Record* (1967)

It's Christmas Time, when there is magic and joy and Church bell chimes.

Christmastime

Billy Corgan   1997

The Smashing Pumpkins   *A Very Special Christmas Volume 3* (1997)

Great "new" Christmas song by a "new" band. In the song they speak of children eagerly awaiting Christmas, later enjoying Christmas as it finally arrives.

Christmastime

Michael W. Smith & Joanna Carlson   1998

Michael W. Smith   *Christmastime* (1998)

Joyous song of Christmastime, with bells ringing and children singing carols.

The Coldest Night of the Year

Cynthia Weil & Barry Mann   **1965**

Nino Tempo & April Stevens   Single (1965)

"B" side of "These Arms of Mine." Song similar to "Baby It's Cold Outside," though the person who has to go out in the snow is male and the woman is trying to get him to leave. It's the "coldest night of the year" and if he leaves, he claims, he might catch the flu.

a	2016	She & Him	Christmas Party

Cool Yule

Steve Allen   **1953**

Louis Armstrong & The Command-   Single (1953)
ers

"B" side of "Zat You, Santa Claus?" Interesting original, with the great Louis Armstrong singing a song written by Steve Allen, famous for many things, like being the first host of *The Tonight Show* and authoring the song "This Could Be the Start of Something Big."

Bette Midler (a) maintains the 40s swing of the song, which is about Santa coming to the US East to West to deliver toys in his "souped-up sled."

a	2005	Bette Midler	Cool Yule

Count Your Blessings Instead of Sheep

Irving Berlin   **1954**

Bing Crosby   *Selections from Irving Berlin's White Christmas* (1954)

From the movie "White Christmas." Basically, the song repeats the phrase in the song title many times, driving home the suggestion to help you sleep. But even with the simple lyrics (accompanied by very pleasant music), it's a very nice song.

Diana Krall (a) provides a very nice rendition, not jazzy like most of her songs, but with her wonderful voice it all sounds great.

a	2005	Diana Krall	Christmas Songs

A Cradle in Bethlehem

Larry Stock & Al Bryan   **1960**

Nat King Cole   *The Magic of Christmas* (1960)

The Story of the first Christmas.

a	1998	Vince Gill	Breath of Heaven: A Christmas Collection

Dance of the Candy Dolls (Dance of the Sugar Plum Fairies)

Pyotr Ilyich Tchaikovsky & Mermann Krasnow   **1954**

Lu Ann Simms & Percy Faith and   Single (1954)
His Orchestra

Version of "Dance of the Sugar Plum Fairies" with lyrics. Lu Amm Simms became an overnight star in 1952 after winning first place on the singing contest *Arthur Godfrey's Talent Scouts.*

Dearest Santa

Bonnie Boyd & Michael Dunn   **1964**

Bobby Vinton   *Kissin' Christmas: The Bobby Vinton Christmas Album* (1964)

The story of Santa Claus visiting a home where children lived but had no home of their own. One boy told Santa that he didn't want toys. Instead, he wanted his own home and family. The song, unfortunately, doesn't say if Santa ever fulfilled his wish!

Decorations

Bob Rivers, Joe Bryant, & Spike O'Neill   **2000**

Bob Rivers   *Chipmunks Roasting on an Open Fire* (2000)

The Beach Boy's hit "Good Vibrations" (1966), with amusing lyrics about Christmas decorations.

Ding-a-Ling the Christmas Bell

Bill Rice & Jerry Foster   **1971**

Lynn Anderson   *The Christmas Album* (1971)

The same year that Lynn Anderson graced us with the mega-hit "Rose Garden," she offered us this Christmas story. A famous Christmas bell once fell, giving him a "funny" ring, and thus he began to be called "Ding-a-Ling." The other bells met secretly, and one said that "Ding-a-Ling" was going to ruin their sound. Hearing this, old "Ding" ran off, only to be found by children who put him atop a tree. That Christmas Eve there was a blinding snow (maybe the same year as Rudolf helped out), so "Ding" rang as loud as he could so Santa could hear him. It was a success!

Do They Know It's Christmas?

Bob Geldof & Midge Ure   **1984**

Band Aid   Single (1984)

This is a song created to raise money for the 1983-1985 famine in Ethiopia, sung by supergroup Band Aid, formed for this effort. Band-Aid's musicians were Phil Collins (drums), John Taylor (Bass guitar), and Midge Ure (various synthesizers). They were accompanied by 37 vocalists, including from the bands Kool & the Gang, Boomtown Rats, Bananarama, Culture Club, Heaven 17, Spandau Ballet, Duran Duran, U2, & Status Quo. As soloists, the band also included Phil Collins, Marilyn (Peter Antony Robinson), George Michael, Sting, Midge Ure, Jody Watley & Paul Young.

The entire process of writing, recording, producing, and releasing "Do They Know It's Christmas" was less than six weeks. The song was recorded in a matter of hours. The single sold a million copies in the first week, topping the UK charts. The song quickly became the fastest-selling single in UK history, a record it would hold until 1997, when it was eclipsed by Elton John's "Candle in the Wind 1997," released in the aftermath of Princess Diana's death. The album raised more than $24 million for relief in Ethiopia, which was desperately needed. The scale of the famine was daunting. The US government estimated it impacted nearly 8 million people—roughly a fifth of Ethiopia's population.[89]

"Do They Know It's Christmas?" was rerecorded and rereleased in 1989 (by Band Aid II), 2004 (by Band Aid 20—its 20th anniversary), 2014 (by Band Aid 30) and 2024 (by Band Aid 40). The 1989 and 2004 versions also raised funds for famine relief, while the 2014 version raised funds for the Ebola crisis in West Africa. The 1989, 2004 and 2014 versions reached number one in the UK, and the 1989 and 2004 versions became Christmas number ones. In 2022 there was a German release.

Song (d) is the German version, which also includes some English lyrics. It included German singing stars, including Art Garfunkel's son, who has become a singing star in Germany.

a	1989	Band Aid II	Single
b	2004	Band Aid 20	Single
c	2014	Band Aid 30	Single
d	2022	Paulina Wagner, Art Garfunkel Jr., et al	Single
e	2024	Band Aid 40	Single

Do You Hear What I Hear?

Noël Regney & Gloria Shayne   1962

The Harry Simeone Chorale   Single (1962)

Many people, including the author, mistakenly assume this Christmas classic has been around for years. But it was written in 1962 during the Cuban Missile Crisis as a powerful plea for peace by a man who had experienced the horrors of war.

A brilliant musical career seemed assured for the French-born Noel Regney. He had studied at Strasbourg Conservatory and at the Conservatoire National de Paris. When WWII arrived, and France was occupied by Germany, Regney was drafted into the German army, much against his will. He hated the Nazis who occupied his homeland. So, while still in the German army, Regney became a member of the French underground. His assignments required him to remain in a German uniform. He collected information and, when possible, warned French resistance fighters of attacks the Germans were planning against them.

One mission would continue to haunt Noel Regney: He was assigned the task of leading a group of German soldiers into a trap where the French fighters could catch them in a crossfire. Although Regney was shot that day, he survived. The French suffered only minor injuries. But the memory of the enemy soldiers falling to the ground, most of them dead, was etched in Noel Regney's mind.

He never commented publicly on what took place that terrifying day. It has been said that he was intentionally wounded by the French to protect him from the Germans, in the belief that his injury would indicate he had no knowledge of the trap that had been set for the enemy.

Not long after this encounter, Regney deserted the German army and lived underground with the French for the rest of the war. "Only then did I feel free," he once observed.

In 1952, Noel Regney moved to Manhattan. He composed music for many early TV shows and commercial jingles, in addition to writing serious musical compositions. He composed the 1963 hit "Dominique" (sung by Soeur Sourire, also known as "The Singing Nun").

In the late 50s, Noel Regney married pianist Gloria Shayne after knowing her for only a few weeks. Their daughter, Gabrielle Regney, says about her mother, "She's an extraordinary pianist and composer who has perfect pitch." Gloria wrote many popular songs recorded by well-known singers, including James Darren, Mike Douglas and Andy Williams.

"My mother's work tends to be more pop; my father's is more classical and avant-garde," says Gabrielle. When her parents collaborated, she says, "Usually, my mother wrote the words and my father wrote the music." But they did the opposite when they composed "Do You Hear What I Hear?" That song came to be as follows.

In October 1962, the Soviet Union and the United States were involved in a crisis centered on missiles the Russians had installed in Cuba. The United States threatened military action if the missiles were not removed. The world trembled and prayed as these two nuclear powers stood eyeball-to-eyeball.

That October, as Noel Regney walked through the streets of New York, a sense of despair was in the air. Regney had endured the horrors of war. He knew the fear and terror of being close to death. The safe and secure life he had built for himself in the United States was on the verge of ending.

Christmas, which was supposed to be a time of peace and goodwill, was approaching. Noel Regney had been asked by a record producer to write a holiday song. "I had thought I'd never write a Christmas song," he recalled. "Christmas had become so commercial. But this was the time of the Cuban Missile Crisis. In the studio, the producer was listening to the radio to see if we had been obliterated.

"En route to my home, I saw two mothers with their babies in strollers. The little angels were looking at each other and smiling. All of a sudden, my mood was extraordinary." A glimpse of these babies filled Noel Regney's heart with poetry. The little ones reminded him of newborn lambs. Thus, the song begins, "Said the night wind to the little lamb...."

As soon as Noel arrived home, he jotted down the lyrics. Then he asked Gloria to write the music to accompany his words. "While walking down the street in New York, my mother heard trumpets playing the melody in her head," explains Gabrielle Regney.

"Noel wrote a beautiful song," Gloria said later, "and I wrote the music. We couldn't sing it, through; it broke us up. We cried. Our little song broke us up. You must realize there was a threat of nuclear war at that time."

The Harry Simeone Chorale performed and released the first recording, and it did well; three years later they would become more famous for "The Little Drummer Boy." But it was the Bing Crosby 1963 recording that brought Noel Regney and Gloria Shayne's song of peace to the nation's attention. In those days, Crosby's recordings were often instant hits; his version sold more than a million copies.

"Do You Hear What I Hear?" carried a beautiful message close to people in all walks of life. It became a popular Christmas carol, but the message of peace was lost on many people. "I am amazed that people can think they know the song and not know it is a prayer for peace," Noel Regney once told an interviewer. "But we are so bombarded by sounds and our attention spans are so short."[90]

There are so many great versions of this great song. Certainly, (d) is one of the most popular and among the best. Bing Crosby (b), as usual, does a lovely job. (j), with Jackie Evancho's voice and a full orchestra to accompany it, is awesome. The most recent on the list, (m), has incredible performances by the Bocelli's, combined with the a cappella group Pentatonix for a glorious outcome. The Instrumentals— (a), (c), (e) and (f)—are all very good, (e) being a lovely New Age version. The rest are all very good, or they wouldn't be listed here.

a	1963	*Living Strings*	*The Sound of Christmas*
b	1963	Bing Crosby with The Ralph Carmichael Chorus and Orchestra	Single
c	1966	*Percy Faith*	*Christmas Is...Percy Faith*
d	1987	Whitney Houston	Exhale
e	2001	*Mannheim Steamroller*	*Christmas Extraordinaire*
f	2002	*Kenny G*	*The Classic Christmas Album*
g	2007	Carrie Underwood	Christmas Music
h	2012	Jordin Sparks	A Very Special Christmas 25th Anniversary
i	2014	Idina Menzel	Holiday Wishes

j	2014	Jackie Evancho, The City of Prague Philharmonic Orchestra, Sally Herbert, Richard Cottle & Shelly Poole	Someday at Christmas
k	2016	Neil Diamond	Acoustic Christmas
l	2019	Celtic Woman	The Magic of Christmas
m	2021	For King & Country	A Drummer Boy Christmas
n	2022	Andrea Bocelli, Matteo Bocelli & Virginia Bocelli (feat. Pentatonix)	(Single)

Do You Know How Christmas Trees Are Grown?

John Barry & Hal David   **1969**

Danish singer "Nina," AKA Nina Magdalene Möller-Hasselblach (in the film), as well as Jackie DeShannon in the same year, 1969   Single (1969, Jackie DeShannon)

From the James Bond film *On Her Majesty's Secret Service* (1969). There are also German and French versions.[91] The answer to the question is that they need sunshine, raindrops, friendship, kindness, and, most of all, love. The song also answers how Santa Claus gets around and how Christmas cards are made, but I don't want to give everything away.

Dominick the Donkey (The Italian Christmas Donkey)

Ray Allen, Wanda Merrell & Sam Saltzberg   **1960**

Lou Monte   Single (1960)

Most have heard this novelty Christmas song. The main point is that Santa's reindeer cannot climb the hills of Italy, so he uses Dominick. Fun song that you can sing to (at least the la-la's).

Dónde Está Santa Claus

Augie Rios   **1958**

Augie Rios   Single (1958)

Another well-known and well-played novelty Christmas song. A Spanish-speaking child is asking, in Spanish mixed with English, "Where is Santa Claus"? He mentions two new reindeer: Pancho and Pedro. Fun song, different from most Christmas music fare.

Driving Home for Christmas

Chris Rea   1986

Chris Rea   Single (1986)

A very pleasant Christmas song that has stayed popular over the years. A man is happily driving home for Christmas and looking forward to getting there—as simple as that.

This great Christmas song is the "B" side of a single, "Hello Friend."

The story behind the song is very interesting and Christmassy. Songwriter Chris Rea explains[92]:

"The story of Driving Home for Christmas is like a classic festive story. It was 1978, coming up to Christmas. It was all over for me: I was just about out of my record contract, and my manager had just told me he was leaving me. I just needed to get home...but the record company wouldn't pay for a rail ticket, and I was banned from driving...My wife...[picked] me up, and we set off back straight away. Then it started snowing. We had £220 and I was fiddling with it all the way home. We kept getting stuck in traffic and I'd look across at the other drivers, who all looked so miserable. Jokingly, I started singing: 'We're driving home for Christmas ...' Then, whenever the streetlights shone inside the car, I started writing down lyrics.

"We eventually got home at 3 AM. It was so cold inside the house that the snow tumbled on to the doormat and didn't melt. There was one letter – from PRS America. My song "Fool (If You Think It's Over)" had been a hit in the US, so there was a cheque for £15,000. We went from being down to our last £220 to being able to buy a house. The [Christmas] song went in my old tin full of unfinished stuff.

"Some years later, my career had turned around and [keyboard player] Max Middleton and I were testing two new pianos. We started joking around, playing this Count Basie-type thing. I pretended I was Nat King Cole. Someone said: "That's a great tune, that. You should get it down." I went back to my tin, and the words to "Driving Home for Christmas fitted perfectly.

"I'd never intended to write a Christmas hit—I was a serious musician! So initially, the song came out on a B-side. Then a DJ flipped it over and started playing it, so Max suggested we re-record it and add some strings. Max played the distinctive jazzy intro, we did a classic 1950s Christmas carol-type arrangement and loved it. At first, it was another radio hit—but then it started re-entering the Top 40 every year."

The original, as is usually the case, is the best version. But the following three are very good. (a) is a very nice rendition with the incomparable Diana Ross; (b) is done very well by the Korgis, a band which produces many remakes of classic rock songs, for collections such as Readers Digest. *They had a hit in 1980 with "Everyone's Gotta Learn Sometime," a hauntingly beautiful song. (c) uses a chorus of young women in the background that makes the song brighter. (d) has a country-western hint to it, which works well with the song.*

a	1994	Diana Ross	Wonderful Christmastime
b	2001	The Korgis	Reader's Digest Music: Wonderful Christmas Time
c	2005	The Bachelors	Christmas with the Bachelors
d	2014	Lee Kernaghan	Driving Home for Christmas

Dysfunctional Family Holidays

Lana Brown   2000

Dysfunctional Family Band   *Dysfunctional Family Christmas*
                                                        (2000)

Warning: this family is *very* dysfunctional.

Every Christmas Eve / Giving (Santa's Theme)

Henry Mancini & Leslie Bricusse   1985

Aled Jones   *Santa Claus: The Movie Soundtrack*
                                                        (1985)

From *Santa Claus: The Movie* (1985). This is a medley of "Every Christmas Eve" and "Giving (Santa's Theme)." Henry Mancini is one of the most successful songwriters in history, and Aled Jones is known for singing a number of great Christmas songs. Very pretty medley about Christmas joy and the bringer of that joy, Santa.

a	1986	Johnny Mathis	Christmas Eve with Johnny Mathis

Every Year, Every Christmas

Luther Vandross & Richard Marx   **1995**

Luther Vandross   *This Is Christmas* (1995)

This song is about a man looking for the love of his life every year at Christmas—he's never met her but hopes one day she will appear, at Christmas. A very unusual song that will make you ponder.

Everybody's Home Tonight

Karla Bonoff & Kenny Edwards   **1979**

Karla Bonoff   *Silent Night* (1979)

Driving home at night, a woman yearns to arrive there, with its warming fire. A bit reminiscent of "Driving Home for Christmas," which was released 7 years later. Karla Bonoff is best known for her 1982 hit "Personally."

Everyone's a Kid at Christmas

Aurora Miller & Ronald Norman Miller   **1967**

Stevie Wonder   *Someday at Christmas* (1967)

A "happy" song about how everybody's a kid of Christmas, and "no one wants to act their age." Uplifting, catchy tune.

The Eyes of a Child

Graham Russell & Ron Bloom   **1987**

Air Supply   *The Christmas Album* (1987)

Very pretty and inspiring song about the joy of youth, where there is laughter and hope and a chance to change the future. It asks the question "does the thrill to achieve match the warm hidden feeling that lies so still and lives in you?" Air Supply was a hitmaker in the 1980s.

Fairytale of New York

Shane MacGowan & Jem Finer   1987

The Pogues featuring Kirsty MacColl   Single (1987)

Great off-beat Christmas tune that has remained popular during the Season. An Irishman spends Christmas Eve in a "drunk tank" of NYC. He thinks of his girl, whom he travelled to NYC with. Then, she sings an Irish-type song about her being with him in NYC. She says he was handsome, promising her Broadway, but he just turned out to be a "bum" and a "punk." She goes on to berate him. He argues with her that he could have been "someone." This description doesn't do justice to the song, which is very entertaining.

Feliz Navidad

Jose Feliciano   1970

Jose Feliciano   *Feliz Navidad* (1970)

Arguably one of the happiest Christmas songs ever written, "Feliz Navidad" was inspired by loneliness. According to Feliciano[93], he wrote the song to express "the joy that I felt on Christmas and the fact that I felt very lonely. I missed my family, I missed Christmas carols with them. I missed the whole Christmas scene."

Translating to "Merry Christmas" from Spanish, "Feliz Navidad" is one of the most downloaded (nearly a million) and aired Christmas songs in the United States and Canada. It has graced every Christmas event I've known and adds a joyous feeling whenever it is played.

Interestingly, the "B" side of this single was Feliciano's version of the Doors' "Light My Fire," which became his biggest hit.

The Instrumentals below vary very much. (a) is done in The Ventures' characteristic old Rock' n' Roll sound, this time reminiscent of "La Bamba"; (c) is New Age; (f) is a beautiful piano piece, by Alexis Ffrench (his last name is not a typo) and (h) is a pretty violin piece with orchestral accompaniment and a disco beat. The improbable matchup of singers in (g) is from The Simpsons *animated TV series. (b), by Penta-tonix, adds an acoustic guitar to their a cappella performance. (d) is done with a Latin beat and Latin background of voices—very pretty. (e) has the usual beautiful voices of Celtic Woman.*

a	2002	*The Ventures*	*Christmas Joy*

b	2002	Pentatonix (feat. La Santa Cecilia)	Holidays around the World
c	2007	*Mannheim Steamroller*	*Christmas Song*
d	2016	Kacey Musgraves	A Very Kacey Christmas
e	2019	Celtic Woman	The Magic of Christmas
f	2020	*Alexis Ffrench*	*Home*
g	2022	Andrea Bocelli, Matteo Bocelli, Virginia Bocelli & The Simpsons	(Single)
h	2022	*Lindsey Stirling*	*Snow Waltz*

The First Christmas Morn

Sue Lane   **1970**

Charley Pride   *Christmas in My Hometown* (1970)

The story of the first Christmas.

First Snowfall

Michael W. Smith   **1989**

Michael W. Smith   *The Christmas Collection* (1989)

Very pleasing Instrumental, with joyous sounds.

Foreigners

Bob Rivers & Twisted Radio, Brian Silva & Dennis Amero   **1987**

Bob Rivers & Twisted Radio   *Bob Rivers & Twisted Radio - Twisted Christmas Boxed Set* (1987)

"*Gloria in excelsis Deo*" with new, nasty lyrics about unwanted foreigners. Skip this one if you don't want to hear about such a thing. Otherwise, listen to this clever, fairly funny spoof.

The Ghosts of Christmas Eve

Robert Kinkel & Paul O'Neill   **1998**

Trans-Siberian Orchestra   *The Christmas Attic* (1998)

Cute song (not Rock, like many Trans-Siberian Orchestra songs) about a little girl who spends Christmas Eve night in the attic, where she finds a trunk "from Christmas past" and explores it, finding it filled with toys, an old wreath and letters. She starts to read the letters, looking to believe in Christmas.

The Gift

Jim Brickman & Tom Douglas   **1997**

Jim Brickman (feat. Collin Raye &   Single (1997)
Susan Ashton)

A love song. The "gift" is the woman the singer prayed for, whom he will hold even when they are grey.

The Gifts They Gave

Pierre de Corbeil & Robert Davis   **1958**

Harry Belafonte   *To Wish You a Merry Christmas* (1958)

Harry Belafonte sings about the first Christmas.

Give Love on Christmas Day

Berry Gordy Jr., Freddie Perren,   **1970**
Deke Richards, Alphonso Mizell &
Christine Yarian

The Jackson Five   *Jackson 5 Christmas Album* (1970)

The Jackson Five's wonderful Christmas song about giving people more than gifts on Christmas Day—giving them love. What the world needs is love; there is no greater gift. Lovely song, great message.

All the following are close to the original, but yet unique and very lovely.

a	1997	SWV	90s Holiday Hits
b	2013	Human Nature	The Christmas Album
c	2015	Taranda Greene	Spirit of Christmas

Goodnight, My Baby

Nick Reynolds   1960

The Kingston Trio   *The Last Month of the Year* (1960)

Song sung to a baby boy, for tomorrow is Christmas Day.

Grandma Got Run Over by a Reindeer

Randy Brooks   1979

Elmo & Patsy   *Grandma Got Run Over by a Reindeer* (1979)

"Elmo" is Dr. Elmo Shropshire, a veterinarian. "Patsy" was his ex-wife, who he claims never sang in this song. Songwriter Randy Brooks was inspired by his uncle, Foster Brooks, a comedian whose single act was to pretend he was drunk (mostly on Dean Martin Roasts, if you recall that). The song has sold over 10 million copies, even though surveys indicate that 20% of people hate or dislike it.[94]

The Greatest Gift of All

John Barlow Jarvis   1984

Kenny Rogers & Dolly Parton   *Once Upon a Christmas* (1984)

After all her guests have left on Christmas Eve, and noting all the gifts under the tree, a woman declares that her husband's love for her is "the greatest gift of all."

Nicolette Larson (a) is best known for her no. 1 hit in 1979, "Lotta Love," written by Neil Young. Larson died on December 16, 1997, at the age of 45, in Los Angeles,

California, because of complications arising from cerebral edema triggered by liver failure. This may have been related to her chronic use of Valium and Tylenol PM.

a	2010	Nicolette Larson	Stars Come Out for Christmas – Special Edition I

(My) Grown-Up Christmas List

David Foster & Linda Thompson Jenner   **1989**

David Foster & Natalie Cole   *River of Love* (1990)

This inspired song was written by pro Christmas songwriter David Foster and Linda Thompson Jenner, then-wife of Bruce (Caitlin) Jenner. The song answers the question, "what would a grown-up put on their Christmas list?" and then answers that question masterfully. Awesome song.

The song was originally written for the 1989 CBC Christmas program *A David Foster Christmas Card.*

In (a) the incomparable Natalie Cole sings this song with the fabulous London Symphony Orchestra, with incredible results. Jane Monheit (b), normally a jazz singer, sings this song in its original way, sans jazz elements. (c) has Kelly Clarkson singing the song with the a cappella group Pentatonix in the background.

a	1999	Natalie Cole (feat. London Symphony Orchestra)	The Magic of Christmas
b	2005	Jane Monheit	The Season
c	2018	Pentatonix (feat. Kelly Clarkson)	Pentatonix - The Greatest Christmas Hits

Hallelujah

Leonard Cohen   **1984**

Leonard Cohen   *Various Positions* (1984)

A simply beautiful song, hard to describe.

As beautiful as the original is, I prefer Pentatonix's version, (a). (a) is simply phenomenal. It seems that the song is perfect for that a cappella group. For a fantastic violin version with background accompaniment and chorus, see (b).

| a | 2016 | Pentatonix | A Pentatonix Christmas |
| b | 2018 | *Lindsey Stirling* | *Warmer in the Winter* |

A Handful of Happy New Years

Krondes & Plano   **1963**

Living Strings   *The Sound of Christmas* (1963)

A joyful Instrumental that may sound familiar to you.

Hang Them on a Tree

Connie Pearce & Arnold Miller   **1961**

June Christy   *This Time of Year* (1961)

The title of this song is disturbing, but the song is not. June sings that she will take the "sorrows of last November" and hang them on a tree and take the "quarrels of last September" and hang them there as well. She will take a year's worth of troubles and tie them to the tree, where they will be shining bright. For her, "time is the best decorator." This is all a unique way of dealing with the bad things of life and putting them away and looking back at them with hope. The song is not maudlin; it does swing and have a fairly upbeat tune. And her voice is marvelous.

Happiest Christmas

Ted Dicks & Myles Rudge   **1969**

Petula Clark   *The Great Songs of Christmas by Great Artists of Our Time, Album Nine* (1969)

Ninth in a series of annual Christmas albums produced for the Goodyear Rubber Company and sold exclusively at their chain of tire shops in the US and Canada. Many of these consisted of previously released tracks, but this track was created especially for the album.

The original with Petula Clark is unavailable for some reason, but fortunately Michael W. Smith, a wonderful songwriter/singer of Christmas music, Christian music and mainstream music, provides us with the version below. He sings that the happiest Christmas is a home Christmas, and the happiest wishes are just old-fashioned wishes. It is a warm song, beautifully executed. [Michael W. Smith appears in this book quite often, in this Chapter and next.]

a	1998	Michael W. Smith	Christmastime

Happy Birthday Jesus

J. P. Pennington & Teddy Gentry   **1996**

Alabama   *Christmas Vol. II* (1996)

Alabama offers this song just for Jesus, who makes us get through bad times. They apologize for the materialism of Christmas, and forgetting what it really means. What we should be giving at Christmas is thanks to Jesus. Very nice song.

Happy Christmas Day

Charley Pride & Sue Lane   **1970**

Charley Pride   *Christmas in My Hometown* (1970)

"Happy" song about a happy Christmas day. Charley sings of a pleasant Christmas day at home but reminds us of Jesus' birth and the warm remembrance of those who have passed.

Happy Holidays

Ronnie Rogers & Swain Schaefer   **1985**

Alabama   *Christmas* (1985)

Not to be confused with "Happy Holidays," written by Irving Berlin in 1942. Alabama sings an upbeat song about the sights and sounds of Christmas, indicating "happy holidays."

Happy Xmas (War Is Over) AKA So This Is Christmas

John Lennon & Yoko Ono   **1971**

John & Yoko/The Plastic Ono Band   Single (1971)

Sung with The Harlem Community Choir in background. A protest song against the war in Vietnam, which did not actually end until two years later, in 1973.

Songs (a) and (c) are known as "Happy Christmas (War is Over)"; song (f) is known as "So This is Christmas." Song (a) is very nicely done, with a children's choir, as in the original. Song (b) is the fullest, with Celine's great voice, good instrumentation, and adult choir background. Song (c) is done very ably by The Moody Blues. Song (d) is sung very nicely by Sarah, and she is also accompanied by a children's chorus. (e) is a solid performance, with a hint of chorus. The only Instrumental on the list, (f), is very beautiful.

a	1992	Neil Diamond	The Christmas Album
b	1998	Celine Dion	These Are Special Times
c	2003	The Moody Blues	December
d	2006	Sarah McLachlan (feat. The Sarah McLachlan Music Outreach Children's Choir and Youth Choir)	Wintersong
e	2011	Scott Weiland	The Most Wonderful Time of Year
f	2015	*Christmas Eve Carols Academy*	*Instrumental Christmas Songs - The Very Best Traditional Christmas Carols*

Hard Candy Christmas

Carol Hall   **1982**

Dolly Parton   Single (1982)

Song from the musical *The Best Little Whorehouse in Texas*. It's a "hard candy" Christmas because life has been hard, and the singer can "barely get through tomorrow." But there is hope expressed by the singer: maybe sorrow won't let them down and they'll be fine.

Tracey Thorn (a) was part of the duo Everything but the Girl, best known for their 1994 hit "Missing."

a	2012	Tracey Thorn	Tinsel and Lights (Deluxe Edition)

Hark! The Herald Trumpet's Sing

"Chip" Louis Davis Jr.   **1993**

Mannheim Steamroller   *A Fresh Aire Christmas* (1993)

Re-imagining of "Hark! The Herald Angels Sing"; very powerful.

("Have a" or "A") Holly Jolly Christmas

Johnny Marks   **1964**

The Quinto Sisters (First Release)   Single (for both) (1964)
Burl Ives (First Recording)

Though Burl Ives' rendition was the first to be recorded, the Quinto Sisters beat him with their release, just barely. Ives' rendition was featured in the 1964 Rankin-Bass stop-motion animated Christmas special, *Rudolph the Red-Nosed Reindeer*, in which Burl Ives voiced the narrator, Sam the Snowman. Originally to be sung by Larry D. Mann as Yukon Cornelius, the song, as well as "Silver and Gold," was given to Ives due to his singing fame. This version was also included on the sound-track album. Ives re-recorded the song for the single. The composer of this song, Johnny Marks, also wrote "Rudolf the Red-Nosed Reindeer," back in 1949. The creator of the fictional character of Rudolf was Marks' brother-in-law, Robert May.

Song (a) below has quite a different sound from the original. It certainly rocks more but doesn't stray much from the charm of the original.

a	2015	Human Nature	The Christmas Album

He'll Be Coming Down the Chimney (Like He Always Did Before)

J. Fred Coots & Al J. Neiburg   **1951**

Gene Autry   Single (1951)

Classic wherein children are assured Santa will get to them like he always has on Christmas Eve.

a	1953	Guy Lombardo and His Royal Canadians	Jingle Bells

Heigh Ho the Holly

Hawley Ades   **1957**

Fred Waring & The Pennsylvanians   *Now Is the Caroling Season* (1957)

The words "Heigh Ho the Holly" appear in a song "Blow, Blow, Thou Winter Wind" which appears in Shakespeare's play *As You Like It*, Act II, Scene VII, written in 1599. This song is not the same as Shakespeare's, however; it just shares this phrase. The song is a short carol celebrating Christmas and "old St. Nick" coming down the chimney.

Holiday for Bells

Bert Kaempfert   1963

Bert Kaempfert   *Christmas Wonderland* (1963)

From *Life in the 1960s: The True Story* (2019, p.63) by this author: "One master of 60s pop would include a man who you have probably never heard of, but you have probably heard his work—Burt Kaempfert (1923-80). Burt graced us with 'Strangers in the Night,' the number 1 hit sung by Frank Sinatra in 1966; 'Danke Schoen' (1962), Wayne Newton's signature song; 'L-O-V-E,' recorded by the late great Nat King Cole in 1966; 'A Swingin' Safari' (1962), and the happy tunes 'Afrikaan Beat' and 'That Happy Feeling' (both 1962).'" This Instrumental reflects his "happy" style.

Holly Leaves and Christmas Trees

Red West & Glen Spreen   1971

Elvis Presley   *Elvis Sings the Wonderful World of*
Christmas (1971)

Great Christmas song from the great Elvis Presley. Elvis sings about the nice things of Christmas, like Christmas trees, holly leaves, Christmas bells and lights. Christmas "seems to come and go" and now, that his Love is not with him, those nice things don't mean so much to him anymore.

(There's No Place Like) Home for the Holidays

Al Stillman & Robert Allen   1954

Perry Como with Mitch Ayres and His   Single (1954)
Orchestra

Christmas classic by a classic Christmas crooner.

The (a) version is a new recording by Como, with a more modern, upbeat sound; this is the version we usually hear on the radio. (b) is a very popular version. (c) is very nicely done.

a	1959	Perry Como with Mitchell Ayres and His Orchestra and The Ray Charles Singers	Season's Greetings from Perry Como
b	1978	The Carpenters	Christmas Portrait
c	2018	Martina McBride	It's the Holiday Season

Home on Christmas Day

Cyndi Lauper, Rob Hyman & William Wittman   **1998**

Cyndi Lauper   *Merry Christmas...Have A Nice Life* (1998)

Cyndi Lauper, superstar of the 1980s, sings this song of separation from loved ones right before Christmas, but she says she'll be home on Christmas Day.

Homecoming Christmas

Ronnie Rogers   **1985**

Alabama   *Christmas* (1985)

Alabama reminisces about Christmas when they were young, but they are coming home and can't wait to be back.

Homeless on the Holidays

Bob Rivers, Joe Bryant & Spike O'Niell   **2000**

Bob Rivers   *Chipmunks Roasting on an Open Fire* (2000)

Spoof of "There's No Place Like Home for the Holidays."

Howdy Doody's Christmas Party

Edward Kean   1951

Howdy Doody ("Buffalo" Bob Smith)   Single (1951) - both sides, a Part 1
and the "Howdy Doody" show cast   and a Part 2

Available as a 10" Vinyl and a 7" Children's Vinyl (colored yellow). *The Howdy Doody Show* ran on NBC from 1947 to 1960 and featured "Buffalo" Bob Smith (decked out as a cowboy), a freckle-faced boy marionette (operated by physically obvious strings) named "Howdy Doody" and characters such as a mute clown called Clarabell, originally played by Bob Keeshan, who would later start his own kid's show *Captain Kangaroo* (1955-84).

The record includes songs for Christmas and the characters from the show.

I Believe in Christmas

Glen Campbell   2000

Glen Campbell   *Christmas* (2000)

He believes in Christmas, but Christmas isn't snow or decorations or even Santa. Love is what it's all about. Christmas would come true if all the love shown in the season would stay awhile. Very pretty song about what Christmas' true meaning.

I Believe in Father Christmas

Music: Greg Lake   1974
Lyrics: Peter Sinfield
Includes orchestrations by Sergei
Prokofiev

Greg Lake   Single (1975)

One of the best Christmas songs to grace the "modern" period. Emerson, Lake & Palmer's keyboardist Keith Emerson had encouraged each member of the band to come up with solo material, so in 1975 Lake teamed up with lyricist Sinfield to create something out of a "Christmassy" chord sequence Lake had written. The result was an anti-consumerist Christmas song that nonetheless was warm and thoughtful. Emerson, however, wanted to add a snippet from a classic piece by Sergei Prokofiev (1891-1953). [Prokofiev had scored music for *Romeo and Juliet* and *Peter and* the *Wolf.*] This "snippet" was a score Prokofiev had written in 1933 for the satirical film *Lieutenant Kijé*, specifically the "Troika" section, which later became one of the first pieces of film music to become an orchestral suite. The "Troika" sequence features a drunken night-time trip in which one of the characters is so addled by drink that he tumbles off a sleigh.[95]

Song (b) is a fantastic New Age version that unfortunately I cannot find the composer of. It begins with sad, haunting strings and segues into a simple part that builds into a pretty crescendo, with an angelic choir, only at its conclusion to return to the sad strings from the beginning. In (c) Sarah Brightman sings in her angelic voice, accompanied by angelic chorus and wonderful instrumentation. (d) presents us with a simple calm version. (e) is powerful.

a	1977	Emerson, Lake & Palmer (Without Orchestra)	Emerson, Lake & Palmer - Works, Vol. 2
b	*2004*	*Unknown*	*The Greatest Christmas Songs*
c	2008	Sarah Brightman	A Winter Symphony
d	2021	Gary Barlow	The Dream of Christmas
e	2024	Sixpence None the Richer	The Dawn of Grace

I Believe in Santa Claus

Dolly Parton   **1984**

Dolly Parton & Kenny Rogers   *Once Upon a Christmas* (1984)

Dolly and Kenny believe in Santa Claus because they believe "that dreams and plans and wishes can come true." They also believe in family, country, neighbors, God and many good things, including forgiving those who hurt you.

I Heard the Bells on Christmas Day

Johnny Marks & Henry   **1956**
Wadsworth Longfellow

Bing Crosby with The Ken Darby Sing-   Single (1956)
ers and Orchestra directed by Buddy
Cole

Based on the 1863 poem "Christmas Bells" by American poet Henry Wadsworth Longfellow (1807-82). On Christmas day, 1863, Longfellow—a 57-year-old widowed father of six children, the oldest of which had been nearly paralyzed in battle as his country fought a war against itself—wrote the poem seeking to capture the dynamic and dissonance in his own heart and the world he observed around him.

He heard the bells that Christmas day and the singing of "peace on earth" (Luke 2:14), but he observed the world of injustice and violence that seemed to mock the truthfulness of this optimistic outlook. The theme of listening to the bells recurred throughout the poem, eventually leading to a settled, confident hope even in the midst of bleak despair.[96]

Johnny Marks, who wrote "Rudolf the Red-Nosed Reindeer," also wrote the music for the special 1964 TV Show of the same name. He included an Instrumental of this song among its background music and included it in the show's soundtrack.

Song (a) is a beautiful, traditional version by Fred Waring and The Pennsylvanians. Seven years later, Frank Sinatra sang with them with great results (d). Harry Belafonte (b) provided a lovely version, with his unique, gentle voice. The lovely instrumental version of (c) is the first part of a medley with "Silver Bells" and "Out of the East." (e) is from the Rudolf *soundtrack, even though it was just a part of background music. (f) is a nice, gentle version with minimal instrumentation. (g) is Burl Ives as his usual great self. (h) is a very simple version, with Jane Monheit's beautiful voice. (i) is a powerful, very modern, version, with a modified tune of the original.*

a	1957	Fred Waring & The Pennsylvanians	Now is the Caroling Season
b	1958	Harry Belafonte	To Wish You a Merry Christmas
c	*1963*	*Living Strings*	*The Sound of Christmas*
d	1964	Frank Sinatra and Fred Waring	12 Songs of Christmas
e	1964	Decca Concert Orchestra	Rudolph the Red Nosed Reindeer (Original 1964 Soundtrack)
f	1965	Living Voices	The Little Drummer Boy
g	1965	Burl Ives	Have a Holly Jolly Christmas
h	2005	Jane Monheit	The Season
i	2008	Casting Crowns	Peace on Earth

I Like a Sleighride (Jingle Bells)

Based on "Jingle Bells," by James Pierpont   1960

Peggy Lee   *Christmas Carousel* (1960)

"Modernization" and "cool" version (for 1960) of "Jingle Bells," written in 1850 by James Lord Pierpont (1822-93).

I Remember (Sky)

Stephen Sondheim   **1966**

Charmian Carr (on TV)   *The Classic Christmas Album* (2001)
Christmas version: Barbra Streisand

This song from a TV episode titled "Evening Primrose" (1966) was never released at the time. It was only released as a very limited edition of only 3,000 copies in 2008. Other renditions, however, were created and released well before that. Barbra Streisand's version precedes the song with a section of Christmas-themed lyrics, and then segues into the "I Remember (Sky)" song itself, which is not a Christmas song but portrays vivid Winter images.

"Evening Primrose," made for TV as a segment of the anthology series *ABC Stage 67*, is a strange but beautiful musical with music by Steven Sondheim about people who escape their lives by living in a department store. The song is sung by the character named Ella (Charmian Carr, the eldest von Trapp girl in *The Sound of Music*), who is describing to a character played by Anthony Perkins (*Psycho*) what memories she has of outside the department store. The show is available on YouTube[97] for free.

I Saw Mommy Kissing Santa Claus

Tommie Connor   **1952**

Jimmy Boyd   Single (1952)

This song was commissioned by Saks Fifth Avenue to promote the store's Christmas card for the year, which featured an original sketch by artist Perry Barlow, who drew for *The New Yorker* for many decades. Jimmy Boyd was only 13 years old when he recorded this song. It reached No. 1 on the Billboard pop singles chart in December 1952. Boyd appeared in several films, including *Inherit the Wind* (1960), with Spencer Tracey. From 1960 to 1962 he was married to actress Yvonne Craig, TV's Batgirl.

The Catholic Archdiocese of Boston condemned the song when it was first released, on the grounds it implied a link between kissing and Christmas, and radio stations followed suit banning it in several markets as well. It wasn't until 13-year-old Boyd went to Boston to meet with Church leaders at the archdiocese and explained the meaning of its lyrics that the ban was lifted.[98]

Of the list below, (c), (d) and (e) are all extremely popular. They can be heard every Christmastime.

a	1953	Guy Lombardo and His Royal Canadians	Jingle Bells
b	1953	Teresa Brewer	Single. Also on *Last Christmas: Holiday Rarities* (2011)
c	1963	The Ronettes	A Christmas Gift for You from Phil Spector
d	1970	Jackson 5	Jackson 5 Christmas Album
e	1987	John Mellencamp	A Very Special Christmas

I Thank You for Your Love

Harvey Schmidt   **1994**

Laurie Beechman   Unknown; appears on *A Broadway Christmas* (1994)

From *The Mummers Play* by Harvey Schmidt and Tom Jones, the team that first won fame as the creators of *The Fantasticks*—the longest-running musical in the history of the world, with more than 21,000 performances given in New York over a period of 58 years. That play's stage is tiny and bare—I know, I've been on it (for an audition).

This very pretty song has a woman thanking her Love for the best Christmas present he has given her—his love. She also thanks God for His love, gracing her with the people she cares for.

I Want a Hippopotamus for Christmas

John Herring (as John Rox)   **1953**

Gayla Peevey - Orch. under dir. of   Single (1953)
Norman Leyden

Gayla Peevy, at age ten, was already a singing star on radio and television in Oklahoma, with a contract with Columbia Records, when she sang this hit novelty Christmas song. Contrary to popular belief, she did not sing the song to raise funds for acquiring a hippopotamus at the Oklahoma City Zoo. Instead, the song came first, and its popularity launched a fundraiser wherein a lot of people supplied small coins to purchase a real hippopotamus named Matilda for Gayla, which she received on Christmas Eve. She did give it away to the Oklahoma City Zoo, moving to California. Matilda lived nearly 50 years.

Interestingly, the song credits, as shown on the record itself, claim the orchestra was under direction of Norman Leyden. However, Gayla fondly recalls being flown to New York City and performing the song under direction of Mitch Miller, who allowed her to modify the song to include names of other animals. As big as her song became, she claimed she never received any royalties for it.[99]

By 2016, however, she had discovered that there was an account under her name with Sony Music from which she could claim royalties and she was also getting revenue for the song through iTunes.[100]

I Wish It Could Be Christmas Every Day

Roy Wood   **1973**

Wizzard   Single (1973)

Roy Wood is a founding member of the Electric Light Orchestra (ELO). This song appears in a special Christmas episode of the TV Series *Black Mirror* from December 2014 called "White Christmas," wherein a digital clone of a real person confesses in cyberspace (a place referred to as a "cookie") that his real counterpart left his daughter to freeze to death. As punishment, a law enforcement officer sets the time inside the character's cookie to run at 1,000 years per minute on an infinite loop. All throughout that time, the song plays constantly from a radio—which he attempts to destroy but keeps reappearing and playing the song, making him to begin to go insane.

Notwithstanding the above, this is a very jolly song about Christmas.

All the versions of this song are quite similar.

a	2007	Paul Winters	All I Want for Christmas
b	2008	Sarah Brightman	A Winter Symphony
c	2013	Leona Lewis	Christmas, with Love
d	2016	Kylie Minogue	Kylie Christmas
e	2017	Cheap Trick	Christmas Christmas

I'm Gonna Be Warm This Winter

Hank Hunter & Mark Barkan   **1962**

Connie Francis   Single (1962)

She's going to be warm this winter because she met a man at a ski lodge that warms her up. Happy song, representative in style for the period.

a	2016	Kylie Minogue	Kylie Christmas

If Every Day Was Like Christmas

Red West   **1965**

Bobby West   Single (1965)

The next year, 1966, Elvis Presley with The Jordanaires and The Imperials Quartet recorded and released this song, with much greater success than the original. He made it into a perennial Christmas classic.

a	1966	Elvis Presley	Elvis Sings the Wonderful World of Christmas

If I Hear Another Song About Christmas

Paul Alter & Sammy Fain   **1994**

Michael Feinstein?   Unknown. Earliest appearance seems to be on *An Intimate Holiday with Michael Feinstein* (2001)

Don't let the song title fool you. The singer claims that nothing thrills him like a Christmas song. Simple tune that alludes to other Christmas songs.

a	2007	Pat Boone	The True Spirit of Christmas

If We Make It Through December

Merle Haggard   **1974**

Merle Haggard & The Strangers   *If We Make It Through December* (1974)

Nice country song. If they make it through December and its cold everything will be fine. They will be somewhere warm, like California. The singer was laid off from his job.

In the Quiet of a Silent Night

First Call   1995

First Call   *Beyond December* (1995)

Pretty song, nicely sung, that uses lyrics from "Silent Night" but to a different, 90s tune.

Is Christmas Only a Tree

Mark Rebek   1955

Bing Crosby   Single (1955)

Song about the true meaning of Christmas, proclaiming it is more than just what it physically appears to be. "B" side of "Christmas Is A-Comin' (May God Bless You)."

It Kinda Looks Like Christmas

Dick Holler   1966

The Royal Guardsmen   Single (1966)

"B" side of the hit Christmas single "Snoopy's Christmas." Gentle, catchy and happy tune about the things you see at Christmas.

It Must Have Been the Mistletoe (Our First Christmas)

Douglas Konecky & Justin Wilde   1984

Barbara Mandrell   *Christmas At Our House* (1984)

Reminiscing about a first Christmas together.

It Wasn't His Child

Skip Ewing   **1988**

Sawyer Brown   *Wide Open* (1988)

Song about the first Christmas, particularly about Joseph, Mary's husband, and how he accepted Jesus, the Son of God, as his own son.

a	1994	Trisha Yearwood	The Sweetest Gift

It's Beginning to Look a Lot Like Christmas

Meredith Wilson   **1951**

Perry Como and The Fontane Sisters   Single (1951)
with Mitchell Ayres and His Orchestra

Popular song every Christmas, usually associated with its original crooner, Perry Como.

Song (c) is a medley with "Silver Bells," "The Christmas Song," and "Santa Claus Is Coming to Town." Song (f) is Celtic New Wave and (h) is a cappella.

a	1951	Bing Crosby with Jud Conlon's Rhythmaires and John Scott Trotter and His Orchestra	Single ("B" Side of "Christmas in Killarney")
b	1963	*Andre Kostelanetz and His Orchestra*	*Wonderland of Christmas*
c	1975	The Sesame Street Cast	Sesame Street: Merry Christmas from Sesame Street
d	1986	Johnny Mathis	Christmas Eve with Johnny Mathis
e	2011	Michael Bublé	Christmas
f	2012	Celtic Angels	New Age Christmas
g	2016	John Farnham & Olivia Newton-John	Friends for Christmas
h	2018	Pentatonix	Christmas Is Here!
i	2018	Martina McBride	It's the Holiday Season
j	2019	Perry Como & The Royal Philharmonic Orchestra	Christmas with the Stars & The Royal Philharmonic Orchestra
k	2023	Tom Gaebel	A Christmas to Remember

It's Christmas (All Over the World)

Bill House & John Hobbs   **1985**

Sheena Easton   *Santa Claus: The Movie Soundtrack*
(1985)

From *Santa Claus: The Movie* (1985), the title says it all. Sheena Easton is one of the most successful British female recording artists of the 1980s.

It's Christmas Again

Henry Mancini & Leslie Bricusse   **1985**

The Ambrosian Children's Choir   *Santa Claus: The Movie Soundtrack*
(1985)

From *Santa Claus: The Movie* (1985).

It's Christmas Time Again

Sonny Burke, Jack Elliott &   **1953**
James Harwood

Peggy Lee   Single (1953)

"One wish came true: you're here with me."

a	1986	Johnny Mathis	Christmas Eve with Johnny Mathis

It's Christmas Time All Over the World

Hugh Martin   **1965**

Sammy Davis Jr.   *The Great Songs of Christmas by
Great Artists of Our Time, Album Five*
(1965)

Wishing a "Merry Christmas" to all in the world, in many different languages. The Album is the fifth in a series of annual Christmas albums produced for the Goodyear Rubber Company and sold exclusively at their chain of tire shops in the US and Canada. Many of these consisted of previously released tracks, but some did contain previously unreleased material as well.

| a | 2023 | Seth MacFarlane & Liz Gillies | We Wish You the Merriest |

It's Gonna Be a Cold, Cold Christmas

Roger Greenaway & Geoff Stephens   **1975**

Dana   Single (1975)

Cute, pretty song about separation from someone's "darling" at Christmas.

It's the Most Wonderful Time of the Year (AKA The Most Wonderful Time of the Year)

George Wyle & Eddie Pola   **1963**

Andy Williams   *The Andy Williams Christmas Album*
                                                                   (1963)

The Christmas classic associated with original crooner Andy Williams.

Aside from the original, Song (a) is probably the most popular version below. Song (e) is a cappella. Song (g) is a vocal with string quartet. Song (p) has a disco beat.

a	1986	Johnny Mathis	Christmas Eve with Johnny Mathis
b	1992	Amy Grant	Home for Christmas
c	1993	David Foster (feat. Johnny Mathis)	The Christmas Album
d	1998	Vince Gill	Breath of Heaven: A Christmas Collection
e	2014	Pentatonix	That's Christmas to Me
f	2016	Kylie Minogue	Kylie Christmas
g	2017	Sleeping at Last	Christmas Collection, Vol. 1
h	2018	Ingrid Michaelson	Ingrid Michaelson's Songs for the Season
i	2018	Martina McBride	It's the Holiday Season
j	2019	Lea Michele	Christmas in the City
k	2019	Andy Williams (with the Roy-	Christmas with the Stars & The

		al Philharmonic Orchestra)	Royal Philharmonic Orchestra
l	2019	Idina Menzel	Christmas: A Season of Love
m	2020	Mandy Moore	Single ("How Could This Be Christmas")
n	2021	The Galway Christmas Singers	Family Christmas: Favorite Carols and Holiday Songs
o	2021	Gary Barlow	The Dream of Christmas
p	2023	Holidayz	Christmas Dance Party 2023
q	2023	Mark Tremonti	Mark Tremonti Christmas Classics New & Old

Jingle Bell Rock

Joe Beal & Jim Boothe   1957

Bobby Helms   Single (1957)

"Jingle Bell Rock," a classic among Christmas music since its inception in 1957, is arguably the first "Rock 'n Roll" Christmas song. But its official authorship may be in doubt. Bobby Helms, who performs the song, and Hank "Sugarfoot" Garland claimed that they wrote "Jingle Bell Rock" together and Garland claimed he was due $100 million in royalties.

Much of the trouble may have resulted from mishandled paperwork. Session guitarists often composed music on the fly, neglecting to write notes. Garland had demonstrated a knack for quick composing when working with Elvis Presley.

Garland recalled a midnight Decca recording session in 1957 when Producer Owen Bradley came to him with "Jingle Bell Hop." He didn't think it was any good and claimed that he and Helms then wrote "Jingle Bell Rock." "We threw a bridge in," he said, "added a couple of verses, changed the words." Basically, it was a whole new song.

Garland and Helms recorded "Jingle Bell Rock" that same night. What was believed to have happened is that the publisher, Decca, treated this as a session where they owned it and controlled it.

Despite the above, Helms never tried to get royalties. He stated that that would "be a joke. You know how the music business is." Garland, however, pursued it.[101] He died in 2004.

Aside from the original, Song (b) is probably the most popular version below.

Song (f) is titled "Jingle Bell Pop" but has the same tune and lyrics and is performed a cappella.

a	1964	Brenda Lee	A Rockin' Christmas with Brenda Lee
b	1990	Daryl Hall & John Oates	Home for Christmas
c	1992	Neil Diamond	The Christmas Album
d	2012	Blake Shelton	Cheers, It's Christmas
e	2017	*Lindsey Stirling*	*Warmer in the Winter*
f	2020	Pentatonix	We Need a Little Christmas
g	2021	Billy Idol	Happy Holidays

Jingle Jingle Jingle

Johnny Marks　　　　　　　　　　　　　　　　　　　　　**1964**

Stan Francis　　　　　　　　　　　*Rudolph the Red Nosed Reindeer Original 1964 TV Soundtrack* (1964)

Stan Francis (1899-1966) was the actor who voiced Santa Claus in *Rudolph the Red Nosed Reindeer* (1964).

Jingo Jango

Bert Kaempfert & Herbert Rehbein　　　　　　　　　**1963**

Bert Kaempfert Orchestra　　　　　　*Christmas Wonderland* (1963)

Like much of Bert Kaempfert's music, this Instrumental is a happy tune.

Having heard them in Hamburg one night, Burt Kaempfert signed the Beatles into their first recording contract, to Bert Kaempfert Productions, for a year. Four months later, the Beatles' recording of "My Bonnie" was released as a single on Polydor Germany. Within days of its release a customer walked into Brian Epstein's Liverpool shop and asked for "the record by the Beatles," a new name to Epstein. When the next day two young women also asked for "My Bonnie," he decided to go and see the Beatles at their home. By the end of the year, Epstein had asked for the Beatles to be released early from their commitment to Bert Kaempfert Productions, something Kaempfert was happy to do as he was too busy with his own music to lose sleep about them moving elsewhere.[102]

Joseph and Mary's Boy

Don Cook & Keith Whitley　　　　　　　　　　　　　**1985**

Alabama   *Christmas* (1985)

The song is about who deserves the credit for the blessings we enjoy—Joseph and Mary's boy, Jesus.

Just One Night

Mac McAnally   **1991**

Mac McAnally   *The Stars Come Out for Christmas* (1991)

The "one night" is the night Jesus was born. The singer describes the nice things at Christmas, and that sometimes we forget it all became possible because of that night.

This album is a compilation of various well-known artists singing Christmas songs[103].

Kay Thompson's Jingle Bells

"Jingle Bells" by James Pierpoint   **1963**
Arrangement by Kay Thompson
and Johnny Mandel

Andy Williams   *The Andy Williams Christmas Album* (1963)

Song based on "Jingle Bells," introducing additional lyrics and music.

Andy Williams was Kay Thompson's protégé. She also provided him "The Holiday Season" (which she recorded in 1945) for this album to sing in a medley with "Happy Holiday," "Happy Holiday" occurring first in the medley. This medley was later sung by others.

Kissin' Christmas

B. Merrill, R. Dante & B. Meshel   **1964**

Bobby Vinton   *Kissin' Christmas: The Bobby Vinton Christmas Album* (1964)

Simple, repetitive song about visitors at Christmas and kissing them all. The song is indicative of Vinton's Polish roots, having a polka-type sound.

Kling, Glockchen

Louis ("Chip") Davis Jr.   **1995**

Mannheim Steamroller   *Christmas in the Aire* (1995)

The title of this song is German for "ring the bell." Pretty Instrumental with bells and children's chorus singing in German.

Last Christmas

George Michael   **1984**

Wham!   Single (1984)

1980s Christmas hit about betrayal of a love given to another the previous Christmas. This song has become a Christmas standard.

Song (a) is a very pretty Instrumental of this song. (b) is done as an early 60s Rock 'n Roll song with great effectiveness. (c) is done as a soft jazz piece—very classy and well-done.

a	2015	*Christmas Eve Carols Academy*	*Instrumental Christmas Songs - The Very Best Traditional Christmas Carols*
b	2017	Gwen Stefani	You Make It Feel Like Christmas
c	2021	Kelly Clarkson	When Christmas Comes Around...

Linus and Lucy

Vince Guaraldi   **1965**

Vince Guaraldi Trio   *A Charlie Brown Christmas Soundtrack* (1965)

From *A Charlie Brown Christmas* TV special (1965), the very familiar theme of characters Linus and Lucy.

Little Altar Boy

Howlett Smith   **1961**

Vic Dana   Single (1961)

Someone who has "gone astray" asks a little altar boy to pray for them.

a	1978	The Carpenters	Christmas Portrait (Special Edition)

Little Christmas Tree

George S. Clinton & Artie Wayne   **1974**

Michael Jackson   Single (1974)

Pretty but sad song about a person seeing nice things on Christmas Eve but where the person's Love used to meet them there is only a little Christmas tree standing now. It's all alone on Christmas Eve as well.

a	2022	Kadhja Bonet	Christmas Holiday

The Little Road to Bethlehem

Michael Head & Margaret Rose   **1983**

Aled Jones   *Diolch â Chân* (1983)

The album title translates from Welsh into "thank you with a song." Along the road to Bethlehem, the traveler hears Mary singing a lullaby to Jesus. The traveler also hears sheep bells as Mary sings.

a	1990	Judy Collins	Christmas Classics

Little Saint Nick

Brian Wilson & Mike Love   **1964**

The Beach Boys   *The Beach Boys' Christmas Album* (1964)

Familiar Christmas classic from The Beach Boys, part of the standard collection of Christmas songs heard every year.

Song (b) is a cappella.

a	2012	Lady A	On This Winter's Night
b	2021	Pentatonix	Evergreen

The Little Star

Connie Pearce & Arnold Miller   **1961**

June Christy   *This Time of Year* (1961)

There was a little star who couldn't grow. Other stars squandered all their light for astronomers, but the little star did not. Then there came a dark night where a special star was needed, but all were tired and dim except for the little star, which became the brightest star ever known.

Though not sung, it is implied this was the Star of Bethlehem.

Look Around You (It's Christmas Time)

Bobby Goldsboro   **1968**

Bobby Goldsboro   Single (1968)

A Dylan-like song that tears down usual conceptions of Christmas: corner Santa's hold a bell in one hand and a bottle (of booze, it would seem) in the other; fathers celebrate Christmas by drinking, while their poor children wait for presents that they know will never come; beggars sell pencils, but nobody has a dime to spare; and more. Not a "celebratory" song, but powerful.

Love on Layaway

Emilio Estefan Jr. & Angie Chirino   **1993**

Gloria Estefan   *Christmas Through Your Eyes (Deluxe version only)* (1993)

This is one of the most popular Christmas songs that came out of the 1990s. Gloria Estefan, formerly of Miami Sound Machine, sings, with a Latin beat, that she just wants her Love on the holidays, not expensive presents.

This may not be Estefan's first release of this song, but the earliest that could be found. She may have had a single or been on a Christmas album with other artists.

Lullaby for Christmas Eve

Pete King & Paul Francis Webster   **1965**

Eddie Fischer   *Mary Christmas* (1965)

The title of this album is not a typo: "Mary Christmas" is a song on the album. Fischer had a two-year-old daughter, Joely, at the time of this recording, so he may have imagined singing the lullaby to her. Of course, Fischer is the father of Carrie Fischer of *Star Wars* fame, who would have been nine at the time of this recording.

Macy's Window

Terry Melcher & Mark Lindsay   **1967**

Paul Revere and the Raiders   *A Christmas Present...And Past* (1967)

Christmastime in a city (presumedly NYC) is described. Megastore Macy's window at Christmastime offered a fascinating display of Christmas toys.

In 1971 the band had a hugely successful cover of the song "Indian Reservation (The Lament of the Cherokee Reservation Indian)."

The Magic Gift

Connie Pearce & Arnold Miller   **1961**

June Christy   *This Time of Year* (1961)

The singer's true love gives her magical gifts, like glasses that made the world look beautiful. But the best magic gift he gave her was his love.

The Magic of Christmas Day (God Bless Us Everyone)

Dee Snider   **1998**

Celine Dion   *These Are Special Times* (1998)

Powerful, majestic and rousing song by the master of such songs. She sings of the joyful celebration of Christmas Day, for all, and asks that "God bless us everyone."

The Man with All the Toys

Brian Wilson & Mike Love   **1964**

The Beach Boys   *The Beach Boys' Christmas Album* (1964)

One of the most popular of the Beach Boys Christmas songs, about "the man with all the toys"—Santa.

Mary Christmas

Ralph Freed & Edward Samuels   **1965**

Eddie Fischer   *Mary Christmas* (1965)

Sentimental song about a girl named "Mary Christmas," who had a magic voice. Her tender kiss that she gave to him was the best Christmas gift he ever received, and he married her—he would have "Mary Christmas" all year round.

Mary, Did You Know?

Buddy Greene & Mark Lowry   **Lyrics: 1984**
                                                         Music: 1991

Michael English   *Michael English* (1991)

Song that asks the question of Mary, the mother of God, if she knew how great her son would be.

All the below are wonderful, but I must admit (c) is my favorite. (e) is a cappella.

198

a	1999	Michael Crawford	A Christmas Album
b	1999	Natalie Cole (feat. London Symphony Orchestra)	The Magic of Christmas
c	2012	CeeLo Green	CeeLo's Magic Moment
d	2014	Pentatonix	The Greatest Christmas Hits
e	2014	Pentatonix (feat. The String Mob)	That's Christmas to Me
f	2020	Carrie Underwood	My Gift

Mary, It's Christmas

Toby Keith & Ron Reynolds   **1995**

Toby Keith   *Christmas to Christmas* (1995)

A man comes home at Christmas and visits a girl named Mary, to spend a little time with her. Apparently, it's been a while since he's been in his hometown, and it looks so pretty to him.

Mary's (Little) Boy Child

Jester Hairston   **1956**

Harry Belafonte   Single (1956)

Beautiful song, sung with a beautiful voice, that graces us every Christmas season.

This song is done beautifully by all below, but (d) is quite special.

a	1966	The Lettermen	For Christmas This Year
b	1970	Jose Feliciano	Feliz Navidad
c	2007	Juice Newton	The Gift of Christmas
d	2010	Little River Band	Stars Come Out for Christmas - Special Edition II
e	2012	Celtic Woman	Home for Christmas
f	2016	Neil Diamond	Acoustic Christmas
g	2019	Harry Belafonte (with the Royal Philharmonic Orchestra)	Christmas with the Stars & The Royal Philharmonic Orchestra

The Merriest

Connie Pearce & Arnold Miller   1961

June Christy   *This Time of Year* (1961)

Not to be confused with the song "We Wish You the Merriest," this song basically has the same idea, wishing to all "the merriest" during "the season."

Merry Christmas

Keith, Alan Bergman & Paul Weston   1964

Jo Stafford   *Joyful Season* (1964)

Soft, sentimental song wishing us "Merry Christmas" (and a Happy New Year) and describing things you see at Christmas.

Merry Christmas (I Don't Want to Fight Tonight)

Joey Ramone   1989

The Ramones   *Brain Drain* (1989)

Popular 80s band The Ramones presents this punkish song that actually talks about nice things, like Santa and children waiting in their sleep for him to come. They don't want to fight with their spouses, that they proclaim their love for. Christmas is not the time for fighting.

A Merry Christmas

Frankie Avalon   1962

Frankie Avalon   *Frankie Avalon's Christmas Album* (1962)

Pretty song with angelic choir that wishes from "our house to your house" and "our hearts to your hearts" a Merry Christmas, with love, joy and happiness.

Merry Christmas All

Vincent Montana Jr. & Andy Kozak   **1976**

The Salsoul Orchestra   *Christmas Jollies* (1976)

Classic 70s Christmas song that doesn't get enough airtime, in my opinion. Few would remember it by name, but many would recognize the song. It doesn't really have the expected disco beat; it has more of a traditional sound. The song describes the nice things about Christmas, in a nice relaxing fashion.

I always liked this song but didn't know its title or who performed it. I came upon it accidentally and had a pleasant "aha!" experience.

Merry Christmas Baby

Brian Wilson & Mike Love   **1964**

The Beach Boys   *The Beach Boys' Christmas Album* (1964)

Lesser-known Beach Boys Christmas song about a man's girlfriend wanting to break up with him after he did her wrong. He wants to convince her to take him back at Christmastime.

Merry Christmas Darling (AKA Merry Christmas, Darling)

Richard Carpenter & Frank Pooler   **1970**

The Carpenters   Single (1970)

One of the most-played Christmas songs that came out of the 70s, with Karen Carpenter's unique voice wishing her darling a Merry Christmas during a period of separation.

The history of this song goes much farther back than its 1970 release. In fact, it goes back to 1944 Wisconsin, when 18-year-old Frank Pooler composed a Christmas love song for his high school sweetheart. The song concerned their separation during that holiday season. Pooler planned to give the song to her as a Christmas present, but before he could do that they broke up. Nonetheless, Pooler had it published by a little-known publishing house and recorded by a now-forgotten singer. However, it was never distributed.

In 1959, Pooler moved to Long Beach, California, where he led the University Choir at California State University–Long Beach. Two of his students were Richard and Karen Carpenter. In 1966, Richard lamented to Pooler, his favorite professor, that he was growing weary of performing the same standard Christmas songs at gigs around town and asked if he had any ideas. Pooler remembered the song he had written many years before and mentioned it, but added he didn't think much of the melody anymore. Richard said he'd take a crack at writing a new tune, and about 15 minutes later he was done, creating a song written by two 18-year-olds a generation apart.

By the fall of 1970, The Carpenters had become a household name. A year after signing with A&M Records, they scored two major hit singles with "Close to You" and "We've Only Just Begun." After completing their second album, *Close to You*, they returned to the studio to record "Merry Christmas, Darling." Richard worked on the arrangement and a saxophone solo was improvised by Bob Messenger. When the recording was completed, Richard called Pooler to the studio to let him hear the tune. In a 2005 interview with *The La Crosse Tribune*, Pooler recalled that at first, he had no idea what he was hearing was the song he had written long ago. "I was totally floored," he said. The single was released on November 20 and went straight to #1 on *Billboard*'s Christmas charts. It would return to that spot again in 1971 and 1973 and quickly became a gold record. In 1978, at Karen's request, the vocals were re-recorded for the release of *Christmas Portrait*, their first Christmas album.

The song was almost recorded in the early 1970s by Elvis Presley, Pooler said. Presley couldn't read music, so in the recording studio he would have the musicians form a circle around him and play him the song, while he walked around the circle trying to get the hang of the song.

"He could not quite pick up on the bridge to 'Merry Christmas, Darling,' so he threw in the towel after three times around the circle," Pooler said, retelling the story Presley had told Richard Carpenter.

In 2002 Pooler met up with the high school sweetheart who had been the inspiration for the song and asked her if she knew he had written the song for her. "No," she said. "Now I have a treasure."

Coincidentally, she was married to a famous musician.[104,105]

Song (a) is soft jazz; (b) is also soft jazz but sung very much like Karen Carpenter. Song (c) is much like the original, with the singer's voice sounding familiar to Karen's.

a	2004	Vanessa Williams	Silver & Gold

b	2005	Jane Monheit	The Season
c	2012	Christina Perri	(Single)
d	2017	*Herb Alpert*	*The Christmas Wish*
e	2018	Carpenters & Royal Philhar-monic Orchestra	Carpenters with The Royal Philhar-monic Orchestra

Merry Christmas Everybody

Neville Holder & Jim Lea   1973

Slade   Single (1973)

So here it is, Merry Christmas, everybody's having fun. Get ready for your family. Are you getting everything ready? Are you hoping that the snow will start to fall?

a	2019	Robbie Williams (feat. Jamie Cullum)	The Christmas Present

Merry Christmas Everyone

Bob Heatlie   1984

Shakin' Stevens   Single (1985)

Description of Christmas fun, like having a Christmas Party. Fast-paced, upbeat.

Song (a) is similar to the original. Song (b) is sung slower, using a softer approach.

a	2021	Esther Graf	(Single)
b	2021	Gary Barlow	The Dream of Christmas

Merry Christmas from Our House to Your House

Mort Greene & George Cates   1956

Lawrence Welk (feat. The Lennon   Single (1957)
Sisters)

Saccharine but nice song about pretty much what the title states. "B" side of "Santa Claus Is Here Again."

Merry Christmas from the Family

Robert Earl Keen   1994

Robert Earl Keen   *Gringo Honeymoon* (1994)

Novelty song. The "Family" is white trash, with the song detailing that. Not for the faint of heart.

Merry Christmas to You

Andy Stone, Troy Powers   1990

Vince Vance & The Valiants   *All I Want for Christmas Is You* (1990)

Pretty song in the style of soft 50s Rock 'n Roll about Christmas and wishing a merry Christmas "to you."

The Merry Christmas Waltz

Ignaz Mosel & Charles Tobias   1953

Guy Lombardo and His Royal Cana-   *Jingle Bells* (1953)
dians

Not to be confused with the popular "(The) Christmas Waltz." This is a short song about "good friends" getting together every year for the Christmas waltz, no matter what the weather.

Miracles

Kenny G & Walter Afanasieff   1994

Kenny G   *Miracles - The Holiday Album* (1994)

Sad but beautiful Instrumental.

The Miracles of Christmas

Aurora Miller & Ronald Norman Miller   **1967**

Stevie Wonder   *Someday At Christmas* (1967) - Bonus Track

Upbeat song about "miracles of Christmas"—a lollipop on the holly, a candy cane in your pocket, all sorts of wonderful things. But we pray on Christmas day that a miracle was born.

Miss You Most (at Christmas Time)

Mariah Carey & Walter Afanasieff   **1994**

Mariah Carey   *Merry Christmas* (1994)

Well-known Mariah Carey Christmas song, using the time-tested theme of separation from a loved one at Christmastime.

Mister Santa

Pat Ballard   **1994**

Amy Grant   *Merry Christmas* (1994)

"Mister Sandman" with Christmas-themed lyrics. Cute.

Mistletoe and Holly

Frank Sinatra, Hank Sanicola & Dok Stanford   **1957**

Frank Sinatra   *A Jolly Christmas from Frank Sinatra* (1957)

Popular Sinatra Christmas tune.

Mistletoe and Wine

Jeremy Paul, Leslie Stewart & Keith Strachan

1977

Twiggy and Natalie Morse   *The Little Matchgirl* (Video) - 1987

First live performance by cast of *Scraps* on December 23, 1977. Hit record by Cliff Richard (1988 single). Joyful song about the great things of Christmas, a time for love and not hate.

The Most Wonderful Day of the Year

Johnny Marks

1964

Videocraft Chorus   *Rudolph the Red Nosed Reindeer (Original 1964 TV Soundtrack)*

Bittersweet song from the 1964 TV Special *Rudolph the Red Nosed Reindeer,* sung by the Misfit Toys on their island.

The Music Box

Kinkel, Oliva, Pachabell & Paul O'Neill

1998

Trans-Siberian Orchestra   *The Christmas Attic* (1998)

Somber song about the gift of a music box made in "Christmas past," next to a couple's first Christmas tree, lit by a candle, but all these things are gone; the candle has long melted.

Must Be Santa

Hal Moore & Bill Fredericks

1960

Mitch Miller and The Gang   *Single* (1960)

Song that begins "Who's got a beard that's long and white? Santa's got a beard that's long and white…" and so on. It must be Santa!

In 2009, Bob Dylan released a crazed polka-like version which mixed in names of US Presidents with the names of the reindeer.[106] The singing duo She and Him (Zooey Deschanel and M. Ward) performed this version in their 2016 Christmas album (*Christmas Party*), with an updated list of Presidents, including Obama and Hillary Clinton, who actually lost the 2016 election to Donald Trump.[107]

I would say that (b) is the most popular version.

a	1961	Mitch Miller	Holiday Sing Along with Mitch
b	1983	Raffi	Raffi's Christmas Album: A Collection of Christmas Songs for Children
c	2009	Bob Dylan	Christmas in the Heart
d	2016	She & Him	Christmas Party

My Christmas Tree

Jimmy Webb   1965

The Supremes   *Merry Christmas* (1965)

Nice but sad song about a girl that has one present under her tree but it's lonely because the best little present she ever had has gone away from her—her honey, her "angel." Yes, another song about loss of a loved one at Christmastime.

My Dear Acquaintance

Peggy Lee & Paul Horner   1983

Peggy Lee   *Christmas with Peggy Lee* (2006)

Pretty, emotional song about one's acquaintance celebrating the new year with that person, wishing a happy new year to the acquaintance and all.

The song was written and recorded for Peggy Lee's flop 1983 Broadway musical, *Peg*, but cut from the show and not released until 2006.

a	2021	Gary Barlow	The Dream of Christmas (Deluxe)

My Kind of Christmas

Jerry Livingston & Paul Francis Webster   **1961**

Johnny Mathis   *Single* (1961)

"My kind of Christmas" is the kind that has all the old-fashioned wonderful things of Christmas around, with peace on Earth and goodwill to men. Joyous tune.

a	2015	Tom Gaebel	A Swinging Christmas

My Little Drum

Vince Guaraldi   **1965**

Vince Guaraldi Trio   *A Charlie Brown Christmas Soundtrack* (1965)

Song that does not appear in the *A Charlie Brown Christmas* TV special. It is an instrumental, with chorus sounds, that is basically a light jazz version of "The Little Drummer Boy."

My Only Wish (This Year)

Brian Kierulf & Josh Schwartz   **2000**

Britney Spears   *Platinum Christmas* (2000)

Popular song at Christmastime sung by Britney Spears. Her only wish from Santa is her baby, nothing else.

The album has songs by various artists. This song appears on other compilation albums, such as *Christmas Hits* (2000).

Nativity Carol

John Rutter   **1987**

The Cambridge Singers   *Christmas Night - Carols of the Nativity* (1987)

Beautiful modern-day carol about the first Christmas. Sir John Milford Rutter is a modern-day composer of mostly choral music, many of them Christmas carols. The Cambridge Singers are his own choir.

New York City Christmas

Nick Vallelonga   **1983**

Nick Vallelonga   *New York City Christmas* (2001)

After the 9/11 tragedy, Nick Vallelonga self-released this album, dedicated to the New York City Police and Firemen. He both wrote and performed "New York City Christmas"; the album includes 1983 demos of this song, so it wasn't actually written for 9/11. Nick is best known for winning two Academy Awards and two Golden Globes for Original Screenplay and Best Picture for *Green Book*, based on the true story of Nick's father Tony Lip (Frank Anthony Vallelonga Sr.), who went on tour of the South with the brilliant pianist Dr. Donald Shirley in 1962. Lip became an actor, appearing in many films and TV shows including *The Godfather*, *The Pope of Greenwich Village*, and *Goodfellas*. Lip also portrayed New York Crime Boss Carmine Lupartazzi on *The Sopranos*. His son Nick appeared in many roles himself, including in the prequel film to *The Sopranos*, *The Many Saints of Newark*.

The Night Before Christmas

Carly Simon   **1992**

Carly Simon   *This Is My Life - Music from the Motion Picture* (1992)

You don't have to be an angel to sing harmony, you don't have to be a child to enjoy the mystery—the heart of this Christmas is in you. From the 1992 non-Christmas movie *This Is My Life*.

The first Christmas album this song appears in was released later the same year by Amy Grant in *Home for Christmas*.

a	1992	Amy Grant	Home for Christmas

No Eye Had Seen

Michael W. Smith & Amy Grant   **1992**

Michael W. Smith   *The Ultimate Christmas Collection*
                                                    (1989)

Gorgeous, moving song about the birth of Jesus. Hard to describe its beauty.

A Not So Merry Christmas

K. Reese, D. Glasser & T. Lesslie   **1962**

Bobby Vee   *Merry Christmas* (1962)

Bobby Vee, sounding very much as he does in other songs, with the theme of lost love at Christmas, making Christmas "not so merry" for him.

Nuthin' for Christmas

Roy C. Bennett & Sid Tepper   **1955**

Art Mooney and His Orchestra - Vocal   Single (1955)
by Barry Gordon

Five renditions, including the original, were released in November 1955. Eartha Kitt's rendition substituted the original innocent lyrics with adult lyrics. Barry Gordon was a very successful child star and is a successful character actor as an adult. In addition, he was the longest-serving president of the Screen Actors Guild. Gordon was only six years old when he recorded this song.

An Old Fashioned Christmas

Sammy Cahn & Jimmy Van Heu-   **1964**
sen

Frank Sinatra and Fred Waring   *12 Songs of Christmas* (1964)

Frank sings of Christmas when he was a child—mom basting a Turkey and an old fireplace. He'd trade "that whole Manhattan skyline" for it.

Sammy Cahn is co-author of "Let it Snow!" and "(The) Christmas Waltz."

An Old Fashioned Christmas

John Bettis & Richard Carpenter   **1978**

The Carpenters   *A Christmas Portrait* (1978)

Sweet song with children's chorus, singing about an old-fashioned Christmas with family and how it's missed.

On Christmas Morning

Kenny Loggins & David Foster   **1989**

Kenny Loggins   *December* (1989)

Song about the wonderful sights and sounds of Christmas morning. The memories come back when he is with his Love.

Once Upon a December

Stephen Flaherty & Lynn Ahrens   **1997**

Liz Callaway   *Anastasia - Music from the Motion Picture* (1997)

Song from the animated movie *Anastasia* (1997), about Anastasia Romanov, ill-fated daughter of the last Tsar of Russia. The song details things "I almost remember," like horses prancing through a silver storm and figures dancing gracefully.

The song in the movie was performed by Liz Callaway and in the end credits by Deana Carter.

The following is a cappella.

a	2020	Pentatonix	We Need a Little Christmas

One Little Christmas Tree

Ronald Miller & Bryan Wells   **1967**

| Stevie Wonder | *Someday At Christmas* (1967) |

Cute but rousing song about a small lone Christmas Tree who wanted to light up a home. An angel gave it a star so it could light up the world so those who are lost can find their way.

a	2017	John Farnham & Olivia New-ton-John	Friends for Christmas

Our Savior Is Born

Steve Wariner   **1990**

| Steve Wariner | *Christmas Memories* (1990) |

Pretty song about the first Christmas.

(Let There Be) Peace on Earth

Jill Jackson & Seymour Miller   **1956**

Champ Butler - Orchestra & Chorus   Single (1956)
conducted by Johnny Mandel

"B" side of "Once Upon a Summertime." Very nice song about brotherhood and peace on Earth. Live each moment with peace eternally.

a	2012	Richard Marx (with Kenny Loggins)	Christmas Spirit

Peace on Earth – Little Drummer Boy

Ian Fraser, Larry Grossman & Buz Kohan   **1977**

David Bowie/Bing Crosby   Single (1982)

From the Bing Crosby TV Christmas Special *Bing Crosby's Merrie Olde Christmas*, recorded on September 11, 1977, and aired on November 30, 1977, a month and a half after Crosby's death on October 14, 1977. Crosby had chosen Bowie as his guest upon the insistence of his children.

[The entire special[108] is available on YouTube, as well as just the performance of the song.[109]]

Song (a) is Celtic New Age. Song (b) is an enhanced version of the original, using samples of Bing and David with a new, full orchestra. Song (c) has nice vocals and simple accompaniment.

a	2015	Celtic Angels	Winterland
b	2019	Bing Crosby, David Bowie & The London Symphony Orchestra	Bing at Christmas
c	2020	ONR	New Christmas Music

Peace, Peace

Richard and Sylvia Powell   1999

Michael Crawford   *A Christmas Album* (1999)

Beautiful song that starts with a children's chorus and segues into "Silent Night," with Michael Crawford's wonderful voice, accompanied by the children's chorus.

Perfect Christmas

Cathy Dennis & Simon Ellis   2000

S Club   Single (2000)

A full orchestral sound is embedded within this song about a girl spending a perfect Christmas with her guy. It's the greatest gift that there could be. Nicely arranged song.

Pie Jesu

Andrew Lloyd Webber   1985

Sarah Brightman and Paul Miles-Kingston   Single (1985)

"Pie Jesu" (English: "Pious Jesus") is the best-known segment of Andrew Lloyd Webber's Requiem Mass simply called "Requiem." Requiem is a Latin Requiem Mass that premiered on February 24, 1985, at St. Thomas Church in New York. The composition, created to commemorate his father, William Lloyd Webber, was inspired by an article Andrew read in *The New York Times* about a Cambodian boy who had to choose between ending the life of his mutilated sister, or being killed himself. Performing and conducting at the piece's premiere were Sarah Brightman & Paul Miles Kingston and Placido Domingo (Conductor). Requiem received a Grammy award in 1986 for Best Classical Contemporary Composition.[110]

"Pie Jesu" was released as a single in March 1985 and reached number three on the UK charts.

Please Come Home for Christmas

Charles Brown & Gene Redd   **1960**

Charles Brown   Single (1960)

Song made very popular by The Eagles in 1978. Most people probably recognize it as the soon as they hear the first few bars on piano start it off.

Song (b) has a different sound to it, with brass replacing much of the piano. Song (c) has more of an early Rock n' Roll beat than the Eagles version. (d) sounds more like the Eagles version than the others.

a	1978	The Eagles	Single
b	1991	Pat Benatar	True Love (CD-only bonus track)
c	2012	Christina Perri	A Verry Merry Perri Christmas (Extra Presents)
d	2013	Human Nature	The Christmas Album

The Prayer

Carole Bayer Sager & David Foster   **1998**

Celine Dion   *Quest for Camelot - Music from the Motion Picture* (1998)

Amazing, emotional song that must be heard to be believed. From the movie *Quest for Camelot* (released internationally as *The Magic Sword: Quest for Camelot*), a 1998 American animated musical fantasy film. The soundtrack also features a version of this song by Andrea Bocelli. Dion's version was chosen because it appears during the body of the movie, and because Bocelli's version is partly translated from English to Italian.

The a cappella version by Pentatonix below (a) is outstanding. There is also a beautiful video[111] *of their performance available.*

a	2021	Pentatonix	Evergreen

Precious Moments / Somewhere in My Memory

Leslie Bricusse & John Williams   **1990**

John Williams   *Home Alone - Original Motion Picture*
                                                     Soundtrack (1990)

From the 1990 motion picture *Home Alone*, this a very pretty Christmas song—not characteristic of the movie.

In song (a), Audrey Smith is Michael W. Smith's daughter.

a	2014	Michael W. Smith (feat. Audrey Smith)	The Spirit of Christmas
b	2021	Darren Criss	A Very Darren Christmas
c	2022	Tasha Layton	This Is Christmas

Pretty Paper

Willie Nelson   **1963**

Roy Orbison   Single (1963)

"B" side of "Beautiful Dreamer," this is a classic Christmas tune.

Song (a) is Roy Orbison's original vocal performance sampled and mixed with a new, full orchestra recording that sounds amazing.

a	2019	Roy Orbison & Royal Philharmonic Orchestra	Christmas with the Stars & Royal Philharmonic Orchestra

Remember (Christmas)

Harry Nilsson   **1967**

Harry Nilsson   *Son Of Schmilsson* (1967)

"Long ago and far away…," this song begins. Life is never how it seems. No direct references to Christmas, but a really nice song.

The Restroom Door Said, "Gentlemen"

Bob Rivers & Twisted Radio, Brian Silva & Dennis Amero   **1987**

Bob Rivers & Twisted Radio   *Bob Rivers & Twisted Radio - Twisted Christmas Boxed Set* (1987)

Raunchy version of "God Rest Ye Merry, Gentlemen."

A Ride in Santa's Sleigh

Leavitt & Giambusso   **1953**

Judy Valentine   Single (1953)

What sounds like a little girl sings about her encounter with Santa on her roof, and the ride he gives her on his sleigh. "B" side of "She Was Five and He Was Ten." Judy Valentine (1923–2022), born Norma Baker, was an American singer and children's television actress. Some of Valentine's most popular recordings include "She Was Five and He Was Ten" (co-written by her husband), "Kiss Me Sweet" and "I'm a Little Teapot." She sang in a child-like soprano. She was married to songwriter and Boston Red Sox P.A. announcer Sherman Feller. Valentine is also known for singing popular radio jingles in Boston.[112]

Ring a Merry Bell

Connie Pearce & Arnold Miller   **1961**

June Christy   *This Time of Year* (1961)

"Never let Christmas" change—ring a merry bell, hang holly, sing a merry song, decorate the tree, and decorate presents.

River

Joni Mitchell   **1971**

Joni Mitchell   *Blue* (1971)

This song is merely set *near* Christmastime, rather than *being about* Christmas; it is actually a song about a recent breakup of a romantic relationship. Although never released as a single, "River" holds second place (after "Both Sides Now") among Mitchell's songs and is the most recorded of her songs by other artists (432 recordings). Linda Ronstadt covered "River" on her 2000 album *Merry Little Christmas*. Sarah McLachlan also covered it on her 2006 album *Wintersong* and released it as a single. Her cover charted at No. 71 on the Billboard Hot 100 and was nominated for a Grammy. In 2021, the song was ranked at No. 247 on Rolling Stone's "Top 500 Best Songs of All Time."[113]

Song (a) begins with "Jingle Bells" and is sung wonderfully. Song (b) gets so much airplay I thought it was originally Sarah's song. It certainly is a memorable rendition.

a	2000	Linda Ronstadt	A Merry Little Christmas
b	2006	Sarah McLachlan	Wintersong

Rockin' Around the Christmas Tree

Johnny Marks   **1958**

Brenda Lee   Single (1958)
Merry Christmas from Brenda Lee
(1962)

Among other Christmas songs, Marks wrote "Rudolph the Red-Nosed Reindeer." He specifically asked Brenda Lee to record "Rockin' Around the Christmas Tree," at age 13. She never found out why. If you watch the *Rudolph the Red-Nosed Reindeer* animated TV classic from 1964, you will note that in one scene there is an instrumental version of this song playing in the background.

In 2023, 65 years after the song was originally released, Lee released a video of the song, which hit No. 1 on the Billboard Top 100. It now holds the record for the longest period of time between an original release and a version topping the Hot 100 charts. This also made Brenda Lee the oldest artist to land number one on the Billboard Hot 100. The song has sold over 15 million copies worldwide and was inducted into the Grammy Hall of Fame.[114]

Song (a) is bubble-gum Rock, which works. Song (b) retains the basic sound of the original but tends to sound more like Country Music. Songs (c) and (e) are jazz-like versions. Song (d) imitates the original well. Songs (f) and (g) have been updated to a modern-type sound.

a	1968	The Archies	The Archies Christmas Album
b	1992	Amy Grant	Home for Christmas
c	2004	LeAnn Rimes	What a Wonderful World
d	2018	Ingrid Michaelson & Grace VanderWaal	Ingrid Michaelson's Songs for the Season
e	2018	Jessie J	This Christmas Day
f	2022	Brenda Lee (Reimagined by Filous)	A Rockin' Christmas with Brenda Lee
g	2023	Miss L. Toe	Christmas Dance Party 2023

Run Rudolph Run (AKA Run Run Rudolf)

Chuck Berry, but credited to Johnny Marks and M. Brodie due to Marks' trademark on the character of Rudolph the Red-Nosed Reindeer   **1958**

Chuck Berry   Single (1958)

This classic Rock 'n Roll Christmas song was released by Chess Records, with the authorship imprinted as "(C. Berry Music — M. Brodie) / ARC BMI." Chuck Berry Music, Inc., Berry's company, is listed as the author as it is on most Chess singles. Chuck Berry Music, Inc. claimed authorship and ARC, the Chess/Goodman publishing company, claimed copyright. But no-one knows whom "M. Brodie" is, and it isn't for lack of searching. Also, it is unsure about Johnny Marks being involved in the creation of this song. According to a Facebook post by Daryl Davis, who played piano behind Chuck Berry in later years, he asked Berry about the authorship. The post states that Berry claimed "he wrote the song himself, but the name 'Rudolph' had been trademarked and the company publishing his songs had been sued for his using it. He was perturbed that the publishing company didn't fight the suit more vigorously, because Johnny Marks had nothing to do with his song and now, he had to share the copyright. He also said that Brodie did not exist, and it was a scheme to make more money for Marks and his publisher. He regretted not pursuing it more at the time. Berry continued to make a lot of money from the song, just not as much as he was entitled to make. It was a bittersweet song for him."[115]

Referring to the story behind "Rudolf the Red-Nosed Reindeer" in Chapter 2, it is interesting to consider that that song was originally owned by Montgomery Ward, and that Montgomery Ward transferred ownership to May in 1947 because of personal hardship. May held on tight to the rights of the song, even though he had been granted them through an act of kindness.

Kim Carnes (a) is best known for 1981's "Bette Davis Eyes." A worldwide hit, it became the best-selling single of the year in the United States, spending nine weeks at No. 1 on the Billboard Hot 100, going Gold, and winning the Grammy Award for Record of the Year and Song of the Year.

a	2010	Kim Carnes	Stars Come Out for Christmas - Special Edition I

Sainte Nuit

André Gagnon   **1992**

André Gagnon   *Noel* (1992)

Beautiful Instrumental based on "Silent Night," which is the translation of the title.

Same Old Lang Syne

Dan Fogelberg   **1981**

Dan Fogelberg   *The Innocent Age* (1981)

Popular song at Christmastime, though it is really a New Year's song. The sax solo (by Michael Brecker) in the outro plays around the melody of the "Auld Lang Syne" traditional.

Santa Baby

Joan Javits & "Tony" Springer   **1953**
(pseudonym for Phillip Springer)

Eartha Kitt with Henri René and His   Single (1953)
Orchestra

Springer was initially dissatisfied with "Santa Baby" and called it one of his weakest works. During a meeting with a group of music publishers in 1953, Springer warned them: "Gentlemen, this is not really the kind of music that I like to write. I hope it's OK. It's the best I could do." [Though he later claimed he wrote the music in five minutes.] However, "Santa Baby" became the best-selling Christmas song of 1953 in the US. Nonetheless, a 2019 poll created by *Evening Standard* revealed it to be the ninth "most annoying festive song" by British listeners. A 2021 YouGov poll in the United States registered it the most annoying Christmas song. In addition, Michael Bublé's version has been named multiple times as one of the worst Christmas songs ever.

In a 2008 interview, Springer told the interviewer that "Philip and Joan (both ASCAP writers) checked into the song title with the publishers from a company called Trinity Music, owned by BMI. At the time, BMI and ASCAP were entrenched in a 'war,'" as Philip described it, so in order to get the song published and settle their differences, they had to create a fictional BMI songwriter who they named "Tony" Springer.[116]

Song (a) is a soft, "beach" version. Cute.

a	2012	Colbie Caillat	Christmas in the Sand

Santa Claus (I Still Believe in You)

John Jarrard, Teddy Gentry, Randy Owen, Greg Fowler & Linda Gentry   **1985**

Alabama   *Christmas* (1985)

Nice, gentle song about the realities of Christmas Eve, but even adults can believe in Santa Claus.

Santa Claus Is Comin' to Town / Santa Man

J. Fred Coots & Haven Gillespie   **1992**

The Manhattan Transfer   *The Christmas Album* (1992)

Cool jazz song that takes "Santa Claus Is Coming to Town" as a base and adds to it.

Santa Mouse

Michael Stephen Brown   **1968**

Burl Ives   *Christmas Album* (1968)

Cute song about Santa's companion, Santa Mouse. He was just a regular mouse until Santa came upon him in a "great big house" on Christmas Eve and decided to dress him as Santa.

Santa Must be Polish

Bobby Vinton & M. Cuthbertson   **1964**

Bobby Vinton   *Kissin' Christmas: The Bobby Vinton Christmas Album* (1964)

A polka Christmas song about how Santa must be Polish, for various reasons. Includes "happy holidays" in Polish.

Santa, the Happy Wanderer

Friedrich-Wilhelm Möller, Florenz   **1953**
Sigismund, & Al Stillman

Santa Claus and His Helpers   Single (1953)

The music is from "The Happy Wanderer" (German: "Der fröhliche Wanderer") or "My Father Was a Wanderer" (German: "Mein Vater war ein Wandersmann"), a popular song in Germany. The original text was written by Florenz Friedrich Sigismund (1791-1877). The present melody was composed by Friedrich-Wilhelm Möller shortly after World War II. The lyrics of "The Happy Wanderer" were changed in this song to portray Santa Claus as the happy wanderer.

Santa's Beard

Brian Wilson & Mike Love   **1964**

The Beach Boys   *The Beach Boys' Christmas Album* (1964)

Popular Christmas song that begins "I wanna meet Santa Claus, the real, real Santa…"

Santa's on His Way

David Anthony   **1999**

George Strait   *Merry Christmas Wherever You Are* (1999)

Easy-going song about Christmas, which is a time of year filled with joy and happiness.

Santa Claus Is Foolin' Around

Bob Rivers, Joe Bryant & Spike O'Niell   **2000**

Bob Rivers   *Chipmunks Roasting on an Open Fire* (2000)

This song excellently captures the sound of "Santa Claus Is Comin' to Town" as performed by Bruce Springsteen in the concert on December 12, 1975, at C. W. Post College in Brookville, Long Island. The words, of course, are different—this time Santa Claus is foolin' around. Very well-done spoof.

Seven Shades of Snow

Connie Pearce & Arnold Miller   **1961**

June Christy   *This Time of Year* (1961)

Snow is mostly colorless, but a change of heart can make it appear different colors, like a rainbow. If your heart can keep its magic, you will see seven shades of snow.

She Won't Be Home

Andy Bell & Vince Clarke   **1989**

Erasure   *Crackers International* (1989)

Pretty but sad song by New Wave group Erasure, about a girl who stays with friends at Christmas, not visiting her family, which makes them feel lonely.

Shopping Bag Menagerie

Sidney Barnes   **1968**

Rotary Connection   *Peace* (1968)

Song about the commercialization of Christmas. Now we give "what only our pocketbooks will allow" and we give our kids gifts when we should be giving them love. We work all year "to purchase happiness" and put it in our shopping bag. Nice message, made at a time when songs questioned many conventional ideas. The tune is nice but, of course, sad. "Heavy" for Christmas, but worth listening to.

Silver and Gold

Johnny Marks   **1964**

Burl Ives   *Rudolph the Red Nosed Reindeer*
                                              (Original 1964 TV Soundtrack) (1964)

Sad song from 1964's *Rudolf the Red-nosed Reindeer* TV special.

Both renditions below are very pretty.

a	2004	Vanessa Williams	Silver and Gold
b	2017	The Perrys	A Very Perry Christmas

Skating

Vince Guaraldi   **1965**

Vince Guaraldi Trio   *A Charlie Brown Christmas sound-*
                                              track (1965)

Nice Instrumental from 1965's *A Charlie Brown Christmas* TV special. Longer version than aired.

Song (a) replaces some piano with a xylophone. Very nice.

a	2020	Warren Wolf	Christmas Vibes

Snoopy's Christmas

Luigi Creatore, George David   **1967**
Weiss & Hugo Peretti

The Royal Guardsmen   Single (1967)

This was a follow-up to the group's 1966 hit, "Snoopy vs. the Red Baron," which peaked at #2 on the Hot 100 during the week of December 31, 1966 (behind The Monkees' "I'm a Believer"). The song references the 1914 "Christmas truce" of World War I. Late on Christmas Eve 1914, men of the British Expeditionary Force (BEF) heard German troops in the trenches opposite them singing carols and patriotic songs and saw lanterns and small fir trees along their trenches. Messages began to be shouted between the trenches. The following day, British and German soldiers exchanged gifts, took photographs and some played impromptu games of football [soccer]. They also buried casualties and repaired trenches and dugouts. The truce was not observed everywhere along the Western Front. Elsewhere the fighting continued, and casualties did occur on Christmas Day. Some officers were unhappy at the truce and worried that it would undermine fighting spirit. After 1914, the High Commands on both sides tried to prevent any truces on a similar scale happening again. Despite this, there were some isolated incidents of soldiers holding brief truces later in the war, and not only at Christmas.[117]

Snow

Irving Berlin   1954

Rosemary Clooney with Percy Faith and His Orchestra and The Mellomen

Rosemary Clooney in Songs from the Paramount Pictures Production of Irving Berlin's White Christmas (1954)

From the movie *White Christmas* (1954), where it was sung by Bing Crosby, Danny Kaye, Rosemary Clooney & Vera-Ellen (dubbed by Trudy Stevens). The song is an ode to snow.

a	2022	Josh Stone	Merry Christmas, Love

Snow Flakes

Bogle, Edwards, Taylor & Wilson   1965

The Ventures

Single (1965)
The Ventures' Christmas Album (1965)

Early Rock 'n Roll Instrumental of "What Child Is This?"

Snow for Johnny

Fred F. Carter & Conway Twitty   1964

Burl Ives   *Have a Holly Jolly Christmas* (Recorded 1964; Released 1965)

Song about a boy from Louisiana who a week from Christmas prays for snow so he can build a snowman. His prayers are answered early Christmas morning.

Someday at Christmas

Ron Miller & Bryan Wells   1966

Stevie Wonder   Single (1966)
Someday At Christmas (1967)

Stevie Wonder's hopeful, rousing Christmas classic about a day men will no longer play with bombs like kids play with toys, and there will be peace on Earth.

a	2016	Jackie Evancho	Someday at Christmas

The Son of Mary

Lyrics: William Chatterton Dix   1958

Harry Belafonte   *To Wish You a Merry Christmas* (1958)

"What Child Is This?" with a different title, sung wonderfully by Harry Belafonte.

Song for a Winter's Night

Gordon Lightfoot   1967

Gordon Lightfoot   *The Way I Feel* (1967)

Really nice song about a common theme—separation from a loved one around Christmastime. He wishes his Love feels as lonely as him. The sound of sleighbells is the only direct connection to Christmastime.

Song (a) is performed slower in tempo and has more of a music background; the original only has guitar.

a	2006	Sarah McLachlan	Wintersong

Soon It Will Be Christmas Day

B. Peters   **1971**

Lynn Anderson   *The Christmas Album* (1971)

Happy, carefree Country Christmas song about the wonderful things at Christmastime. Nice tune.

Sorry to See You Go

Connie Pearce & Arnold Miller   **1961**

June Christy   *This Time of Year* (1961)

Nice, swinging song that is basically an ode to the past year, which she is sorry to see go.

The Sound of Christmas

Riley C. Hampton & Ramsey Lewis   **1961**

Ramsey Lewis Trio   *The Sound of Christmas* (1961)

Wonderful Instrumental that captures the essence of Christmas. Though it's a jazz song, it has bells and plenty of strings—just a really nice song for Christmastime.

Star of Wonder

Terre Roche   **1990**

The Roches   *We Three Kings* (1990)

This song about the Star of Bethlehem is performed a cappella by the Roches, who are a wonderful chorus of voices. Very much like a carol.

Step into Christmas

Elton John & Bernie Taupin   **1973**

Elton John   Single (1973)

The classic Christmas song by Elton John, this tune gets a lot of airplay every year. Very, very upbeat.

Some years ago, I was fortunate to star in a musical play named after this song. I played Santa Claus and other characters that Santa was disguised as. Fortunately, I didn't have to sing or dance—I was onstage with wonderful dancers from a dance school on Long Island, trained in part by a former Radio City Music Hall Rockette, who was also in the play. Proceeds were donated to the school.

A Strange Way to Save the World

David Clark, Don Koch, & Mark Harris   **1993**

4HIM   *Christmas - The Season of Love* (1993)

The "strange way to save the world" is Christ's birth and Crucifixion. This is a very nice song about the first Christmas, from Joseph's point of view.

a	1999	Michael Crawford	A Christmas Album

Sweet Little Jesus Boy

Robert MacGimsey   **1958**

John Raitt   *Under Open Skies* (1958)

Song about baby Jesus, who at the time we didn't know would "take our sins away" and didn't know himself what lie ahead for him.

a	1994	Trisha Yearwood	The Sweetest Gift

Take a Walk Through Bethlehem

Wally Wilson, John Barlow Jarvis   **1994**
& Ashley Cleveland

Trisha Yearwood   *The Sweetest Gift* (1994)

Song about the true meaning of Christmas, while we shop or watch another Christmas TV special. If you close your eyes, you can take a walk through Bethlehem.

Tennessee Christmas

Gary Chapman & Amy Grant   **1983**

Amy Grant   *A Christmas Album* (1983)

Nice song that describes Christmas in Tennessee, which is the "only place to be" for Christmas.

a	2008	Point of Grace	You're Here

Thank God It's Christmas

Brian May & Roger Taylor   **1984**

Queen   *The Works* (1984)

Rock sensation Queen's Christmas song. Thank God it's Christmas, but let it be Christmas every day. We live in "troubled days."

That Holiday Feeling

Bill Jacob, Joe Guercio & Patty   **1964**
Jacob

Steve Lawrence & Eydie Gorme con-   *That Holiday Feeling!* (1964)
ducted by Joe Guercio

Steve and Eydie's signature Christmas song.

a	2023	Seth MacFarlane & Liz Gillies	We Wish You the Merriest

That Man Over There

Meredith Willson   **1963**

Paul Reed and Chorus   *Here's Love - The New Musical [Original Broadway Cast]* (1963)

"That man over there" is Santa Claus…or is it? This song is from the 1963 Broadway Musical *Here's Love*, later to be retitled *Miracle on 34th Street - The Musical*. Based on the 1947 film *Miracle on 34th Street*, it tells the tale of a single mother, Doris Walker, who doesn't want her six-year-old daughter Susan's head filled with romantic notions. Their neighbor Fred Gailey tries to woo Doris by charming Susan and taking her to see Santa Claus at Macy's, where Doris works. Doris is not impressed—but when it turns out Macy's Santa may in fact be the real Kris Kringle, a wave of love spreads across New York City that "melts even the most cynical hearts." The author, Meredith Wilson (author of *The Music Man!*), also wrote the song "It's Beginning to Look a Lot Like Christmas," which he worked into the play. The character in the play that sings "That Man Over There," is R. H. Macy, the founder of Macy's department store in New York City.[118]

a	1994	Lindsay Ridgeway	A Broadway Christmas

That Spirit of Christmas

Mable John, Parnell Davison & Joel Webster   **1985**

Ray Charles   *The Spirit of Christmas* (1985)

Ray Charles sings of the spirit of Christmas, which has families get together, giving each other gifts. He asks why can't this spirit last all year?

That's What I Want for Christmas

Earl Lawrence   **1963**

Nancy Wilson   Single (1963)

Nancy Wilson (1937-2018) was a jazz singer whose career spanned more than a half-century. This single was released on November 18, 1963—four days before

President John F. Kennedy was assassinated. In this sweet song all she wants for Christmas is the love of her special guy, who should let people see that he loves her.

a	2024	Stella Cole	Snow!

There's a New Kid in Town

Don Cook, Curly Putman & Keith Whitley   **1985**

Keith Whitley   Single (1985)

"B" side of "A Christmas Letter." The "new kid in town" is Jesus, in this lovely song telling us about the birth of Jesus in Bethlehem. A female voice (unidentified) tells of the Three Wise Men. The duo completes the song.

There's Always Tomorrow

Johnny Marks   **1964**

Janis Orenstein   *Rudolph the Red Nosed Reindeer (Original 1964 TV Soundtrack)* (1964)

Hauntingly beautiful song of Hope. Janis Orenstein (1948-2010) was the actress who voiced the doe Clarice (based on a friend of the author of the screenplay, Romeo Muller) in the 1964 TV Special *Rudolph the Red Nosed Reindeer*. Clarice was Janis Orenstein's only voice role in her career, when she was just 15 years old. She sang at the New York World's Fair at age 15 in 1964.[119] She studied at the Royal Conservatory of Music in Toronto beginning at age 6, at the Julliard School in New York and the Glyndebourne Festival Opera in England, as well as at the Faculty of Music at the University of Toronto.[120]

The album contains both Vocal and Instrumental versions.

a	2014	Aidia	All is Bright

There's Another Santa Claus

Bob Rivers & Twisted Radio, Joe Bryant, Spike O'Neill & Terry Gangstad   **1993**

Bob Rivers & Twisted Radio

Bob Rivers & Twisted Radio - Twisted Christmas Boxed Set (1993)

Novelty Christmas song using the music of "Here Comes Santa Claus" with new lyrics.

There's Someone Who's Knocking

James Butz & Vincent Montana Jr.   **1976**

The Salsoul Orchestra   *Christmas Jollies* (1976)

Children sing about someone who's knocking at their door, who turns out to be Santa Claus. The song has a disco beat.

This Christmas

Donny Hathaway & Nadine McKinnor   **1971**

Donny Hathaway   *This Christmas* (1971)

Popular Christmas song most would recognize from its beginning with brass instruments. This Christmas will be a very special Christmas, with its wonderful trappings and someone special.

Song (a) is performed without the brass from the original. It is more subdued. Song (b) is more like the original.

| a | 1993 | Gloria Estefan | Christmas Through Your Eyes |
| b | 2020 | Francesca Battistelli | This Christmas |

This Time of the Year

Cliff Owens & Jesse Hollis   **1964**

Brenda Lee   *Merry Christmas from Brenda Lee* (1964)

Brenda Lee lovingly sings of "this time of year when Christmas is near." Children dream of toys, choirs sing carols, and Santa is on his way.

a	1985	Ray Charles	The Spirit of Christmas

This Time of Year

Connie Pearce & Arnold Miller   1961

June Christy   *This Time of Year* (1961)

Pretty song with Christy's great voice describing Winter cold, church bells, and "lovers clinging." She, however, is alone at Christmas, having lost her lover. She's decided to forget him, but stays secluded, ignoring her friends.

A Time for Peace

Eric Robertson & Greg Adams   1976

Roger Whittaker   *A Time for Peace - The Roger Whittaker Christmas Album* (1976)

This beautiful, rousing song describes Christmas, a special time for peace and love. He hopes this feeling will never end but it will come back next Christmas.

Tonight Is Christmas

Keith Worsham, Stan Munsey, Jr.,   1985
Donnie Matthews & Steve Baccus

Alabama   *Christmas* (1985)

The factories are shut down, malls are closed, and streets are empty...tonight is Christmas, and we celebrate Jesus' birth, with the hope of peace and harmony. Across the sea, there are two armies facing each other, but their shooting will cease. Nice song.

Toy Parade

Bert Kaempfert & Heinz Mihm   1963

Bert Kaempfert   *Christmas Wonderland* (1963)

"Happy" Instrumental that you could whistle to.

Traditions of Christmas

Chip Davis   1988

Mannheim Steamroller   *A Fresh Aire Christmas* (1988)

Instrumental of a music box playing a pretty, gentle tune.

Song (a) has the same tune as the original but is played with a New Age orchestra. Beautiful.

a	1997	*Mannheim Steamroller*	*My Little Christmas Tree*

The Tree

Peggy Lee   1960

Peggy Lee   *Happy Holiday* (1960)

Children sing of buying a Christmas tree, and Peggy then sings along with them, singing how they will get it and decorate it.

The Twelve Gifts of Christmas

Allan Sherman   1964

Allan Sherman   *For Swingin' Livers Only* (1964)

Non-PC spoof of "The Twelve Days of Christmas."

The Twelve Pains of Christmas

Bob Rivers & Twisted Radio, Brian Silva & Dennis Amero   1986

Bob Rivers   *Bob Rivers & Twisted Radio - Twisted Christmas Boxed Set* (1987)

Spoof of "The Twelve Days of Christmas," with different lyrics. The author remembers this dating back to the early 1970s but can find no evidence of that. It makes references to the 70s sitcom *All in the Family*, so it must go back that far. This is a harmless spoof, with much of it still applying to today (except for writing Christmas cards).

Twinkle Twinkle Little Me

Ron Miller & William O'Malley   **1965**

The Supremes   *Merry Christmas* (1965)

Cute song about the star upon your tree. Nice.

Song (a) starts with the beginning of "Twinkle, Little Star."

a	1967	Stevie Wonder	Someday at Christmas
b	2015	Tom Gaebel	A Swinging Christmas

The Twisted Chipmunk Song

Bob Rivers, Joe Bryant & Spike O'Niell   **2000**

Bob Rivers   *Chipmunks Roasting on an Open Fire* (2000)

Spoof of "The Chipmunk Song (Christmas Don't Be Late)."

Under the Christmas Tree

John Bettis & Albert Hammond   **1989**

Albert Hammond   Single (1989)

Don't forget to put love under the Christmas tree. Nice song.

Albert Hammond is a prolific songwriter, who wrote hits such as "The Air that I Breathe" (1972), "99 Miles from LA" (1975), "To All the Girls I've Loved Before" (1984), "Don't Turn Around" (1986) and "One Moment in Time" (1988).

Upon a Christmas Eve

Arranged by Steve Vaus   **1988**

Michael Johnson   *Stars Come Out for Christmas - Special Edition II* (2010)

Describes walking around on Christmas Eve, with snow and decorations. An angel comes to him and tells him that to bring Jesus home he just had to believe. On Christmas morning a thousand bells ring out and he realizes that Jesus is born within him.

The Very Best Time of (the) Year

John Rutter   **1985**

Unknown. There is a rendition by Michael Crawford, as part of a medley with "It's the Most Wonderful Time of the Year"   Crawford medley in *A Christmas Album* (1999)

Richly orchestrated and beautifully sung song, including children's chorus, about the joys of Christmas, like family and friends together. It then smoothly segues to "It's the Most Wonderful Time of the Year."

Walkin' Round in Women's Underwear

Bob Rivers & Twisted Radio, Joe Bryant, Spike O'Neill & Terry Gangstad   **1993**

Bob Rivers & Twisted Radio   *Bob Rivers & Twisted Radio - Twisted Christmas Boxed Set* (1993)

Raunchy lyrics are sung to the tune of "Walking Around in a Winter Wonderland."

Walking in the Air

Howard Blake   **1982**

Peter Auty   *The Snowman* (1982)

From the British short animated film *The Snowman* (1982). The song is not listed in the first release of the album, but it is part of the track "The Complete Sound Track of the Film." Pretty and richly orchestrated song about "walking in the air" and floating across the sky, not directly about Christmas.

a	2010	Celtic Woman	The Best of Christmas

A Warm Little Home on the Hill

Ron Miller & Bryan Wells   1967

Stevie Wonder   *Someday At Christmas* (1967)

About a utopian Christmas, complete with a "warm little home on the hill" filled with presents, blankets of snow, bells ringing, a choir singing, and a family filled with love and peace. Lovely.

We Are Santa's Elves

Johnny Marks   1964

Videocraft Chorus   *Rudolph the Red Nosed Reindeer*
(Original 1964 TV Soundtrack)
(1964)

Song sung by elves in Santa's castle in the 1964 Christmas TV Special *Rudolph the Red Nosed Reindeer*. Cute song, but Santa says it "needs work."

We Need a Little Christmas

Jerry Herman   1966

The New Christy Minstrels   *Christmas with the Christies* (1966)

This classic Christmas song originated from Jerry Herman's 1966 Broadway hit *Mame*, first performed on stage with Angela Lansbury in the title role, and then played by Lucille Ball in the film version. After the stock market crash of 1929, Auntie Mame tries to hurry up the Christmas preparations, even though it's still November and the snow hasn't yet started to fall, hoping it will help take her mind off her lost fortune.[121]

Song (a) is probably the most popular, though (b) is also very popular. (c) is quite different than the original, sounding a bit like a samba, if I'm correct. (d) starts with some bars of "Joy to the World" and is very nicely done. (e) and (g) are pretty close to the original. (f) is done at a slower tempo. (h) is a cappella.

a	1966	Percy Faith	The Essential Percy Faith - The Christmas Recordings
b	1986	Johnny Mathis	Christmas Eve with Johnny Mathis
c	1994	Lynette Perry	A Broadway Christmas
d	2007	Kimberley Locke	Christmas
e	2007	Legacy Five	A Little Christmas
f	2012	Ages and Ages	Holidays Rule
g	2019	Idina Menzel	Christmas: A Season of Love
h	2020	Pentatonix	We Need a Little Christmas

We Wish You the Merriest

Les Brown   1961

Les Brown

An All-Star Christmas - "We Wish You the Merriest" (1961)

Another Christmas classic. Les Brown was probably mostly known for his appearances with Bob Hope for over 50 years. Bob would often refer to "Les Brown and His Band of Renown."

a	1964	Bing Crosby, Frank Sinatra and Fred Waring & His Pennsylvanians	12 Songs of Christmas
b	2019	Idina Menzel (feat. Josh Gad)	Christmas: A Season of Love
c	2023	Seth MacFarlane & Liz Gillies	We Wish You the Merriest

We Wish You Weren't Living with Us

Bob Rivers & Twisted Radio, Brian Silva & Dennis Amero   1987

Bob Rivers & Twisted Radio

Bob Rivers & Twisted Radio - Twisted Christmas Boxed Set (1987)

Spoof of "We Wish You a Merry Christmas."

We're a Couple of Misfits

Johnny Marks   1964

Billie Mae Richards ("Rudolph")   *Rudolph the Red Nosed Reindeer*
Paul Soles ("Hermey")   *(Original 1964 TV Soundtrack)*
(1964)

Song sung by Rudolf the Red-Nosed Reindeer and Hermey the Elf in the 1964 Christmas TV Special *Rudolph the Red Nosed Reindeer*.

Welcome Christmas

Albert Hague & Ted Geisel   1966

Boris Karloff & Thurl Ravenscroft   *Dr. Seuss' How the Grinch Stole Christmas! (1966 TV Soundtrack)*
(1966)

Song sung by the Who's of Whoville on Christmas Day, even though their presents and decorations had been stolen by the Grinch. From Dr. Seuss' *How the Grinch Stole Christmas!* 1966 TV Special. Ted Geisel is "Dr. Suess."

Song (a) is a "find." Very nicely done, including lyrics in Whospeak.

a	2023	Walk Off the Earth	A Christmas Album

Welcome to Our World

Chris Rice   1999

Amy Grant   *A Christmas to Remember* (1999)

Welcome to our world, infant Jesus. Make yourself at home. Bring us peace and sustenance. Rob our sin and make us holy.

a	1998	Michael W. Smith	Christmastime
b	2007	Legacy Five	A Little Christmas

What Can I Give You This Christmas?

Ralph Blane   **1966**

The Lettermen   *For Christmas This Year* (1966)

A man ponders what he can give to his girl at Christmas; he is not a man of means. All he can give her is heart and his own true love, that will last all year.

What Christmas Means to Me

Anna Gordy Gaye, George Gordy   **1967**
& Allen Story

Stevie Wonder   *Someday At Christmas* (1967)

Popular song at Christmas. Mistletoe, snow and ice and choirs singing Christmas carols are part of what Christmas means to him. But mostly it means he loves his darling even more.

a	2022	Joss Stone	Merry Christmas, Love

What Do the Lonely Do at Christmas?

H. Banks & C. Hampton   **1977**

The Emotions   *Sunshine!* (1977)

A girl has nobody at Christmastime. It will be joy to the world but it's going to be sad for her.

Whatever Happened to Christmas?

Jimmy Webb   **1968**

Frank Sinatra   Single (1968)

Christmas has gone and left with no traces. Whatever happened to the giving and magic in the snow? And whatever happened to you?

Aimee Mann (a) co-founded the new wave band 'Til Tuesday and wrote their top ten single "Voices Carry" (1985). Her voice is very calm in this song and sounds wonderful.

a	2006	Aimee Mann	One More Drifter in the Snow

When a Child Is Born (Original Italian name: *Le rose blu*)

Music: Dario Baldan Bembo, Maurizio Seymandi, Ciro Dammicco & Alberto Baldan Bembo
Original Italian Lyrics: Alberto Salerno & Francesco Specchia
English Lyrics: Fred Jay

Original Italian: 1972
English: 1974

Italian: Ciro Dammicco
English: Michael Holm

Mittente: Ciro Dammicco (1972) [Italian]
Single (1974) [English]

Very pretty song about the birth of Jesus, and how it changed everything—hate to love, war to peace and more. There are also Swedish, Czech, Danish, Dutch, German, Finnish, French, Hungarian, Portuguese & Spanish versions.

All the below are wonderful renditions. (d) provides the fullest orchestral accompaniment.

a	1981	Kenny Rogers	Christmas
b	2003	The Moody Blues	December
c	2013	Susan Boyle (with Johnny Mathis)	Home for Christmas
d	2019	Johnny Mathis & The Royal Philharmonic Orchestra	Christmas with the Stars & The Royal Philharmonic Orchestra
e	2020	Val Doonican	Christmas Gold

When my Heart Finds Christmas

Harry Connick, Jr.

1993

Harry Connick, Jr.

When My Heart Finds Christmas (1993)

When my heart finds Christmas "my eyes will shine like new." I hope your heart finds it too. Let our children's love surround us.

Where Are You Christmas? AKA Christmas, Why Can't I Find You?

James Horner, Will Jennings &   **2000**
Mariah Carey

Taylor Momsen & (separately) Faith Hill

Dr. Seuss' How the Grinch Stole Christmas - Original Motion Picture Soundtrack (2000). Two tracks:
"Christmas, Why Can't I Find You?" (Momsen)
"Where are You, Christmas?" (Hill)

Very popular and beautiful song from the 2000 movie *Dr. Seuss' How the Grinch Stole Christmas*. Performed by the character, Cindy Lou Who, in the film.

a	2018	Pentatonix	Christmas Is Here!

Where Can I Find Christmas

Doug Goodwin   **1986**

Johnny Mathis (with the International Children's Choir)

Christmas Eve with Johnny Mathis (1986)

Sung in a medley with "Christmas Is for Everyone." A children's choir sings "Where can I find Christmas?" Is it something I can see? Mathis answers that it is a happy feeling deep inside that you get when you are kind.

From the animated Christmas TV special *The Bear Who Slept Through Christmas* (1973).

A Whistle and a Whisker Away

L. Hayes & B. Hayes   **1971**

Lynn Anderson   *The Christmas Album* (1971)

As Lynn is singing to children, she warns they better listen to their parents as Santa Claus is just a "whistle and a whisker away."

The White Snows of Winter

Tom Drake & Bob Shane   **1960**

The Kingston Trio   *The Last Month of the Year* (1960)

The white snows of Winter fall into a quiet town. But the man's Love cannot be found. He left her in October and has been to the sea and back to the land, "crowning" many hills (I assume in battle). Fortunately, he does find his Love again, in the town.

Who Would Imagine a King

Mervyn Warren & Hallerin Hilton Hill   **1996**

Whitney Houston   *The Preacher's Wife: Original Soundtrack Album* (1996)

From the 1996 film, *The Preacher's Wife*. Parents think much of their children, that they could be anything when they grow up, but who would imagine a king, like Jesus? The Wise Men came to Jesus with gifts, but Jesus gave us all the wonderful gifts he could bring.

Why Can't You Be Here for Christmas

Unknown   **1990**

Vince Vance And the Valiants   *All I Want for Christmas Is You* (1990)

A woman waits for her darling to come home, but admits he boldly told her he won't be home. She ponders this and wonders if she should get ready for Christmas alone. She thinks of him being with another girl.

Winter Light

Eric Kaz, Linda Ronstadt & Zbigniew Preisner   **1993**

Linda Ronstadt   *Dedicated to the One I Love* (1993)

Ronstadt's angelic voice is superb in this song about a night where "love's shadow will surround you" and that she will follow until "you love me too."

Winter Melody

Donna Summer, Giorgio Moroder   **1976**
& Pete Bellotte

Donna Summer   *Four Seasons of Love* (1976)

Love is gone with nothing left for me but loneliness. I never knew that love could hurt so bad. He's not coming home. Pretty, but sad, soft disco song.

Winter's Got Spring Up Its Sleeve

Connie Pearce & Arnold Miller   **1961**

June Christy   *This Time of Year* (1961)

This is a song that paints the Winter in a negative light—it makes you sad and sentimental, bringing up memories you would rather forget. But Spring will be coming, and you will awaken to a bright new world.

A Winter's Tale

Mike Batt & Tim Rice   **1982**

David Essex   Single (1982)

Song about separation from a loved one at Winter. The snow covers up the footsteps of the one he loves and now can no longer follow. The "Winter's tale" is of one more love that has failed, which in the scheme of things won't ever be noticed. He wishes her the best in his loneliness.

a	2003	The Moody Blues	December

Wonderful Christmas Time AKA …Christmastime

Paul McCartney   **1979**

Paul McCartney   Single (1979)

Happy song about celebrating Christmas. The video[122] of this song was made at the Fountain Inn in Sussex, England, which dates back to the 16th century.[123] In 2010 it was estimated by Forbes that McCartney receives $400,000-$600,000 annually from this song. That means by 2010 McCartney had seen about $15 million from the song since its release.[124]

It appears that nobody made a rendition of this classic until the 21st century, of which 8 renditions are listed below.

Song (a) has differences in instrumentation. Song (b) sounds like a "modernized" version. Song (c) has more of a traditional sound. Song (d) exhibits some influences from The Beach Boys, especially as it begins. Song (e) sounds a lot like the original. Song (f) is a swinging traditional Christmas song, with large orchestra using much brass. Song (g) is a cappella. Song (h) is the prettiest, with Perri's very soothing voice and minimal accompaniment.

a	2001	The Korgis	Reader's Digest Music: Wonderful Christmas Time
b	2008	Demi Lovato	All Wrapped Up
c	2012	Lady A	On This Winter's Night
d	2012	The Shins	Holidays Rule
e	2016	Kylie Minogue	Kylie Christmas
f	2021	Gary Barlow	The Dream of Christmas
g	2021	Pentatonix	Evergreen
h	2023	Christina Perri	Songs for Christmas

The Wonderful World of Christmas

Charles Tobias & Al Frisch   1968

Robert Goulet   *Robert Goulet's Wonderful World of Christmas* (1968)

Song describing the wonderful things of Christmas. The next release of this song was by Elvis Presley, in *Elvis Sings the Wonderful World of Christmas* (1971).

| a | 1971 | Elvis Presley | Elvis Sings the Wonderful World of Christmas |

Wreck the Malls

Bob Rivers & Twisted Radio, Brian Silva & Dennis Amero   **1987**

Bob Rivers & Twisted Radio   *Bob Rivers & Twisted Radio - Twisted Christmas Boxed Set* (1987)

Spoof of "Deck the Halls."

You Make It Feel Like Christmas

Neil Diamond   **1992**

Neil Diamond   *The Christmas Album* (1992)

Song about lovers in love. His lover makes him feel like Christmas. Even when things go wrong, he hears the sound of Christmas in her song. Wake up the kids and let's light up the tree on Christmas day.

You're a Mean One Mr. Grinch

Albert Hague & Ted Geisel   **1966**

Thurl Ravenscroft   *Dr. Seuss' How the Grinch Stole Christmas! (1966 TV Soundtrack)* (1966)

Famous spoken song from the 1966 TV Christmas Special *Dr. Seuss' How the Grinch Stole Christmas!* Thurl Arthur Ravenscroft (1914-2005) was an American actor and bass singer. He was the voice ("That's great!") behind Kellogg's Frosted Flakes animated spokesman Tony the Tiger for more than five decades. He also did voicework for Disney and his voice can be heard today on a number of attractions at Walt Disney World in Florida.

2000 Miles

Chrissie Hynde   **1984**

The Pretenders   *Learning to Crawl* (1984)

Classic Christmas song from the 1980s.

Song (a) is a beautiful symphonic version with Chrissie Hynde's vocals.

a	2018	Pretenders (Symphonic Version)	80's Symphonic

4 21st Century (So Far)

T he 21st century has seen the creation of numerous Christmas songs that have become modern classics, blending traditional holiday themes with contemporary sounds. In the latter part of the 20th century many artists had avoided Christmas releases. Mariah Carey didn't want to record a Christmas album in the 1990s because, in her twenties, when her career was doing phenomenally well, she considered Christmas albums to be for older artists who had been put out to pasture. She was convinced, however, to release a Christmas album in 1994, *Merry Christmas*, which included the single "All I Want for Christmas Is You," released the same year. The single was an immediate success, reaching number six on the Billboard Hot Adult Contemporary chart in the United States and number two in the United Kingdom and Japan. It would become the bestselling Christmas song of all-time in the US and certified Diamond in Australia, Canada, Sweden, and the US. The album has sold 5.7 million copies in the United States as of December 2019 and has been certified nine-times Platinum by the Recording Industry Association of America (RIAA).

Mariah Carey's success with Christmas music inspired many artists with extremely successful careers to follow suit in the 21st century, including Kelly Clarkson, Carrie Underwood, Ariana Grande, Justin Bieber, Taylor Swift, Destiny's Child, Sia and many others. Many major artists now release holiday albums as a rite of passage, adding their name to the Christmas music tradition.

Christmas music in this century was popular in many genres, including Pop, Rock, Alternative Rock, R&B, Soul, and Country. Country was particularly well-suited for Christmas music, as much of it concerned traditional and old-fashioned values, and a plethora of Christmas Country albums were produced. The blending of country music with mainstream pop has led to Christmas hits like Blake Shelton and Gwen Stefani's "You Make It Feel Like Christmas" (2017).

Digital Streaming in the 21st century made it easier for artists to release their works and many lesser-known artists released their renditions of Christmas classics as well as their own compositions. Social media and streaming platforms like Spotify, Apple Music, Amazon Music, Pandora and TIDAL have reshaped how Christmas music is consumed and popularized. Viral hits, such as Mariah Carey's annual resurgence of "All I Want for Christmas Is You," thrive on these platforms. TikTok trends have also helped older and newer Christmas songs gain a fresh audience.

Many Christmas songs in the 21st century have seen a reviving of nostalgia. Many artists incorporate vintage styles (e.g., jazz, swing, and Motown influences) to evoke the golden era of Christmas music. Examples include Michael Bublé's

Christmas album (2011), and Seth McFarlane & Sara Bareilles in their Christmas Albums *Holiday for Swing!* (2014) and *We Wish You the Merriest* (2023). Re-recording traditional Christmas songs remains popular, with stars like Pentatonix, Kelly Clarkson, Ariana Grande and Sarah MacLachlan putting their unique spin on beloved tunes, like Sarah MacLachlan's "Let It Snow" (2016). Ingrid Michaelson's version of "Looks Like a Cold, Cold Winter" (2018) actually "swings" more than the 1950 Bing Crosby original. Billy Idol put aside his punk rock image to sing traditional Christmas songs, as well as singing new songs that sound traditional. Lyn Lapid, in "Old Fashioned Christmas" (2024), a new but wonderfully old-fashioned song, pines for a time when lovers stay together and asks Santa to take her back in time. Animated films like *The Polar Express* (2004) and *Frozen* (2013) have delivered iconic family-friendly Christmas songs, blending holiday themes with universal appeal.

There has also been a resurgence of creating new Christmas songs. These songs often blend contemporary pop, R&B, or rock with festive themes, such as Justin Bieber's "Mistletoe" (2011) and Taylor Swift's "Christmas Tree Farm" (2019). Christmas songs now often focus on themes of love and modern relationships, with tracks like Ariana Grande's "Santa Tell Me" and Leona Lewis's "One More Sleep" (both 2013) capturing romantic holiday moments. However, there has been a glut of Christmas songs concerning missing a loved one at Christmas, or Christmas being meaningless because a loved one is not around, for a variety of reasons. Some of these are done very well (like Ingrid Michaelson's good-natured "Happy, Happy Christmas" of 2018), but many lack any real soul or inventiveness.

This is not to say that soul or inventiveness are rare in 21st century Christmas songs. Leslie Odom provided us in 2020 with both the sublime "Heaven and Earth," wherein he expresses that his love for his family could move Heaven and Earth, and "Snow," about the blissfulness of a Christmas with family. In 2018, with Ingrid Michaelson, Odom performed an amazing slow rendition of Carey's "All I want for Christmas is You" that gave it a fresh, new, meaning. "Text Me Merry Christmas" (2013) by Straight No Chaser and Kristin Bell made a great statement about the absurdity of modern life and our dedication to cell phones, while "Thank You Note" (2021) by Salem Ilese makes a statement about the commercialization of Christmas, expressing that the only present she wants is a thank you note on a Post-it for her "presence" all year. Sia "takes the cake" for inventiveness, in the entirety of her *Everyday Is Christmas* album (2017), which is a collection of all new songs, each written by her. Meanwhile, Pentatonix, with their a cappella sound, reinterpreted classics in amazing ways.

New Christmas songs were introduced in the 21st century by familiar artists from the 20th century. In some cases, they retained their well-known sounds and in others they changed to traditional sounds. In addition to Billy Idol, mentioned above, we had songs from The Pet Shop Boys, Erasure, Alabama, Enya, Cher (with Cyndi Lauper), Amy Grant, Christopher Cross, Patty Smyth, Neil Diamond, Nick Lowe, Sixpence None the Richer, Melissa Etheridge, America, Nicolette Larson. Barry Manilow, Jon Bon Jovi, Juice Newton, Olivia Newton-John, Carole King, Barenaked Ladies, The Moody Blues, LeAnn Rimes, The Oak Ridge Boys, Tori Amos,

Glen Campbell, Sam Phillips, Richard Marx & Kenny Loggins, Robert Plant, ABBA, Rick Astley, Elton John, Daryl Hall & John Oates, Andrew Gold, Whitney Houston, Cheap Trick, Pat Boone, The Monkees, Def Leppard, and James Taylor.

With the technology of voice sampling, there are now new song renditions released that are voiced by deceased artists. *Christmas with Elvis and the Royal Philharmonic Orchestra* (2017) provides rich renditions of Elvis Christmas songs with a full orchestra. *Christmas with the Stars & Royal Philharmonic Orchestra* (2019) provides beautiful renditions of songs by Harry Belafonte, Doris Day, Andy Williams. Dean Martin, Roy Orbison and Perry Como. *Bing at Christmas* (2019) blends Bing Crosby with Pentatonix and the London Symphony Orchestra for an amazing "White Christmas." Olivia Newton-John "is back" in 2024 in *Angels in the Snow (Reimagined)*, singing a version of "All Through the Night" that incorporates her 1970s sound.

Ain't Santa Cool

Randy Owen, Ronnie Rogers & Danny Wells　　　　　　　**2017**

Alabama　　　　　　　　　　　　*American Christmas* (2017)

Mellow song of how "cool" Santa is, speeding across the sky and making his way around the globe. He slides down the chimney and eats a little of the cookies and milk left for him. He leaves presents for the children, the singer naming his own.

All I Really Want for Christmas (AKA A Family Guy Christmas)

Kevin Ryder and Gene "Bean" Baxter　　　　　　　**2001**

Kevin and Bean　　　　　　　　　*Swallow my Eggnog* (2001)

Performed in *Family Guy* episode "Road to the North Pole" (2010) by *Family Guy* cast with new lyrics. That version was made available for download in 2010.

All I Want for Christmas Is New Year's Day

Hurts (Theo Hutchcraft & Adam Anderson)　　　　　　　**2010**

Hurts　　　　　　　　　　　　　Free download

Everyone waits for Christmas, but he waits for New Year's Day, which is going to take his blues away. He wants to say goodbye to the year before, knowing the next year will be different. This is actually an upbeat, pleasant song, filled with hope.

All My Bells Are Ringing

Lenka Kripac　　　　　　　　　　　　**2008**

Lenka Kripac　　　　　　　　　　　Single (2008)

Cute song with a cute vocal and chorus. Another song about missing a loved one at Christmastime.

All Over the World

Pet Shop Boys (Tennant & Lowe)   2009

Pet Shop Boys   *Christmas* (Pet Shop Boys EP) (2009)

The song starts with Tchaikovsky's "March from the Nutcracker" and returns to that theme throughout the song, in which they sing that it is a song for boys and girls that you hear all over the world. Nicely done.

All Year Long

Michael W. Smith & David Hamilton   2004

Michael W. Smith   *It's a Wonderful Christmas* (2004)

This pretty song is about the wonders of Christmas. He offers a prayer that peace comes into our hearts, and he wishes us luck—the kind that lasts all year long.

Almost There

Michael W. Smith, Amy Grant & Wes King   2014

Michael W. Smith with Amy Grant   *The Spirit of Christmas* (2014)

Song about Mary, the mother of God, carrying Jesus inside her as she treks to a place to give birth to him. She's almost there…she's almost there…Emotional ending.

Amid the Falling Snow

Enya, Roma Ryan, & Nicky Ryan   2008

Enya   *Christmas Secrets* (2008)

Pretty song by Enya in her unique style. She ponders about the falling snow. If she falls, would she make a sound in the darkness? Would she reach the ground?

a	2019	Celtic Woman	The Magic of Christmas

The Angel Song

Chris Eaton   **2001**

Jaci Velasquez   *Christmas / Navidad* (2001)

The singer is amazed that the God who made all the beauty in the world also made her. The mystery of Christmas is revealed to her, taking her back to pure, sacred peace. A savior was born to us, and we'll never be alone. Hauntingly beautiful.

Angels in the Snow

Amy Sky & Steve MacKinnon   **2005**

Amy Sky   *Images of Christmas* (2005)

She and her Love lie in wonder as they make angels in the snow. She will always think of him as her angel in the snow. Nice song.

Amy Sky wrote a number of songs for Olivia Newton-John (a) in her later years.

a	2007	Olivia Newton-John	The Wish

Angels in the Snow

F. Alqaisi, J. Saint John, L. Crasta,   **2023**
M. Schick, S. Hudson & JHart

Cher (with Cyndi Lauper)   *Christmas* (2023)

New Christmas hit by Cher. We will always be together, angels in the snow.

Another Merry Christmas

Amy Grant & Ed Cash   **2016**

Amy Grant   *Tennessee Christmas* (2016)

Loved ones are separated at Christmas: Mary's in a nursing home and Billy's home from overseas, but "still fights a war no one sees." Jill hangs four stockings, now just three, and wonders if they'll ever be another Merry Christmas. But an old nativity set silently reminds her that God is with us, on another Merry Christmas.

Aurora

Chuck Myers   **2019**

Caranua   *A Celtic Christmas* (2019)

An aurora drifts across the sky, which we gaze upon in wonder, awakening new sensations of color and light.

Back Home for Christmas

Mimi Webb, et al   **2023**

Mimi Webb   Single (2023)

She wants her Love back home for Christmas. She doesn't want to spend Christmas Eve at home alone.

Because It's Christmas

Daniel Tashian   **2020**

Daniel Tashian   *Because It's Christmas* (2020)

Cute, happy tune with a dad and his kids singing about the good things at Christmastime.

Behold Him

Jeff Pardo & Molly Reed   **2020**

Francesca Battistelli   *This Christmas* (2020)

A family prepares for its first Christmas without someone. They turn to God for comfort, for they are not truly alone, and in this moment should behold Jesus Christ.

Being Home for Christmas

Ryan Carbrary, Timothy Kim, et al   **2020**

Ivan & Alyosha   *A Very Merry Christmas with Ivan & Alyosha* (2020)

Remembering Christmas when he was a boy and looking forward to it now. There's nothing like being home for Christmas. Nice upbeat tune.

Believe

Glen Ballard & Alan Silvestri   **2004**

Josh Groban   *The Polar Express: Original Motion Picture Soundtrack* (2004)

This song from the wonderful 2004 computer-animated film *The Polar Express* was nominated for Best Original Song at the 77th Academy Awards. It was sung at that show by original performer Josh Groban with Beyoncé. It received a Grammy Award in 2006.

Believe

Unknown   **2013**

Clyde Bawden & Jason Barney (feat. Dianne Michelle)   *Glen Beck Presents: Believe Again* (2013)

Pretty song about believing in Christmas, sung beautifully by Dianne Michelle. The producer of this album, Glenn Beck, is a leading American media personality, political commentator, author, and founder of the radio network known as *TheBlaze*.

Believe

Mariah Counts & Ryan Benyo   **2023**

Mariah Counts   Single (2023)

Simple, peppy tune with a somewhat 50s sound that tells you if you want presents from Santa all you have to do is believe.

Bells of Christmas

Alan Jardine & Ron Altback   2001

Gentleman League and Miss OD   *A Christmas Record* (2001)

Very pretty song about the bells of Christmas and children singing, for Christ is born.

The Bells of Christmas

GENTRI   2021

GENTRI (feat. Hailey Hyde)   *Season of Light* (2021)

The Christmas bells will bring you home; love comes with Christmas Day. Very nice song.

The Best Christmas

George Green & Steve Dorff   2007

Christopher Cross   *A Christopher Cross Christmas* (2007)

A man thinks of carefree Christmases during his childhood, but the best Christmas of all is when a child is born to him. Christopher Cross won five Grammy Awards for his 1979 eponymous debut album. The singles "Sailing" (1979), and "Arthur's Theme (Best That You Can Do)" from the 1981 film *Arthur* peaked at number one on the U.S. Billboard Hot 100. "Sailing" won three Grammys in 1980, while "Arthur's Theme" won the Oscar for Best Original Song in 1980.

Best Christmas Ever

Robbie Williams   2019

Robbie Williams   *The Christmas Present* (2019)

A child lies in bed awaiting the arrival of St. Nick, but he has heard in school that he is not real. He decides to believe anyway and has the best Christmas ever. Many years have passed since then and he has children. He knows Santa is still real, for it is he and his beloved wife. It will be the best Christmas ever. Nice song, with children's chorus.

The Best Side of Life

Marc Lennard & JoJo HF   **2005**

Sarah Connor   *Christmas In My Heart* (2005)

The best time of the year is when she goes home and sees her Love. The best side of life is when they are together. Triumphant song.

Sarah Connor (born Sarah Lewe) of course has no connection with the character in *The Terminator* movie franchise. She is a German pop singer who has enjoyed international success.

Blame It on the Mistletoe

Michael Davey and Courtney   **2018**
Turnbull

Coreen Orender   Single (2018)

In 1995 Toby Keith released a song with this title. Four different songs were released in the 21st century with the same title. This 50s-style song blames a girl falling in love on the mistletoe and other Christmas traditions, like Bing Crosby on the radio. Cute, pleasant song.

Blame It on the Mistletoe

Gabriella Henderson, Jez Ashurst,   **2020**
Julie Frist & Tre Jean-Marie

Ella Henderson & A J Mitchell   Single (2020)

Instantly famous song that may become a Christmas standard. Kiss me and we'll blame it on the mistletoe.

Song (a) is a beautiful piano Instrumental.

a	2020	iSingKeys	Single

Blame It on the Mistletoe

Amanda Shires & Brittney Spencer   **2022**

Amanda Shires (feat. Lawrence Rothman)   Single (2022)

Amanda Shires, sounding like Dolly Parton, blames the mistletoe on kissing a man and making love to him.

Blame It on the Mistletoe

Sarah Connor et al   **2022**

Sarah Connor   *Not So Silent Night* (2022)

A woman is infatuated with a man, who she needs a few more hours with in bed. She blames it on…the mistletoe.

Blessed

Lindy Robbins, Toby Gad & Nicole Cohen   **2021**

Kelly Clarkson   *When Christmas Comes Around...* (2021)

She is blessed, looking in the eyes of her children and surrounded by the love she's been given. She doesn't want to take this for granted and forget to be grateful.

Bring on Christmas Day

Josh Stone   **2022**

Josh Stone   *Merry Christmas, Love* (2022)

Just bring on Christmas Day, throw your fears away. Open up your door and ask for nothing more. Nice song, jubilant.

Broken

Patty Smyth   2015

Patty Smyth   *Come on December* (2015)

During Christmastime, a woman is "broken" after losing someone. Once you are broken, how can you unbreak?

Smyth joined New Wave group Scandal as lead vocalist in 1981. The band released a self-titled debut EP the next year. Featuring the song "Goodbye to You," it went on to become Columbia Records' biggest selling EP. She is not singer Patti Smith.

Can't Stop Christmas

Robbie Williams et al   2019

Robbie Williams   *The Christmas Present* (2019)

No matter what bad things may happen, including friends that disappear, nothing is going to stop Christmas. People need something to believe in. Nice, upbeat song despite some sad lyrics.

Candy Cane Lane

Sia Kate Isobelle Furler & Greg Kurstin   2017

Sia   *Everyday Is Christmas (Snowman Deluxe Edition)* (2017)

Take a trip down Candy Cane Lane, with all its colors. Christmas is waiting for you. Catchy tune that became instantly popular. The video[125], mimicking the old stop-motion animation process, is cute as well. Sia introduced a number of fresh Christmas songs in recent years.

Canon of Christmas

Alex Economy   **2011**

Alex Economy   *Christmas At the Studio: Guitar Studio of Arlington* (2011)

New Age version of "Pachelbel's Canon."

Carol of the Meows

Peter Wilhousky   **2004**

Guster   *Single* (2004)

Following the tradition started by Don Charles & The Singing Dogs in 1955, whereby "dogs" sang "Jingle Bells," this novelty song has "cats" singing "Carol of the Bells." Guster is an American alternative rock band.

Carolin'

Francesca Battistelli et al   **2020**

Francesca Battistelli   *This Christmas* (2020)

Let's go caroling, walking through a winter wonderland. A number of other Christmas songs are mentioned in this one.

Charlie Brown Christmas

Mariah Carey, Vince Guaraldi, et al   **2010**

Mariah Carey   *Merry Christmas II You* (2010)

This song begins with the "Linus and Lucy" theme from the 1965 *A Charlie Brown Christmas* TV Special, with sounds of happy children in the background. It segues into Mariah singing a wonderful rendition of "Christmastime is Here," from the same source.

Cheer for the Elves

Gwen Stefani, Justin Tranter, & busbee   **2018**

Gwen Stefani   *You Make It Feel Like Christmas* (2018 deluxe edition)

An ode to Santa's elves. They work hard but stay away from Santa's spotlight. Let's give a cheer for the elves.

a	2022	Blake Shelton	Cheers, It's Christmas (Super Deluxe)

Cherry Cherry Christmas

Neil Diamond   **2009**

Neil Diamond   *A Cherry Cherry Christmas* (2009)

Have a Cherry, Cherry Christmas—which seems to mean have a merry, merry Christmas. Sing songs of harmony, not a "song sung blue." ["Song Sung Blue" was a 1972 hit song by Neil Diamond.] Fun song mixing "merry with "cherry" throughout.

Christmas 2066

Sarah Connor et al   **2022**

Sarah Connor   *Not So Silent Night* (2022)

She is an optimist, who "likes to think that things turn out good," so she imagines Christmas 2066, rocking in a chair with 22 grandkids. Friends send postcards from Mars and Santa drops presents from a floating car. She and her lover will be old, but Christmas will be perfect as long as they spend it together.

Christmas Angels

Michael W. Smith & Jonas Myrin   **2007**

Michael W. Smith   *It's a Wonderful Christmas* (2007)

Christmas angels sing of the child born in a manger, king of kings, hope for our nations. We sing "Joy to the World," the Lord has come. Great production values, with full orchestra, filled with energy.

Christmas at the Airport

Nick Lowe   **2013**

Nick Lowe   *Quality Street: A Seasonal Selection for All the Family* (2013)

It's Christmas and he is snowed in at the airport. He beds down in a closet and when he wakes up everyone is gone. He should be with his family, eating turkey, but settles for a "burger in a bin." Despite this depressing landscape, it's a rather "happy" tune. Lowe is best known for the hit "Cruel to be Kind" (1979).

Christmas Bells

Bogachuk Alexandr Alexandrovich   **2023**

Alex Lead   *Disco Christmas* (2023)

Beautiful New Age (with a disco beat) Instrumental that will make you mellow.

Christmas Bells, Carousels & Time

Paul O'Neill, Robert Kinkel & Jon Oliva   **2004**

Trans-Siberian Orchestra   *The Lost Christmas Eve* (2004)

Pretty but short Instrumental with a lot of bells and chimes.

Christmas Blues

Sabrina Claudio, Abel Tesfaye, Kaveh Rastegar, Mikhail Beltran & Nasri Atweh   **2020**

Sabrina Claudio (feat. The Weeknd)   *New Christmas Music* (2020)

Very pretty song about a girl who only wants her Love under the tree. If she doesn't have him, she'd have Christmas blues.

Christmas C'mon

Lindsey Stirling, Jon Levine, &   **2017**
Autumn Rowe

Lindsey Stirling (feat. Becky G)   *Warmer in the Winter* (2017)

The song starts with Lindsey Stirling playing a violin solo and segues into vocals by Becky G., with Lindsey's violin in the background. The song is about a girl who has made it through a year in her relationship and is celebrating Christmas now with him.

As of May 10, 2023, Lindsey Stirling's *Lindseystomp* YouTube channel exceeded 13 million subscribers and over 3 billion total views. In 2010, at the age of 23, Stirling was a quarterfinalist on season five of *America's Got Talent* but was buzzed by Piers Morgan and received negative comments from Sharon Osbourne.

Christmas Calling (Jolly Jones)

Norah Jones   **2021**

Norah Jones   *I Dream of Christmas* (2021)

Norah Jones treats us to her lovely voice in a lovely song. She pines to be with someone special at Christmas. Is Christmas calling out to her, so she can be "Jolly Jones"?

Christmas Canon

Johann Pachelbel, Paul O'Neill,   **2016**
Jon Oliva, & Robert Kinkel

Trans-Siberian Orchestra   *The Ghosts of Christmas Eve* (2016)

Based on Pachelbel's "Canon," written anywhere between 1680 and 1706. This is an Orchestral version, with Chorus; the Trans-Siberian Orchestra did a rock version on their album *The Lost Christmas Eve* (2004).

Christmas Canon Rock

Johann Pachelbel, Paul O'Neill, Jon Oliva, & Robert Kinkel   **2004**

Trans-Siberian Orchestra   *The Lost Christmas Eve* (2004)

Incredible rock version of Pachelbel's "Canon."

Christmas Card

Chad Gilbert, Jordan Pundik, Cyrus Bolooki, & Ian Grushka   **2021**

New Found Glory   *December's Here* (2021)

He can't find a perfect Christmas card (in 2021?) with words worthy to describe how he feels about someone.

Christmas Come Early

Frederick Heider, Bobby Strand, Brock Baker, Molly Kate Kestner & Dave Lubben   **2021**

Kelly Clarkson   *When Christmas Comes Around…* (2021)

She wants Christmas to come early this year, for she is down. She doesn't need snow or songs on the radio, only Christmas itself. She needs something to believe in and just a little peace for her family.

Christmas Comes Too Early

Grace Baldridge & Zach Fisher   **2022**

Semler   Single (2022)

Pretty 50s-style rock 'n roll song about a guy who will miss his girl as she visits her family on Christmas.

Christmas Day

Stefano Fresi   2012

Stefano Fresi   *70s Christmas* (2012)

Pretty, easy-going Instrumental.

Christmas Day

Michael W. Smith, Wes King & Cindy Morgan   2014

Michael W. Smith (feat. Jennifer Net-   *The Spirit of Christmas* (2014)
tles)

Very pretty song about Christmas day and all the wonderful things about it, in an idyllic setting, with children's chorus.

Christmas Day

Ed, Scott, Franni & Martin Cash   2021

Chris Tomlin & We the Kingdom   *A Family Christmas* (2021)

Soft rock song about celebrating God and his arrival on Earth on Christmas day.

Christmas Dream

Neil Diamond   2009

Neil Diamond   *A Cherry Cherry Christmas* (2009)

Neil sings about a Christmas dream, where men and women, sons and daughters wait like children for their gifts on Christmas day. It changed him, making him become what he should be. Nice, happy tune.

Christmas Dream

Louise Goulet   **2016**

Louise Goulet   *Christmas Christmas: Magical Holiday Favorites* (2016)

Pretty Instrumental, with a New Age sound.

Christmas Dream

Emily Frost, Jennifer Decilveo, John Hanson, & Whakio Taahi   **2023**

Christina Perri   *Songs for Christmas* (2023)

The best way to describe this song is to call it adorable. Christina Perri, with her beautiful soft voice, sings to her baby daughter about her anticipation of enjoying her first Christmas with her. She has been waiting all her life for this and describes the wondrous things of Christmas to her. Perri is singing about her true-life baby daughter.

Christmas Dreams

Francesca Battistelli, Ian Eskelin & Tony Wood   **2012**

Francesca Battistelli   *Christmas* (2012)

Jazz song about midnight on Christmas Eve. Everyone is asleep and the tree is unplugged. The kids are dreaming Christmas dreams, dreams of wonder and magic that they will look back on all their life.

Christmas Eve

Ritchie Blackmore & Candice Night   **2002**

Blackmore's Night   *Winter Carols* (2002)

This song is about the magic (like reindeer taking flight) of Christmas Eve and wishes peace and love to everyone. It is a very festive song.

Blackmore's Night is a band that performs what is called "medieval folk rock" or "neo-medieval folk rock." It is hard to describe this esoteric kind of music, except that it sounds great. It has certainly a medieval sound to it, using what sounds like medieval instruments. This form of music started in the 1960s and 1970s but did not come into prominence until the late 1980s. Jethro Tull was an early Rock band that introduced medieval sounds. Bands specializing in neo-medieval music are particularly plentiful in Germany, although it also enjoys some popularity in North America and many European countries.

Blackmore's Night's music is very upbeat, to the extent that many songs can be considered "drinking" songs. It is full of life and happiness. The band is a husband-and-wife team with various background performers that are just temporarily in the band. Ritchie Blackmore plays guitar and some strings. Candice Night is the lead vocalist, who writes the lyrics and plays woodwinds. Her voice is beautiful, perfect for this genre.

Christmas Eve

Stefano Fresi   2012

Stefano Fresi   *70s Christmas* (2012)

Very pretty Instrumental that sneaks in other Christmas themes. The album is called *70s Christmas,* but I can't find any reference to this and other songs on this album that dates to the 70s, so I consider the release date to be 2012.

Christmas Eve

Tatsuro Yamashita   2014

Pentatonix   *That's Christmas to Me* (2014)

A Cappella group Pentatonix sings about someone praying to see their Lover on Christmas Eve, but that's just not going to happen, unlike previous Christmas Eves.

Christmas Eve

Kelly Clarkson & Jason Halbert   2021

Kelly Clarkson   Bonus Track of *When Christmas*

Comes Around… (2021)

Very upbeat song about Christmas Eve. In this song, fortunately, she is still sharing Christmas Eve with her "baby."

Jessica Ashley Karpov, known as just "Jessica Ashley" or Harloe, co-produced four songs for Kelly Clarkson. I worked for some years with her mother. Her daughter spoke very fondly of Kelly.

Christmas Eve Carols for Family Dinner

Christmas Eve Carols Academy   2021

Christmas Eve Carols Academy   *Christmas Eve Carols for Family Dinner: Angelic Instrumental Carols,* [etc.] (2021)

Soothing Instrumental that would actually make a nice background for a Christmas family dinner.

Christmas for All the Children of the World

Daniel Berthiaume   2009

Daniel Berthiaume   *O Holy Night* (2009)

Beautiful New Age Instrumental.

Christmas for Two

Leigh Ann Bingham & Kate Ellen York   2008

Sixpence None the Richer   *The Dawn of Grace* (2008)

Leigh Nash's voice is just so adorable, it hardly matters what song she is singing with her band Sixpence None the Richer. This is an easygoing song about a girl and her guy enjoying Christmas together and not needing anything else.

The name of the New Wave / Alternative Rock band Sixpence None the Richer was inspired by a passage from the book *Mere Christianity* by C. S. Lewis discussing how children buying gifts for their parents with the parents' money means the parents are "none the richer" monetarily but yet clearly there is value in the act.

Christmas for You and Me

Elizabeth Bannister Holcomb, Elli
Holcomb & Nathan Dugger
                                                2016

Amy Grant   *Tennessee Christmas* (2016)

Pretty song with a nice beat about Christmas being for a husband and wife, after all the decorations and presents are taken care of. After Christmas is over, and the kids have unwrapped their presents, it's still Christmas for the two.

Christmas in America

Melissa Etheridge   **2008**

Melissa Etheridge   *A New Thought for Christmas* (2008)

A woman goes through all the motions of getting ready for Christmas, but her feelings are focused on her missing Lover, who is in "someone else's land." She asks Santa to send her baby home, far away from harm. It sounds like he or she is a soldier serving overseas, based on the lyrics, which includes "whatever happened to Peace on Earth?" and "I pray that you're alright."

Christmas in California

Lee Bunnell & Andrew Gold   **2002**

America   *Holiday Harmony* (2002)

America sings about Christmas in California, with surf and sand. America re-used some of the melodies from their famous songs on this album.

Christmas in the City

Jay Leonhart   **2012**

Sandy Bainum   *This Christmas* (2012)

Sandy lovingly sings of Christmas in the city (probably New York).

Christmas in My Heart

Kay Denar & Rob Tyger   **2005**

Sarah Connor   *Christmas In My Heart* (2005)

It's Christmas in her heart when she is with her Lover. She wants him to stay with her at Christmas.

Christmas in New York

Shilelagh Law   **2002**

Shilelagh Law   *Together in the End* (2002)

This song is about the first Christmas in NYC after the tragedy of 9/11. It's Christmas in New York again, and everything looks great. But there is one last thing he must do: go to the church and ask God to bless the New York PD, the FDNY, the troops overseas, the hard hats removing debris of the World Trade Center, and those who died in the attack. Nice song that was kindled by the unfortunately short-lived patriotism experienced in the US, especially NYC, after 9/11.

Christmas in New York

Lea Michelle, Adams Ariders, Nik-   **2019**
ki Anders, & Peer Astrom

Lea Michelle   *Christmas in the City* (2019)

Wonderful, energetic song about the sights and sounds of NYC on Christmas, like Rockefeller Center's big lit tree and skaters playing on the ice, Radio City and the Rockettes, Broadway, Macy's, St. Patrick's cathedral and more.

Lea Michele Sarfati began her career as a child actress on Broadway, appearing in productions of *Les Misérables* (1995–1996), *Ragtime* (1997–1999), & *Fiddler on the Roof* (2004–2005).

This song has a fantastic video[126].

Christmas in Our Hearts

Rina Cañizan & Jose Mari Chan   **2022**

Pentatonix (feat. Lea Salonga)   *Holidays Around the World* (2022)

Whenever there are people giving gifts and cards, he believes that Christmas is truly in their hearts. Let Jesus guide us and may the spirit of Christmas be always in our hearts. We should rejoice this holiday season.

Christmas in the Sand

Colbie Caillat, Jason Reeves, &   **2012**
Kara DioGuardi

Colbie Caillat   *Christmas in the Sand* (2012)

She loves Christmas in the snow but prefers Christmas in the sand. She saw Santa in a bathing suit trying to catch a wave. He washed up next to her and gave her a present, saying "It's Christmas in the sand." She thinks she had too much to drink, or maybe it was the sun or the sea, but the Christmas in the sand seemed real.

Christmas in the Year 2000

Daniel Berthiaume   **2009**

Daniel Berthiaume   *O Holy Night* (2009)

Very pretty New Age Instrumental.

Christmas Is

Francesca Battistelli, Ian Eskelin   **2012**
& Tony Wood

Francesca Battistelli   *Christmas* (2012)

Christmas Is…a lot of things. The good things include music, family in town, and Snoopy and Charlie Brown. The not so good things are finding a place to park at the mall, burning the turkey and saying thanks for gifts you will return. There are more good and not so good things, but Christmas is the good news of hope for the whole world because Christmas is Jesus.

Christmas Is a Time for Giving

Canellas, Day, Schwenk & York-man   **2010**

Nicolette Larson   *Stars Come Out for Christmas - Special Edition I* (2010)

Pretty song sung sweetly by Nicolette Larson about helping people at Christmastime who have nothing, or you have a little more than them. Jesus was born with nothing.

Christmas Is All Around

Reg Presley   **2003**

"Billy Mack," character portrayed by   *Love Actually Soundtrack* (2003)
Bill Nighy

This song was written for the 2003 movie *Love Actually*. It was created using the melody from the 1967 Troggs hit "Love Is All Around," written by Reg Presley, lead singer of the Troggs, who claimed he wrote it in about ten minutes. The lyrics were changed to Christmas-orientated ones. It was performed in the movie by actor Bill Nighy as fictional rock star Billy Mack.

Christmas Is Almost Here

Zachary Marsh   **2023**

Super Simple Songs   Single (2023)

Song aimed for children about the anticipation of Christmas.

Christmas Is Just Around the Corner

Barry Manilow & Bruce Sussman   **2007**

Barry Manilow   Single (2007)

Christmas is just around the corner, so write your letters to Santa and do your shopping and wrapping. From the animated Christmas Special *Cranberry Christmas* (2008), which Manilow narrated.

Christmas Isn't Christmas

Jon Bon Jovi   **2023**

Jon Bon Jovi   Single (2023)

There's nothing wrong, but this year Christmas isn't right. This Christmas is without "you." How am I supposed to let you go? Promise me you'll come home soon because Christmas isn't Christmas without you.

Christmas Isn't Christmas 'til You Get Here

Kylie Minogue & Karen Ann Poole   **2016**

Kylie Minogue   *Kylie Christmas* (2016)

A girl anticipates the arrival of her Lover on Christmas. In the end he does indeed arrive. Nice song.

Christmas Joy

John Durrill, Gerald McGhee, Melvin Taylor & Donald Wilson   **2017**

Alabama   *American Christmas* (2017)

Many things at Christmas bring joy, like presents under the tree. Pleasant, happy song.

Christmas Joy

Yvonne Abel, Thomas Jobmann, Sven Greiner & Helmut Hoinkis   **2013**

Yvonne Abel   *Christmas All Over the World* (2013)

Very pretty song about the wonderful things about the Christmas season, including celebrating the birth of Christ.

Christmas Kids

Bogachuk Alexandr Alexandro-vich   **2023**

Alex Lead   *Disco Christmas* (2023)

Pretty, relaxing Instrumental with a disco beat.

Christmas Lights

Guy Berryman, Jonny Buckland,   **2010**
Will Champion & Chris Martin

Coldplay   Single (2010)

It's Christmas night and there's been another fight with his girl. Now she's left, and Christmas just doesn't really feel like Christmas anymore. As Christmas lights keep shining on, he reflects on how he still loves her and always will.

Christmas Lights

Ingrid Michaelson   **2019**

Ingrid Michaelson   *Stranger Songs* (2019)

The album contains music that is inspired by the Netflix television series *Stranger Things*. This song specifically relates to the first season episode "Chapter Three: Holly, Jolly," in which a character communicates via pulses in Christmas lights.

Christmas Magic

Perri Louise Edwards, Tre Jean-   **2024**
Marie, Jez Ashurst & Nina Nesbitt

Perri   Single (2024)

She misses a special someone and asks Santa to work his Christmas magic to get her one true love back. That is her one wish.

Christmas Makes Me Cry

Kacey Musgraves, Shane McAnally & Brandy Clark   **2016**

Kacey Musgraves   *A Very Kacey Christmas* (2016)

Christmas makes her cry because of the people she misses and not having anybody to kiss under the mistletoe. It's another year that she can't make it home. It's always sad meeting her parents, who get greyer and greyer, but she's never able to make it home.

Christmas Morning

Mark Tremonti & Carey Deadman   **2023**

Mark Tremonti   *Mark Tremonti Christmas Classics New & Old* (2023)

He sings about an idyllic Christmas morning. Pretty tune.

Christmas Needs Love to Be Christmas

Steven McClintock & Tim James   **2007**

Juice Newton (with Steve McClintock)   *The Gift of Christmas* (2007)

Despite all the great things about Christmas, Christmas needs love to be Christmas. It needs hearts full of joy. The greatest gift is love. Very pretty tune.

"Juice" (Judith Kay) Newton, a country singer from New Jersey, charted 14 top 10 hits across the Billboard Country, AC, and Hot 100 charts in the 80s, with many of the recordings achieving crossover success and six of the songs hitting the No. 1 position. "Angel of the Morning," a hit for Merrilee Rush in 1968 and covered by many other artists, had its highest-selling and highest-charting version by Juice Newton in 1981.

Christmas On My Radio

Olivia Newton-John & Amy Sky   **2007**

Olivia Newton-John   *Christmas Wish* (2007)

Song in the style of 1950s music about her love of Christmas songs on the radio. Many Christmas songs are mentioned outright or alluded to— "Away in a Manger," "The First Noel," "Silver Bells," "Jingle Bells," "The Christmas Song" and more.

Christmas Paradise

Louise Goffin, George Noriega &   **2011**
Jodi Marr

Carole King   *A Holiday Carole* (2011)

Carole King prefers Christmas with her honey in "paradise"—which has palm trees, coconuts, rum and sand to build castles with. She mentions paradise as being perhaps in San Juan or Rio. "Feliz Navidad" plays on the beach.

Carole King is one of the most successful songwriters in American history. She wrote or co-wrote 118 pop hits appearing on the Billboard Hot 100 over the latter half of the 20th century.

I found the Broadway play Beautiful, *a musical about Carole King's early success, very entertaining.*

Christmas Peace

Louise Goulet   **2016**

Louise Goulet   *Christmas Christmas: Magical Holiday Favorites* (2016)

New Age Instrumental inspired by "Silent Night."

Christmas Pics

Jim Creeggan   **2004**

Barenaked Ladies   *Barenaked for the Holidays* (2004)

Laid back song in Barenaked Ladies style about taking pictures of everyone visiting on Christmas day.

Christmas Prayers

Neil Diamond   **2016**

Neil Diamond   *Acoustic Christmas* (2016)

As he enjoys Christmas day, he says Christmas prayers to those he has known—grandparents, parents, aunts, uncles, friends, siblings, sons and daughters.

Christmas Saves the Year

Jodh Dun & Tyler Joseph   **2020**

Twenty One Pilots   *New Christmas Music* (2020)

You rest assured, Christmas saves the year, even if the world is crumbling down. Everyone wants to make it home this year, because they have someone waiting for them. Interesting animated video[127], in the style of stop-motion figures.

Christmas Secret

Enya, Roma Ryan & Nicky Ryan   **2006**

Enya   *Amarantine (Christmas Edition)* (2006)

Gorgeous New Age Celtic song about a woman waiting for someone. If he doesn't come, what will she do? Who will she tell her secrets to?

Christmas Snowfall

Stefano Fresi   **2012**

Stefano Fresi   *70s Christmas* (2012)

Pretty Instrumental.

Christmas Sweater

Gary Barlow, Jane Goldman,   **2021**
Lorne Balfe, Matthew Vaughan &
Michael Bublé

Gary Barlow   *The Dream of Christmas* (2021)

Put your Christmas sweater on, the uglier the better. You will light up everyone's faces.

Christmas Through the Years

Matthew West & AJ Prius   **2021**

Matthew West   *We Need Christmas* (2021)

He sings about Christmas through the years with his Love, whom he met when they were young. Now they have kids of their own. One chapter ends and another begins.

Christmas Time Again My Friend

Mac Powell, Scott Butler & Alec   **2023**
Butler

Mac Powell   *Christmas* (2023)

Catchy tune about Christmastime, which when he was a kid, he thought toys would make it better, but now he realizes it's all about being together. He mentions classic Christmas songs, as well as Rudolf and Charlie Brown on TV.

Christmas Time Is Here Again

Rolf Lovland   **2021**

Secret Garden & Catherine Iversen   *Sacred Night - The Christmas Album*
                                                              (2021)

Once a year good things come to show, all because a child was born a long, long time ago. Bells are ringing and children are singing that Christmas time is here again. Includes children's chorus, making for a very lovely song.

Christmas Time Is in the Air Again

Mariah Carey & Marc Shaiman   2010

Mariah Carey   *Merry Christmas II You (2010)*

Christmas time is in the air again and she is still deeply in love with her man. Even the Grinch and Scrooge warm up this day when they see them. The dream is to share this Christmas cheer throughout the year.

Christmas Time With You

Lindsay Stirling, Frawley. Nathan Fertig, Jason Reeves & Dave Barnes   2022

Lindsay Stirling (feat. Frawley)   *Snow Waltz* (2022)

All a woman wants is a little Christmas time with her Love. She doesn't want any presents, and Santa can skip her roof.

A Christmas To Remember

Gerald Beckley & Lee Bunnel   2002

America   *Holiday Harmony* (2002)

A Christmas to remember lay ahead. Remember to not make all the little mistakes made in Christmases gone by, like what ornaments to set up how to bake the cookies. Nice, easygoing song.

Christmas Treat

Horatio Sands & Jmmy Fallon   2009

Julian Casablancas   Single (2009)

A song with an 80s New Wave style. They wish it were Christmas today, in the good, old USA. They don't want to hear any negativity about Santa coming.

Christmas Tree Farm

Taylor Swift   **2019**

Taylor Swift   Single (2019)

In my heart is a Christmas tree farm, where every wish comes true.

Christmas Valentine

Ingrid Michaelson, Jason Mraz &   **2018**
Dave Barnes

Ingrid Michaelson & Jason Mraz   *Ingrid Michaelson's Songs for the Season* (2018)

A really cute Christmas song about a loving couple in NYC. The refrain of "baby, just be mine, a kinda sorta Christmas valentine…" is just so wonderful and happy. A great Christmas song because it is so happy and nice.

Christmas Valentine

Francesca Battistelli, Jeff Pardo &   **2020**
Molly Reed

Francesca Battistelli   *This Christmas* (2020)

A nice song about love at Christmas. She doesn't want any presents; all she wants is something money can't buy—a Christmas Valentine.

Christmas Whisper

Billy Paul Williams   **2007**

Billy Paul Williams   *The Santa Affair Vol. 1 - A Christmas Lounge* (2007)

New Age Instrumental with bars of "Carol of the Bells" repeating in it. Cool and different.

Christmas Wish

Otha Young & Juice Newton   **2007**

Juice Newton   *The Gift of Christmas* (2007)

Sweet song wishing all you hold near a Merry Christmas and Happy New Year. May the peace of the Christ child remain in your heart and remain in your life.

Christmas Without You

Andrew Tierney, Harvey Mason Jr., Kenneth Crouch & Damon Thomas   **2013**

Human Nature   *The Christmas Album* (2013)

It doesn't feel like Christmas without you. A familiar theme but sounding different with a 50's-style sound. Nicely orchestrated.

Christmas Yay!

Paul Field   **2022**

Peachy Keen   *Christmas Yay!* (2022)

An energetic Christmas song targeted for children, with a nice happy beat, but including lyrics about the first Christmas.

Christmastime (Oh Yeah)

Kevin Hearn   **2004**

Barenaked Ladies   *Barenaked for the Holidays* (2004)

Mellow song about a man walking down his street and seeing Christmassy things happening around him, like people getting presents and carolers singing "oh yeah." It's Christmastime.

Christmastime Is Killing Us

Seth MacFarlane, Ronald Jones &   **2010**
Danny Smith

Family Guy cast   Single (2010)

Christmastime is killing Santa and the elves, as people ask for too much at Christ-mastime. "Christmastime Is Killing Us" is a song from the season nine episode "Road to the North Pole" of the animated television series *Family Guy*. The song was performed by Santa's voice actor Bruce McGill (an actor with numerous film and TV credits), Stewie's voice actor Seth MacFarlane, and a studio chorus as the elves. The song was nominated for a 2011 Primetime Emmy Award for Outstanding Music and Lyrics, as well as for a 2012 Grammy award in Best Song Written for Visual Media category.[128]

Cold December Night

Michael Bublé, Bob Rock & Alan   **2011**
Chang

Michael Bublé   *Christmas* (2011)

He has asked for many different things for Christmas, but now he knows what his heart wants—a girl to fall in love with him. It is something that will last forever. He will wear her like a Christmas sweater and walk her proudly to the mistletoe.

Song (a) is a Celtic New Age version.

a	2012	Celtic Angels	New Age Christmas - Relaxing Christmas Classics

Cold in December

Josie Dunne   **2018**

Josie Dunne   *New Christmas Music* (2020)

Missing a loved one at Christmastime. It seems colder in December without him. An overused theme in Christmas songs, but nicely done.

The Colder It Feels

Gary Barlow   2021

Gary Barlow (feat. Sheku Kanneh-Mason)   *The Dream of Christmas* (2021)

Missing someone that's been gone for years, since a "Winter of pain." Every year the colder it feels.

Coldest Winter

Kanye West & Roland Orzabal   2008

Kanye West   *808s & Heartbreak* (2008)

Her love for him is a thousand miles separated from him. Memories are made in the coldest Winter. Will he ever love again? If Spring can take the snow away, can it melt away all our mistakes? He thinks he won't ever love again.

Song (a) is an a cappella version.

a	2016	Pentatonix	A Pentatonix Christmas

Come on Christmas

Gary Barlow   2021

Gary Barlow   *The Dream of Christmas* (2021)

Can someone save him? It's been a rough year, and nothing heals the soul like Christmastime. He hopes and prays he can leave that year behind. Seeing faces and sharing love and good will start to heal his pain and make his heart beat again. Nice beat, and something different.

Count on Christmas

Benj Pasek & Justin Noble Paul   2018

Bebe Rexha   *Gift Wrapped, Vol. 4: Winter Won-*

derland (2018)

It doesn't matter if you're feeling down, you can count on Christmas to find the feeling that you always found on that holiday. Energetic, happy song.

Cozy Little Christmas

Katy Perry, Greg Wells & Ferras Alqaisi   **2018**

Katy Perry   Single (2018)

Katy Perry's popular Christmas song about a girl who doesn't need anything for Christmas but her lover, who lights her fire and revs her up more than any present can do. She just wants a cozy little Christmas with him.

Crazy for Christmas

Lindsey Stirling, Bonne McKee, David Marup & Mette Kathrine Mortensen   **2022**

Lindsey Stirling (feat. Bonnie McKee)   *Snow Waltz* (2022)

Bonnie McKee gets a great accompaniment from Lindsey Stirling and her violin in this song about someone who is "crazy for Christmas" and starts celebrating it early. It drives her mad that everyone else can wait until December. Why not make it last, she asks. She goes all out for Christmas, like decorating with 50,000 lights.

Cried Out Christmas

Kylie Minogue, Karen Ann Poole & Matt Prime   **2016**

Kylie Minogue   *Kylie Christmas* (2016)

She doesn't want her lover to keep her waiting because it would be a cried-out Christmas without him.

Darkest Night

Robbie Williams et al   **2019**

Robbie Williams   *The Christmas Present* (2019)

Even if it is the darkest night of the coldest year, Christmas is still Christmas. He wants sex, love and drugs on that day. Decent, rousing song, even if some lyrics are naughty and not nice.

Dear Mrs. Claus

Michael Rubin, James Terranova   **2022**
and Tom Diognardi

King Falcon   Single (2022)

No-one ever writes Mrs. Claus letters, so he is sending one her way. She sits at home while Santa rides his sleigh, and she knows better than to wait for him. Energetic Rock or New Wave song that is fun to listen to.

December 25

Francesca Battistelli & Jason   **2012**
Walker

Francesca Battistelli   *Christmas* (2012)

50s-style song about December 25, a great time of the year.

December 25th

Charlie Puth & Jacob Kasher   **2024**
Hindlin

Charlie Puth   Single (2024)

A song about lost love on Christmas day. December 25th is the day he misses her the most. He stays inside and spends Christmas alone.

December Lights

Joe Stilgoe   **2019**

Joe Stilgoe   *Joe Stilgoe's Christmas Album*
                                                              (2019)

Very pretty song about Christmastime. The lights will lead the way to bring the joy we always need at Christmas. Bells will ring across the town.

December Snow

Justin Hayward   **2003**

The Moody Blues   *December* (2003)

Someone brought their love in October and in November took all he had. His life is now like December snow. He wants time to take his sadness from him. He wants to hold on to warm September, and not experience October again.

December We'll Remember

Francesca Battistelli, Ian Eskelin   **2020**
& Dave Barnes

Francesca Battistelli   *This Christmas* (2020)

It's Christmastime again, and family visit—a big old family. They all have a great time, singing carols and talking to each other.

December's Here

Chad Gilbert, Cyrus Bolooki, Jor-   **2021**
dan Pundik & Ian Grushka

New Found Glory   *December's Here* (2021)

He's counting the days to December. He's been cooped up for 8 months in a "real ghost town." He's very sentimental about Christmas. He's seen *Home Alone* and *Elf* about a thousand times, and *Christmas Vacation* about a million times. Very upbeat song, with a New Wave or Rock sound.

A Different Kind of Christmas

Allan Rich, Jud J. Friedman,   **2004**
LeAnn Rimes & Pete Amato

LeAnn Rimes   *What a Wonderful World* (2004)

It's a different kind of Christmas in a different kind of world. The lights around the tree don't burn as bright, there's a sadness in the voices singing carols, and all around the world it is not a silent night. She wishes she were a kid again, in her daddy's arms, feeling secure.

DJ Play a Christmas Song

Sarah Hudson, Jessie Saint John,   **2023**
Brett McLaughlin, James Abra-
hart, Mark Schick & Lionel Crasta

Cher   *Christmas* (2023)

Recent Christmas song hit, by Cher, who wants the DJ to play a Christmas song so she can dance all night long. That's the only thing she wants this year.

Do You Want to Build a Snowman?

Kristen Anderson-Lopez & Robert   **2013**
Lopez

Kristen Bell, Agatha Lee Monn & Katie   *Frozen* (2013)
Lopez

From the animated movie *Frozen* (2013).

Doesn't Feel Like Christmas

Lily Williams, Ben Abraham, &   **2023**
Michael Blum

Lily Williams   *Overallidays* (2023)

Cute song about it not feeling like Christmas when you are decorating palm trees. It doesn't feel like Christmas 'til you're home. Lily Williams has a soft, gentle voice that is very appealing.

Don't Be a Jerk (It's Christmas)

Tom Kenney & Andy Paley   **2009**

Tom Kenny (as "SpongeBob   *SpongeBob's Greatest Hits* (2009)
SquarePants")

Don't be a jerk at Christmas. SpongeBob offers many examples of bad and illegal behavior. From the Nickelodeon cartoon series *SpongeBob SquarePants*.

Don't Fight It's Christmas

Chad Gilbert, Jordan Pundik, Cy-   **2021**
rus Bolooki, & Ian Grushka

New Found Glory   *December's Here* (2021)

Not to be confused with "Merry Christmas (I Don't Want to Fight Tonight)" by The Ramones in 1989. This song is about not showing anger at Christmas. Examples given of frustrating things are getting stuck in traffic, being cut off in traffic, standing in shopping lines and the cold weather.

Don't Go Pullin' on Santa Claus' Beard

Anderson East & Aaron Raitiere   **2019**

The Oak Ridge Boys   *Down Home Christmas* (2019)

You can lean on Santa's belly, sit on his knee, wrap your arms around him and give him a peck, but don't go pullin' on Santa's beard.

Don't Need a Reindeer

Justin Hayward   **2003**

The Moody Blues   *December* (2003)

I don't need a Reindeer. I don't need the snow. Tell me you love me and I'm ready to go.

Don't You Know that It's Christmas

Sarah Connor, Joe Walter & Pascal Reinhardt   **2022**

Sarah Connor   *Not So Silent Night* (2022)

Catchy tune about people feeling melancholy at Christmas, tired of shopping and getting trapped into the hustle just like the year before. Just take some time and be kind, because it's Christmas.

The Dream of Christmas

Gary Barlow   **2021**

Gary Barlow   *The Dream of Christmas* (2021)

Hear the dream of Christmas roar. It brings your most beloved near and in just one day the heart will heal. Let the dream of Christmas become real. Beautiful uplifting song with great orchestration.

Elf's Lament

Barenaked Ladies   **2004**

Barenaked Ladies (with Michael Bublé)   *Barenaked for the Holidays* (2004)

Great, happy tune about Santa's elves "toiling through the ages making toys on garnished wages." Elves make toys but have aspirations. They decide to petition Santa. If he doesn't give in to their demands, they will just stop making toys—toys that most kids consider junk and throw away, though.

Evergreen

Sam DeRosa, Eric Leva, Scott Hoying, Kirstin Maldonado, Kevin Olusola & Jesse Thomas   **2021**

Pentatonix   *Evergreen* (2021)

A mother's love is evergreen. A mother's love gave us everything. Through hard times they struggled, but she never made it show and she "kept food on the table, and gifts under the tree."

Evergreen

Matt McGinn, Michael Matosic,   **2024**
Jon Hume & Emily Falvey

Tiera Kennedy   Single (2024)

This song has an excellent sound, though it is bittersweet. Christmas is over, so Santa won't be at the mall anymore, there won't be any more Christmas songs on the radio, the lights will be packed away and the tree will be taken down. But for the rest of our lives, we'll get to keep all of the pictures and good memories—because Christmas is evergreen.

Every Day's Like Christmas

Chris Martin, Mikkel Erikesen &   **2016**
Tor Erik Hermansen

Kylie Minogue   *Kylie Christmas* (2016)

Really nice song about a love being so strong that every day is like Christmas. Before, every day was ordinary, and she was "down and disused." Great production values.

Every Time It Snows

Olivia Newton-John & Amy Sky   **2007**

Olivia Newton-John (with John Seca-   *Christmas Wish* (2007)
da)

Every time it snows, a woman misses a special someone the most. Carolers and revelers sing songs that are bittersweet. Lights are sparking but they lack a glow. Everything reminds her that he's too far from home.

Fairytales

Robbie Williams et al   **2019**

Robbie Williams (feat. Rod Stewart)   *The Christmas Present* (2019)

Angels are singing from far away, and we start believing in fairytales. Even when we're drifting apart it's the season to make a new start.

Faith Noel

Paul O'Neill & Robert Kinkel   **2004**

Trans-Siberian Orchestra   *The Lost Christmas Eve* (2004)

Instrumental that is a Rock version of "The First Noel," followed by new material, and then a Rock version of "Adeste Fidelis."

Favorite Time of Year

Carrie Underwood, Hillary Lindsey   **2020**
& Chris DeStefano

Carrie Underwood   *My Gift* (2020)

New Christmas hit that is a lively song about a couple enjoying Christmas together, snuggled up together sitting by the fire while "love pours out like snow from the sky."

Finding Christmas

GENTRI   **2016**

GENTRI   *Finding Christmas* (2016)

He doesn't need a perfect tree or nicely wrapped gifts; all he needs is his lover to be with him, because she brings Christmas to life. Nice.

First Snow

Paul O'Neill   **2016**

Trans-Siberian Orchestra   *The Ghosts of Christmas Eve* (2016)

Instrumental that starts off with a mellow sound and segues into a great Rock tune.

Footprints

Edward Robertson   **2004**

Barenaked Ladies   *Barenaked for the Holidays* (2004)

Nice gentle song about a man following footprints in the snow so closely one would think he was walking hand-in-hand with the owner of the footprints. He stands frozen, though, as he approaches her. Now it's Christmas Eve and the two have gotten together. He made his move, and he is happy. She might have left him in the cold, but she didn't.

For Believers

Otha Young   **2007**

Juice Newton   *The Gift of Christmas* (2007)

Sweet song about a woman telling her children to close their eyes and go to sleep. The angels will fly, but only for believers. When she was a child, she saw them.

For Christmas Sake

Chad Gilbert, Jordan Pundik, Cy-   **2021**
rus Bolooki & Ian Grushka

New Found Glory   *December's Here* (2021)

A man's reminiscence of Christmas when he was five years old, hoping for his favorite toys to arrive. His parents worked hard all year to give him a morning he would not forget. But all he got was a skinny skateboard. His parents couldn't afford better, so he just smiled at them, which he is sure was priceless to them. So, he stays young for Christmas's sake.

Forever Christmas Eve

Greg Barnhill & Phil Swann   **2002**

Lee Ann Womack   *The Season for Romance* (2002)

Christmas is so magical—why can't it always be forever Christmas Eve? She wants to stay together with her Love, asking "mister brand new year" to let them stay right there and spare them a little cheer.

From a Distance (Christmas Version)

Julie Gold   **2005**

Bette Midler   *Cool Yule* (2005)

Christmas version of Bette Midler's hit "From a Distance" (1990). Beautiful.

The Garland

Caroline Brooks, Kerri Ough &   **2019**
Susan Passmore

Good Lovelles   *Evergreen* (2019)

Nice, easy song with a good beat and cute vocals about an idyllic family Christmas. There's an evergreen wrapped up in a garland and a Christmas tree at the center of the family, who is counting their blessings by the light of the tree.

A Gift of Love

Barry Manilow & Bruce Sussman   **2007**

Olivia Newton-John (feat. Barry Ma-   *Christmas Wish* (2007)
nilow)

Really nice, triumphant song with great vocals and lush orchestration about the gift of Love given to us "on this silent night." Love makes it summer at the coldest time of year.

Giving Christmas Away

Tasha Layton, Tony Wood & Keith Everette Smith   **2021**

Tasha Layton   *This Is Christmas* (2021)

Nice song about a woman who is "blown away" by the blessings she has at Christmastime, which include friends and precious family. But she knows for so many it is hard this time of year, and she wants to give them hope and peace. So, she is "giving Christmas away" to them, through acts of kindness and love.

Glorious

Ed Cash, Scott Cash, Franni Cash, Martin Cash & Andrew Bergthold   **2021**

We the Kingdom   *A Family Christmas* (2021)

Very lovely and triumphant song about the first Christmas, which was glorious. It gave hope to every man and woman. Emmanuel loved Mankind and is glorious.

Good King Joy

Lowell Mason, Paul O'Neill & Robert Kinkel   **2016**

Trans-Siberian Orchestra   *The Ghosts of Christmas Eve* (2016)

Complex song that starts softly with "Joy to the World," turns to Rock, then gives us a rendition in Rock of "Good King Wenceslas," and then of "Joy to the World" again and back to "Good King Wenceslas." The remainder of the song is an original composition, to be finally followed by "Joy to the World," as it began. Fantastic instrumentation, with vocals.

Greatest Gift

Sally Gentry & Mark Narmore   **2017**

Alabama   *American Christmas* (2017)

He reminiscences of when his dad would tell him stories of the first Christmas. He then sings about the true meaning of Christmas, which is not about Santa, candy canes, lit-up trees or the hustle and bustle of Christmas, but is about the greatest gift that ever came to life—God's son, Jesus, whose birthday we celebrate on Christmas.

Green Christmas

Steven Page & Edward Robertson   **2004**

Barenaked Ladies   *Barenaked for the Holidays* (2004)

He describes winter scenes at Christmastime, but it's a green Christmas "in this town" because of everything he misses. A Christmas without the white of snow is just not the same. Nice beat.

Hallelujah (Light Has Come)

BarlowGirl   **2008**

BarlowGirl   *Home for Christmas* (2008)

Haunting song with great vocals from the point of view of Mary, Jesus' mother. Who is she to hold the one that will bring us life? He will save us and set us free. She sings for her baby, whom kings have come to.

A Hand for Mrs. Claus

Kristen Anderson-Lopez & Robert Lopez   **2019**

Idina Menzel & Ariana Grande   *Christmas: A Season of Love* (2019)

Also released as a single, this song was written by the songwriting team that wrote songs for *Frozen*, specifically for Idina Menzel and Ariana Grande. Every December we aways remember Santa, Rudolf, Frosty and the Grinch, and they are all OK, but how about a hand for Mrs. Claus? She gets everything done for Christmas Eve to happen. She's better than Santa and reads all the letters. "She runs the operation with no appreciation." Send a little Christmas love her way.

Happiness (Is Christmas)

Charlie Midnight, Jay Landers, &   **2021**
Clark Gesner

Kristin Chenowith   *HAPPINESS is...Christmas!* (2021)

This darling song begins with "Christmastime is Here" from *A Charlie Brown Christmas* TV Special (1965) and segues into a lot of "happiness is..." lyrics that describe the many great things about Christmas, like: spending fun times with the whole family, being home on Christmas day, listening to reindeer, decorating, listening to carolers, building a snowman, sleigh rides and much more.

Happy Christmas

Colbie Caillat & Tobias Gad   **2012**

Colbie Caillat   *Christmas in the Sand* (2012)

When it is almost Christmas everyone is wishing for everything they've always wanted, but maybe we worry too much about that and not enough about giving, as some people have nothing at all. We should show random acts of kindness, remember the homeless, give hope to the hopeless and love to the loveless.

Happy Holiday

Billy Idol & Brian Tichy   **2021**

Billy Idol   *Happy Holidays* (2021)

Not to be confused with the song "Happy Holiday" written by Irving Berlin in 1942, and don't expect the New Wave / Punk styles of Billy Idol from the 1980s. In this song he wishes a happy holiday to all, clean and simple. Enjoy the fun of Christmas and remember Christ was born this day.

Happy People

Tom Gaebel   **2015**

Tom Gaebel   *A Swinging Christmas* (2015)

Happy people are all around at Christmas, enjoying its sights and sounds. This swinging song is a monument to the Christmas songs of the 60s, catching their flavor exactly.

Happy, Happy Christmas

Ingrid Michaelson   **2018**

Ingrid Michaelson   *Ingrid Michaelson's Songs for the Season* (2018)

Ingrid Michaelson graces us with her wonderful voice in a wonderful song that is bittersweet; it is apparently one of separation with a lost Love. She is not bitter about that loss and tells him to live well and let go. She promises him that she'll have a happy, happy Christmas and wishes him the same.

Harps of Gold

Tori Amos   **2009**

Tori Amos   *Midwinter Graces* (2009)

Those who don't have much still sing at Christmas, songs like "Adeste Fideles," especially the line "Gloria, gloria in excelsis Deo" and smile through the pain.

The Heartache Can Wait

Brandi Carlile & Phil Hanseroth   **2007**

Brandi Carlile   Single (2007)

Her lover is talking about leaving right around Christmas. She wants her lover to stay, because the heartache can wait. She wants "one last truce" that can make it through December. She wants one more Christmas to spend together, because it gives her lover one more chance to be inspired.

Heaven & Earth

Leslie Odom, Jr., Rafael Casal,   **2020**
Theron "Neff-U" Feemster & Paul

Duncan

Leslie Odom, Jr.   *The Christmas Album* (2020)

He loves a young woman, and on this Christmas, love can move Heaven and Earth. He loves a young mother, holding his baby, and he feels God's word lately. Very sublime.

Heaven Everywhere

Francesca Battistelli   **2012**

Francesca Battistelli   *Christmas* (2012)

At Christmastime there's a little bit of Heaven everywhere. Somehow there's a little more of love. The Heaven can be seen on a man who has finally found hope and the tears of a mother whose child has come home. It's the grace we show to a world that shows hope, as well as the joy that we feel and love that we share. Very nice tune.

a	2020	Aspen Meadow Band	A Modern Classic Christmas

Here Comes Christmas

T. Chase, S. Rucker & J. Roberts   **2012**

Alvin & The Chipmunks   *Chipmunks Christmas* (2012)

Here comes Christmas, the happiest time of the year. There is a fireplace glowing, a winter chill in the air, family near you and friendship to cheer you, and much more. There is good will to those everywhere. Sing and rejoice on this happiest time of year.

Holiday Party

Andy Albert, Dan Smyers & Jordan Reynolds   **2022**

Dan + Shay   Single (2022)

Great modern Christmas tune. He wants a holiday party at home with someone special. When friends ask them to meet them elsewhere, they'll just stay home. He just wants to be alone with his honey, pour some drinks, hang some lights on a tree and play karaoke. They will spend Christmas at a holiday party at home wrapped up in a blanket for two.

Holiday Records

Chad Gilbert, Jordan Pundik, Cyrus Bolooki & Ian Grushka   **2021**

New Found Glory   *December's Here* (2021)

They will be wearing out holiday records on Christmas Eve, listening to the Beach Boys, Bruce Springsteen and Mariah Carey. Everyone is invited and come when you can; you won't miss anything because they will play the records over again.

Holiday Season

Louis Biancaniello, Jordan Omley & Suzie Ali Omley   **2022**

Station Little (feat. Elle Winter)   Single (2022)

We've got so much love to go around as the snow is falling around. It's the holiday season and are thankful for so many reasons. We all need something to believe in. Have you made anyone's day today? It will make you feel great inside; it's the best surprise every time. Very nice, upbeat song.

Holidays Are Near

Andre O. Mayeux   **2007**

Juice Newton   *The Gift of Christmas* (2007) - Deluxe edition only

Shoppers have smiling faces, love is the air; children's eyes are so bright, it must mean that holidays are near. It is the best time of year for family and friends, and we hope it will never end. She hears the bells of Christmas, reminding her that the holidays are near. Happy, upbeat song about Christmastime.

Home

Robbie Williams et al   **2019**

Robbie Williams   *The Christmas Present* (2019)

Nicely orchestrated song about how time flies and then the holidays are here. He travels at night just to be home again with his family. He has always said the wasted times are the minutes he is away from them. He'd love to stay home and be all together with his family.

Home

Michael Bublé, Alan Chang & Amy Foster-Gillies   **2011**

Blake Shelton (feat. Michael Bublé)   *Cheers, It's Christmas* (2011)

He is away from home, and he's got so far to go. He needs to go home, even though he is surrounded by strangers and Christmas lights, and he shouldn't feel so alone. He can close his eyes and see all the nice things at home. The reasons that he's so far away are not enough; he knows he needs his family more.

Home for Christmas Eve

Clyde Bawden & Jason Barney   **2013**

Clyde Bawden & Jason Barney   *Glenn Beck Presents: Believe Again* (2013)

She's got to go back home for Christmas Eve. She wants to go back to a quiet place where angels steal the night.

The Hope of Christmas

Matthew West & AJ Pruis   **2020**

Matthew West   Single (2020)

He wants to go back to when he was eight to "those innocent Decembers." These days peace on Earth is hard to find. He needs God to remind him that He is the hope of Christmas, the light when the world is dark. May the sick find healing's touch and may every heart find room for God, the one who came to save us.

This Single was included the following year in West's album *We Need Christmas* (2021).

How Christmas Is Supposed to Be

Gary Barlow   2021

Gary Barlow (feat. Sheridan Smith)   *The Dream of Christmas* (2021)

On Christmas, he's fighting with his significant other, which is not how Christmas is supposed to be. He's hoping that next year things will be better, with them respecting each other. He wants them both to agree this is not how Christmas is supposed to be. And they do—the only gift he needs is her love, and Christmas again is what it's supposed to be.

I Have Wanted You (for Christmas)

Raul Malo & Alan Miller   2018

The Mavericks   *Hey! Merry Christmas!* (2018)

Upbeat song about wanting someone for Christmas since the holiday began, in fact "since the dawn of Man." He wanted her to be his baby and every year that comes true. She is his prize.

I Still Believe in Santa Claus

LeAnn Rimes   2018

LeAnn Rimes   *It's Christmas, Eve - Original Motion Picture Soundtrack* (2018)

She still believes in Santa Claus, not for any logical reason but because it keeps the kid in her alive. Adults grow up too fast and lose their imagination. And she still has faith in God above. Nice, happy song from the movie *It's Christmas, Eve* (2018).

I Wanna Be With You (On Christmas Day)

Brady Parks   2023

The National Parks   Single (2023)

He wants to spend Christmas in the forest, desert or the ocean, as long as he is with his honey on Christmas day. The song is in the style of the 60s/70s.

I'll Be Stoned for Christmas

Bob Rivers   **2002**

Bob Rivers & Bob Rivers Twisted Radio   *White Trash Christmas* (2002)

Spoof of "I'll Be Home for Christmas," the singer imitating a drunk Dean Martin.

I'll Be Stoned for Christmas

Dent May   **2014**

Dent May   Single (2014)

Pleasing New Wave song about a man looking forward to going out on Christmas night with his old High School friends and getting stoned. There is an angel on the treetop but a devil on his mind.

If You Believe

Joss Stone   **2022**

Joss Stone   *Merry Christmas, Love* (2022)

Santa won't let children down who believe in him. If you believe, then you will see a reindeer run and the angels singing and using their drum.

In Stiller Nacht

Unknown   **2014**

Pink Martini & The von Trapps   *Dream a Little Dream* (2014)

This song is not "Silent Night," but is a beautiful song in German, a cappella. The "von Trapps" are descendants of the von Trapp children, made famous in *The Sound of Music* (1965).

Instrument of Peace

Amy Sky, Marc Jordan & Stephan Moccio   **2007**

Olivia Newton-John   *Christmas Wish* (2007)

Olivia sings beautifully, promising that all the negative and bad things in life will be changed into positive, good things. Hauntingly, she sings that in dying she hopes to be made into an "instrument of peace." She died 15 years after this song was released.

Isn't That What Christmas Is For

Caleb Liechty, Bekah Liechty, Josh Liechty, Skylar Mones & Toby Gad   **2022**

Girl Named Tom   *One More Christmas* (2022)

She'll ask for a little less this Christmas and give a little more. She will count her blessings and open the door to lonely souls and hearts that have been torn. Isn't that what Christmas is for? When she was a child, she asked for things she wanted, while others were wishing for things they needed. Her mom told her it was better to give than to receive.

It Ain't Christmas

Molly Kate Kestner, Phil Bentley & Taylor Bird   **2020**

Anna Clendening   *New Christmas Music* (2020)

A woman waits for her darling to come home. Everything is set up for Christmas, but something is missing—him. She stays up late in case he gets a flight home. It "ain't Christmas" until he's home. Finally, he arrives.

It Doesn't Feel Like Christmas

Sam Phillips   **2019**

Sam Phillips   *Cold Dark Nights* (2019)

She hopes that her Love will be with her this time next year. It doesn't feel like Christmas with him so far away. Familiar theme but done with Sam Philips' unique style.

It Doesn't Often Snow at Christmas

Pet Shop Boys (Tennant & Lowe)   **2009**

Pet Shop Boys   *Christmas* (Pet Shop Boys EP) (2009)

Great Pet Shop Boys tune, done in their usual grand style. Christmas is not all it's cracked up to be—families fighting around a plastic Christmas tree, nothing good on TV, and it's hardly ever snowing. But he'll still "have a glow" at Christmas being with the one he loves.

Last Pet Shop Boys single to have entered the UK top 40.

It Must Be Christmas

Chris Young, Johnny Bulford &   **2016**
Will Doughty

Chris Young   *It Must Be Christmas* (2016)

Everything around him indicates that it must be Christmas. When you believe in Santa Claus, and you give gifts "just because" and you drive all night only to be near the ones you love it must be Christmas.

It Really Is (A Wonderful Life)

Chely Wright   **2007**

Chris Young   *My Holiday* (2007)

This song is the opposite of many songs that deal with missing loved ones at Christmas. Instead, it is about having someone at Christmas and seeing Christmas in a new, happier light.

It's A Wonderful Life

Robbie Williams et al   **2019**

Robbie Williams (feat. Poppa Pete)   *The Christmas Present* (2019)

Christmas song with a classic 60s/70s sound, with full orchestra. A man and his friends have a great time at Christmas, drinking gin and juice and eating goose. He's counted their blessings, and they are blessed, sure enough, enjoying a wonderful life.

It's Christmas

Alvin Love III   **2024**

CeCe Winans   *Joyful, Joyful: A Christmas Album* (2024)

Really nice Christmas song with a full sound. She's so glad it's Christmas, even though it's a hustle.

It's Christmas Eve

LeAnn Rimes & Darrell Brown   **2018**

LeAnn Rimes   *It's Christmas, Eve - Original Motion Picture Soundtrack* (2018)

A woman is with a loved one on Christmas Eve, right where she wants him to be. From the movie *It's Christmas, Eve* (2018).

It's Christmas Time

Olivia O'Brien, Roget Chahayed,   **2021**
Taylor Dexter, Wesley Singerman,
Sam Fischer & Tia Scola

Olivia O'Brien   Single (2021)

A woman always dreads December and the holidays; it doesn't snow, it just rains, and all her spirit has gone away. But this year she wants things to be different—she wants to feel like a kid again. So, she'll stop being bitter and smile. She doesn't need a lot of gifts under the tree on Christmas Eve because she'll be working then anyway. She's going to enjoy Christmas, even hop in a sleigh.

It's Christmas Time (Let's Just Survive)

Kathleen Edwards   **2019**

Kathleen Edwards   *A Dualtone Christmas* (2019)

Christmastime isn't that wonderful, but she'll just survive. She visits her parent's house, drinking homemade wine that tastes like crap and listening to Mom's criticizing Dad's mashed potatoes. There are so many things that go wrong and are unpleasant. She meows. Very amusing situations are in this song.

The album is of songs by various artists.

It's Finally Christmas

Mark Hall & Matthew West   **2017**

Casting Crowns   *It's Finally Christmas* (2017)

Lights are twinkling down the block and dad's looking for the perfect tree while mom bakes cookies. They listen to Nat King Cole as grandpa falls asleep and grandma reminiscences. All the crazy families knock on the door. These and more things mean that it's finally Christmas.

It's Only Christmas Once a Year

Norah Jones   **2021**

Norah Jones   *I Dream of Christmas* (2021)

A woman anxiously awaits someone special to arrive at her home. Last year he was not with her and Christmas was not as bright as it could have been. She pleads that we gather all our loved ones and hold them close because one never knows when you'll part. She asks her loved one to say he's coming home for Christmas—it is only once a year.

A Jazzy White Christmas

Irving Berlin (original version)   2006

Anne Miranda   *I Love This Holiday* (2006)

As the title declares, this is a jazzed-up version of "White Christmas." It includes a medley with "Up on the Housetop."

Jingle Bell Dreams

Chris Craker   2022

Lullaby Planet   *Snowflakes* (2022)

Lovely piano piece that includes bars of "Jingle Bells."

Jolly Time of Year

Sarah Connor, Ali Zuckowski & Max Wolfgang   2022

Sarah Connor   *Not So Silent Night* (2022)

Very upbeat, classic-style Christmas song about Christmastime. Very nice yuletide tune.

Journey of the Angels

Enya & Roma Ryan   2008

Enya   *And Winter Came* (2008)

Beautiful New Age Celtic song about angels flying dark winter skies to reach the newborn king, Christ. One is sorrow, one is peace, one will give him sleep. One is comfort, one is grief, and one will take the tears he weeps.

Joy

Cindy Morgan   **2009**

Cindy Morgan   *You're Here* (2009)

She wishes joy to the young Jesus, who has come down to Earth from Heaven. Triumphant song.

Joy

Tracey Thorn   **2012**

Tracey Thorn   *Tinsel and Lights* (2012)

Joy—you loved it as a kid, and you need it more than you ever did. That's why the carols make you cry. We'll gather up our fears and face down all the coming fears. In their faces we throw our Joy.

Just to Be With You (This Christmas)

Ross Bon   **2013**

Nick Lowe   *Quality Street: A Seasonal Selection for All the Family* (2013)

Easygoing, old-fashioned song about having Christmas anytime or anywhere, just to be with someone special at Christmas. He'll accept a lump of coal from Santa. There's nothing he wouldn't do to see her this Christmas. He could never be blue if he's with her this Christmas.

Kid at Christmas

Calum Scott, Christina Perri, et al   **2024**

Calum Scott & Christina Perri   Single (2024)

I still feel like a kid at Christmas. I still get the same old feeling waking on Christmas morning and I've still got wishes on my wish list. If I believe, then it's still true.

Kid on Christmas

Meghan Trainor, Trannie Anderson, Jared Conrad, Scott Hoying, Kevin Olusola & Matt Sallee　　　　　　**2023**

Pentatonix (feat. Meghan Trainor)　　　*The Greatest Christmas Hits* (2023)

Stay being a kid on Christmas; you are never too old to be a kid on Christmas. May your heart be evergreen in December. Never lose your wonder and every year grow younger.

Kissing in the Cold (Mistletoe Version)

Brian Higgins, Ben Taylor, et al　　　　　　**2024**

Florrie　　　　　　Single (2024)

Kissing in the cold, I treasured you like gold. So naïve we thought it would last. If I could go back, then you should know that there's a part of me that wants you even now. I miss the old you. Very nicely performed song in terms of vocals and instrumentation.

The Last Christmas

Matthew Preston Slocum & Steve J Hindalong　　　　　　**2008**

Sixpence None the Richer　　　　　　*The Dawn of Grace* (2008)

On this last Christmas without Jesus, she thinks of the first Christmas with Jesus that is coming.

Last Time by Moonlight

Enya & Roma Ryan　　　　　　**2008**

Enya　　　　　　*And Winter Came* (2008)

Another beautiful New Age Celtic song by Enya and her usual lyricist, Roma Ryan. She thinks of walking with someone at midnight during winter, in the snow, and how wonderful it was. It is important to remember, though, that "no one knows the way love goes" and the way life goes, and that this may be the last time they are together like this.

Let It Shine

Amy Sky   **2006**

Amy Sky   *The Lights of December* (2006)

She lights a candle as she watches the snow fall and prays for peace with all her might. She prays that impossible dreams come true and that someday the whole world will make it shine.

Let It Snow

Brian McKnight & Wanya Morris   **2024**

MaKenzie   Single (2024)

Not the traditional "Let It Snow." It's another Christmas holiday, and it's a joyous thing, because we are together. When our bodies meet, I don't care about the weather. So, let it snow…

Let There Be Peace on Earth

Richard Marx   **2012**

Richard Marx (Duet with Kenny Log-   *Christmas Spirit* (2012)
gins)

Let there be peace on Earth, the peace that was meant to be, and let it begin with me. Let me walk with God, our Father, and our brothers, in perfect harmony.

Let's Get Christmas Going

Bryan Adams & Robert John   **2022**
"Mutt" Lange

Bryan Adams   *Let's Get Christmas Going* (2022)

Everything indicates that Christmas is coming, so let's get it going.

Let's Not Go Shopping

Robbie Williams et al   **2019**

Robbie Williams   *The Christmas Present* (2019)

At Christmastime there's so much to do but he'd rather just spend time with his darling. So, he suggests that they don't go shopping, and expresses excuses not to. It's much more pleasant to stay home.

The Light of Christmas Day

Charles Duncan   **2015**

Robert Plant & Alison Krauss   Single (2015)

They are only hours away from the light of Christmas day, but somehow, they are all ready. They await the shouting and singing of their children when Christmas arrives. From the Christmas comedy-drama *Love the Coopers* (2015).

Light of the World (Sing Hallelujah)

Ed Cash, Scott Cash, Franni   **2005**
Cash, Martin Cash & Andrew
Bergthold

We the Kingdom   *A Family Christmas* (2005)

Sing hallelujah, God became one of us and has done so many things for us. Adore Him and bow down before Him. He was born for the Cross, to suffer and save us. He is the light of the world.

Lights of Christmas

John Kavanaugh   **2010**

Voices of Orange County High School   *Orange County High School of the*
of the Arts & Susan Egan   *Arts: Home for the Holidays* (2010)

She sees the lights of Christmas in your eyes. It gives her feelings of joy and wonder. She sings of the wonders of Christmastime.

Lights of December

Amy Sky **2008**

Amy Sky *The Lights of December* (2008)

In the lights of December, she tries to surrender to the joys of receiving and giving.

Like a Snowman

Stephin Merritt **2006**

Kiki & Herb *Broadway's Greatest Gifts - Carols for a Cure - Volume 8 (2006)*

There's only one way to get through the winter, as all the broken-hearted know.

a	2012	Tracey Thorn	Tinsel and Lights

A Little Bit of Love

Jimmy Barnes, Joy Williams & Jerry Lynn Williams **2009**

Joy Williams *More Than I Asked For* (2009)

A happy, catchy tune about someone who feels so lucky at Christmas having all the people sharing it with her. She cherishes the moment, as without them she would never have known a little bit of love goes a long way. A little bit of love changes everything.

A Little Peace on Earth

Legacy Five **2007**

Legacy Five *A Little Christmas* (2007)

Lately he's been praying for a little peace on Earth. It's hard to imagine a silent night in a busy world that never sleeps but he realizes that's just what we really need. He hears a church bell ringing and asks the Lord if this Christmas He could help us get along for just awhile.

Little Star of Bethlehem

Olivia Newton-John, Stephan Moccio & Amy Sky   **2007**

Olivia Newton-John   *Christmas Wish (2007)*

Little star of Bethlehem, she prays, you will cast your light upon the world. It is a flame of peace and hope. Show the hungry hearts and souls bound in chains that we hear their cry, and care.

Little Things

Björn Ulvaeus & Benny Andersson   **2021**

ABBA   *Voyage* (2021)

As far as I know, this beautiful song is the only Christmas song ever written by supergroup ABBA. The music and lyrics are wonderful. It's about the little things, like a simple touch, that can achieve so much. It's a lovely Christmas morning that you awaken with your companion, and you decide to stay in bed awhile before waking the kids.

Love This Christmas

Rick Astley   **2020**

Rick Astley   *Love This Christmas* (2020)

What do you want, what would you like for Christmas? All we need is love this Christmas.

The album has songs by various artists. Rick Astley's debut single "Never Gonna Give You Up" in 1987 was a No. 1 hit in over 25 countries, winning the 1988 Brit Award for Best British Single. His 1988 single "Together Forever" also topped the US Billboard Hot 100 and was one of his eight songs to reach the UK Singles Chart Top 10.

The Magic of Christmas

Ezra Nicolas Proch & Samuel Beecher Proch   **2022**

Willow City   Single (2022)

If you had to explain to extraterrestrials what's with December 25th, what would you say? He says it's magic, and it would probably drive them insane.

Make It to Christmas

Alessia Caracciolo & Jon Levine   **2019**

Alessia Cara   Single (2019)

Song about a failing relationship that she wants to give another try at Christmas; she doesn't want to spend it alone. She begs for another chance and is afraid that a break-up will ruin future holidays for her. She just begs and begs…

Make It to Christmastime

Tasha Layton, Tony Wood & Keith Everette Smith   **2021**

Tasha Layton   *This is Christmas* (2021)

There are so many things to do to get ready for Christmas, but she will be fine when she makes it to Christmastime.

Make Way

Matthew West & AJ Prius   **2021**

Matthew West   *We Need Christmas* (2021)

Make way for the King of Kings, born in a manger on Christmas day. Make room for the promised one.

Make You Mine This Season

Alex Hope, Sara Keirsten Quin &   **2020**
Tegan Rain Quin

Tegan and Sara   *Happiest Season* (2020)

Somebody broke your heart under a Christmas tree. But have I been good enough to make you mine this season? Album is music from and inspired by the Hulu original film *Happiest Season*.

Maybe This Christmas

Tracey Thorn   **2012**

Tracey Thorn   *Tinsel and Lights* (2012)

Maybe this Christmas will mean something more; maybe this year love will appear deeper than any before. Maybe forgiveness will bring us back together, and a star that shined before will shine once more.

Merry Christmas

Bryan Adams & Jim Vallance   **2011**

Bryan Adams   *Christmas* (2011)

He's so very glad he's with that special someone at Christmas. He doesn't care about the celebrations; he only wants to stay with her by the fire.

Merry Christmas

Ed Sheeran & Elton John   **2021**

Ed Sheeran & Elton John   Single (2021)

There's been pain this year, but it's time to let it go and celebrate Christmas together. We've both known love, but this love we have is the best of all. While we're here, let's spare a thought for the ones who have gone.

Merry Christmas Darlings

Rick Nielsen, Tom Petersson, &   **2017**
Robin Zander

Cheap Trick   *Christmas Christmas* (2017)

Very happy tune about Christmas celebrations.

Merry Christmas Everybody

Neville Holder & James Lea   **2015**

Train   *Christmas in Tahoe* (2015)

Merry Christmas, everybody's having fun. They sing about a family Christmas, with all its quirks. Good song for Christmas.

Merry Christmas Wherever You Are

Melissa Sheppard   **2018**

Meiko   Single (2018)

It's been "about a decade or so" since she last saw her boyfriend. They had good times, and she was his girl—they had it made. Merry Christmas, wherever you are, she says, and she hopes he thinks of her.

Merry Christmas, Happy Holidays

JC Chasez, Justin Timberlake,   **2016**
Veit Renn & Vincent Paul Degior-
gio

Pentatonix   *A Pentatonix Christmas* (2016)

This song is a happy song about the holidays. They look forward to everything most want from Christmas.

Merry Christmas, Happy New Year

Ingrid Michaelson, Dave Barnes &   **2018**
Zooey Deschanel

Ingrid Michaelson & Zooey Descha-   *Ingrid Michaelson's Songs for the*
nel   *Season* (2018)

Nice, happy holiday song sung by two talents very familiar with performing Christmas songs (Deschanel usually teams with M. Word in She and Him). Ingrid sings that she feels like a kid again falling in love with someone. Zooey describes the great feeling of being in love at Christmas. Ingrid and Zooey wish each other a Merry Christmas at the end. Cute.

Merry Something to You

Gerald Casale & Josh Freese   **2010**

Devo   *Gift Wrapped, Vol. II: Snowed In*
                                                              (2010)

Devo visits from the 80s to sing this short, quirky song wishing Christians, Muslims and Jews to celebrates their own holidays and believe what they want (but they say nothing's really true).

Various artists on the album.

Messiah

Francesca Battistelli, Jeff Pardo &   **2020**
Molly Reed

Francesca Battistelli   *This Christmas* (2020)

She sings about the first Christmas, wherein we were delivered a messiah to save us all. Oh come, let us adore him (with the theme from "Adeste Fideles"). Rousing song.

A Million Stars

Rolf Løvland   **2021**

Secret Garden & Cathrine Iversen   *Sacred Night - The Christmas Album*
                                                                    (2021)

Cathrine Iversen (first name not misspelled) joins New Age sensation Secret Garden to sing this pretty song about the first Christmas.

Mistletoe

Justin Bieber, Nasri Atweh and   **2011**
Adam Messinger

Justin Bieber   *Under the Mistletoe* (2011)

This song reached the top ten in Canada, Denmark and Norway, and peaked at 11 in the US, while also reaching the top forty in nine other countries. It set the record for the highest debut for a Christmas song in Billboard Hot 100 history.

Under the Mistletoe is the first Christmas album and second studio album by Justin Bieber. The album debuted at number one on the US Billboard 200 chart and the Billboard Top Holiday Albums chart, selling 210,000 copies in its first week, becoming the first Christmas album by a male artist to debut at number one.[129]

More Than I Asked For

Joy Williams   **2009**

Joy Williams   *More Than I Asked For* (2009)

The boy that she met at Christmas is more, more, more than she asked for.

A Mother's Christmas Wish

Olivia Newton-John & Amy Sky   **2007**

Olivia Newton-John   *Christmas Wish* (2007)

At Christmas a mother wishes her child love and someone who cares. She hopes that time will be kind to her and that all her dreams come true. She looks forward to when her child will have children of her own. She knows her child will realize then what she's been to her—the greatest gift of all. A child was born on Christmas day to lead the way.

Mr. Right

Leona Lewis, Richard Stannard,   **2013**
Jez Ashurst, Ash Howes & kamille

Leona Lewis   *Christmas, With Love* (2013)

Being without her lover she finds Christmas blue. He's 2,000 miles away and she's lonely. She asks Santa for one thing—her "baby," Mr. Right. She feels that she is the only one without a man and can't stand to watch other couples.

As of 2021, Lewis has sold over 35 million records worldwide.[130] She is the first British female solo artist to reach the top five with eight singles, surpassing Olivia Newton-John's record of seven.

My Holiday

Mindy Smith   **2007**

Mindy Smith   *My Holiday* (2007)

Some will say her tree is not real, but it makes her holiday feel like Christmas. Some will say it's not about gift-giving, but it makes her holiday feel like Christmas.

Naughty & Nice

Jesse Shatkin & Sia   **2017**

Sia   *Everyday Is Christmas (Snowman Deluxe Edition)* (2017)

Sia has been a great force in this century for creating popular and fresh Christmas songs. All tracks on this album are written by Sia (full name Sia Furler).

Not much to this song—she can be naughty or nice, and so can her lover. She makes her point with a number of examples. The song has a great rowdy sound.

Nearly Christmas

Joel Richard Evans & Martha   **2020**

Rosalind Hannah Bean

Nursery Rhymes 123   *Christmas for Kids* (2020)

Very gentle and pleasant song aimed at juveniles. It's nearly Christmas, and she can hardly wait. Everything is great. A lot of la-la's. Great for stressed out adults.

A New Christmas Song

Stefie Shock   **2017**

Florence K. (feat. Stefie Shock)   *Everyday Is Christmas (Snowman Deluxe Edition)* (2017)

Relaxing song with very pleasant beat and refrain that just wishes a Merry Christmas to her love. She is excited and happy to experience the sights and sounds of Christmas, but it does remind her of those that don't have love that night, and she says to always give love.

A New Kingdom

Lyrics: Kay Denar & Rob Tyger Music: Adapted from "Leise rieselt der Schnee" (author unknown)   **2005**

Sarah Connor   *Christmas In My Heart* (2005)

Very pretty song about the new kingdom that began when Christ was born. She adds that all her wishes come true when she thinks of her lover, for love is the gift that he brings.

"*Leise rieselt der Schnee*" (which translates as "the snow falls softly") is one of the most famous Christmas songs in the German language. It was composed in 1895 by the Protestant pastor Eduard Ebel (1839-1905). The composition of the melody is also often attributed to Ebel, but this is probably not true. The melody is probably derived from a folk tune.

A New York Christmas '21

Rob Thomas   **2021**

Rob Thomas   *Something About Christmas Time* (2021)

Follow your angel and come down to the city. Bring all your compassion and all your forgiveness. We'll celebrate each and every day on this New York City Christmas. Though 9/11/2001 is not mentioned, it is interesting that this song was released on the 20th anniversary of that event.

There are a number of songs about New York City on Christmas. This is one of my favorites. And though not mentioned, I think it relates well to 9/11.

No Child Should Ever Cry on Christmas

John Oates   **2006**

Daryl Hall & John Oates   *Home for Christmas* (2006)

Sad but beautiful song with rich orchestration. No child should ever cry on Christmas or ever be afraid. May the Holy Star above shine a silver light of loving and turn the world around.

This album was the final studio album of Hall & Oates.

Noel

Stephen Nelson   **2019**

GENTRI   *Noel* (2019)

The song begins with "Carol of the Bells" and carries this theme throughout. Noel, come and see what God has done. He was born to suffer to save us. It's a story of amazing love.

North Star

Caitlyn Smith, Mary Steenburgen   **2021**
& Troy Verges

Tori Kelly   *Music from Zoey's Extraordinary Christmas (Original Motion Picture Soundtrack)* (2021)

She has lost someone to the stars (Heaven) while she remains on Earth. She misses him but says part of him is still with her and in a way she's with him. At Christmas she always looks up at the stars because she can feel his love. She's never been to Heaven, but it doesn't seem that far because he's her North Star.

The movie that this song is from is based on the NBC series *Zoey's Extraordinary Playlist.*

Not Christmas

Robbie Williams et al   **2019**

Robbie Williams   *The Christmas Present* (2019)

He knows that his babe is worried that he won't show up on Christmas night. But he flatly refuses to go; he fears too many judgements and apologies if he does. He's not going to line up to take abuse. He doesn't want to do Christmas anymore with her.

Nothin's Gonna Bring Me Down (At Christmas Time)

Randy Travis   **2007**

Randy Travis   *Songs of the Season* (2007)

Great song about nothing going to bring him down at Christmastime—not wind, not snow, or even frozen pipes or a dead car battery. Even though he's broke from all the gifts he bought, he doesn't care. He just wants to snuggle with his honey; Santa can skip his street.

Nothing for Christmas

Chad Gilbert, Jordan Pundik, Cyrus Bolooki & Ian Grushka   **2021**

New Found Glory   *December's Here* (2021)

He wants to keep holding on to his honey and forget about their troubles. He wants to spend Christmas with her. He got what he wanted—her—and doesn't want her to buy him anything else.

Officially Christmas

Dan Smyers, Dave Barnes, Jordan Reynolds & Nicolle Galyon   **2021**

Dan + Shay   Single (2021)

Holiday magic is everywhere—and it's officially Christmas. He's officially wishing for something not found in a store—his girl. He's officially hers. Nice song, upbeat.

Old Fashioned Christmas

Lyn Lapid, David Kingston & Annie Schindel   **2024**

Lyn Lapid   EP (2024)

A wonderfully old-fashioned (circa 60s) song about an old-fashioned Christmas. She isn't happy with the present, when someone says "I love you" and then just disappears. She asks Santa to take her back in time, where someone will take her hand, take her dancing to a 50s band and promise her he'll will forever be hers. He will miss her when apart and will be the first to call.

On Christmas Day

Billy Idol   **2021**

Billy Idol   *Happy Holidays* (2021)

He almost lost his love, but on Christmas day he believes in her and he's glad to be with her. On Christmas Day the sun is shining.

On Christmas Eve

Andrew Gold   **2010**

Andrew Gold   *Stars Come Out for Christmas - Special Edition I* (2010)

Song starts with street sounds from a Victorian Christmas. A harpsicord is used in the song, to add to that Victorian feeling. The song is about celebration of Christmas Eve back then. It really puts you in that time. Nice.

On This Christmas Day

John Lodge   **2003**

The Moody Blues   *December* (2003)

Very pretty song about a man who sees a picture of someone in the paper that he doesn't even know the name of but becomes enamored with her. Wherever he goes, and whatever he says on this Christmas day he will think of her and be with her.

On This Winter's Night

Charles Kelley, Dave Heywood,   **2012**
Hillary Scott & Tom Douglas

Lady A   *On This Winter's Night* (2012)

This song is from a great Christmas album by Lady A, and this is the best song from that album. It is very beautiful, beginning with soothing harp-like sounds and segueing into the song (the harp-like sounds appear later again in it). The orchestration and vocals are awesome. It describes a perfect winter night, with stars that shine like silver bells and snowflakes fall like frosting. Strangers look like neighbors, and he is in the arms of the one he loves. On this winter's night they remember what Christmas really is, the birth of Jesus. A children's chorus appears near the end of the song. Very moving.

Lady A was originally known as Lady Antebellum. On June 11, 2020, joining widespread commercial response to the George Floyd protests, the band announced it would abbreviate its name to its existing nickname "Lady A" to remove the term "Antebellum." The next day, it was widely reported that the name "Lady A" had already been in use for more than 20 years by Seattle-based Anita White, an African American activist and singer. She soon submitted a demand that either the band be renamed, or that her act would be renamed for a $5 million fee plus a $5 million donation to be split between Seattle charities, a nationwide legal defense fund for independent artists, and Black Lives Matter. On July 8, 2020, the band filed a lawsuit against White, to affirm its longstanding trademark of the name. On September 15, White filed a countersuit asserting her claim to the "Lady A" trademark and rejecting the notion that both artists could operate in the same industry under the same brand identity. She sought damages for lost sales and a weakened brand, along with royalties from any income the band received under the "Lady A" name. In February 2022, it was reported that White and the band had settled their lawsuit; the terms of that settlement have never been disclosed.[131,132]

One Child

Mariah Carey & Marc Shaiman   **2010**

Mariah Carey   *Merry Christmas II You* (2010)

She tells the story of visitation by angels experienced by Mary and Joseph. She then tells the story of the first Christmas. Jesus is one child that can change the world. Very nice song, jubilant.

One Last Christmas

Robbie Williams et al   **2019**

Robbie Williams   *The Christmas Present* (2019)

A man approaches the door of his child. He wants his child to give him one last Christmas. He details how he doesn't deserve the child's kindness or forgiveness— he's done something terrible in the past, he's let his child down and hurt his child, including abandonment. If it were him, he'd slam the door.

One More Sleep

Leona Lewis, Richard Stannard,   **2013**
Jez Ashurst, Iain James & Brad-
ford Ellis

Leona Lewis   Single (2013)

Popular "recent" Christmas tune. She's waiting for her baby to come home for Christmas. One more sleep and she'll be a day closer to seeing him. Also found on *Christmas, with Love* (2013) and *Christmas Music* (2013), the latter by various artists.

One Wish (For Christmas)

Barry J. Eastmond, Gordon   **2003**
Chambers & Freddie Jackson

Whitney Houston   *One Wish: The Holiday Album*
(2003)

Her one wish for Christmas is joy and peace on Earth. We would all come together as one. Christmas is not about material things. What you've got to think about is the love Christmas brings.

Osama Got Run Over By a Reindeer

Bob Rivers & Bob Rivers & Twist-ed Radio   **2002**

Bob Rivers   *White Trash Christmas* (2002)

Spoof of "Grandma Got Run Over by a Reindeer" by "Elmo and Patsy" (1979), using the same music but with different lyrics. This song was written shortly after the tragedy that occurred on 9/11/2001 and Osama bin Laden, mastermind of the terror attack, was at-large. He would not be found and killed until May 2, 2011, by a United States military special operations unit.

Our Father of Life

Robin Zander, Rick Nielsen & Tom Petersson   **2017**

Cheap Trick   *Christmas Christmas* (2017)

Teach us Lord, our Father of Life, to protect our children from all evil and how we can live in peace. Christmastime is time for family, friends and cheer.

Our First Christmas

Chad Gilbert, Jordan Pundik, Cy-rus Bolooki & Ian Grushka   **2021**

New Found Glory   *December's Here* (2021)

It's the first Christmas for a man and a woman, and the man feels it's going to be better than all before. He's doing everything to make it perfect, like learning how to bake from YouTube.

Pick Out a Christmas Tree

Dan Smyers, Dave Barnes, Jordan Reynolds & Nicolle Galyon   **2021**

Dan + Shay   Single (2021)

It's time to pick out a Christmas Tree, tie it to the car, bring it back home and plug it in and watch it glow.

Pink and Glitter

Tori Amos   **2009**

Tori Amos   *Midwinter Graces* (2009)

Classy, old-style sexy song about the joy of being with her lover at Christmastime. The joy isn't about presents and toys. Shower the world in pink. Very nicely done.

Please Santa Please

Kirstin Maldonado, Kevin Olusola,   **2023**
Emma Lee & Karen Kosowski

Pentatonix   *The Greatest Christmas Hits* (2023)

A "special someone" is on his way to meet her, and she is very impatient. The only wish on her list is a kiss underneath the mistletoe. She begs Santa to fulfil that wish.

The Polar Express

Alan Silvestri & Glen Ballard   **2004**

Tom Hanks   *The Polar Express: Original Motion Picture Soundtrack* (2004)

The theme from the 2004 animated classic *The Polar Express*, a great Christmas movie. Trains and Christmas have always gone together to me. The song and the movie are great fun.

Pop Disco Christmas

Bogachuk Alexandr Alexandro-   **2023**
vich

Alex Lead   *Disco Christmas* (2023)

Not too heavy on the disco, this is a very pleasing Instrumental with a Christmas feel.

Present Without a Bow

Kacey Musgraves, Leon Bridges,   **2016**
Austin Jenkins & Luke Laird

Kacey Musgraves (feat. Leon Bridg-   *A Very Kacey Christmas* (2016)
es)

This time of the year is meant for two, so she pleads her honey don't let her go and leave her alone on Christmas. Christmas would not shine without him. He admits that being without her would be like a present without a bow.

Promises to Keep

John Oliva, Paul O'Neill & Robert   **2016**
Kinkel

Trans-Siberian Orchestra   *The Ghosts of Christmas Eve* (2016)

A children's chorus beautifully sings this gentle song about a dream being alive that will always survive as long as we can see that the dreams we find in life are those we tend to seek, and Christmas has its promises to keep.

Put a Little Holiday in Your Heart

Greg Wojahn, Roger Wohahn &   **2023**
Scott Wohahn

Cher (with Cyndi Lauper)   *Christmas* (2023)

Put a little holiday in your heart. There's a man on the corner who doesn't have a name and is ignored by people, but if you share a simple kindness with him, it could set your heart aflame and you'll get more than you ever gave away.

Quiet Christmas Background Music

Marco Rinaldo   **2021**

Christmas Eve Carols Academy   *Christmas Eve Carols for Family Dinner: Angelic Instrumental Carols, Piano Carols for Magic Atmosphere,*

Christmas Bells Carols for Baby's First Christmas (2021)

The title says it all. It is a very pleasant Christmas Instrumental that can serve as a background for any Christmas occasion.

The Quiet of Christmas Morning

Johann Sebastian Bach   2003

The Moody Blues   *December* (2003)

The music here was written by Johann Sebastian Bach in 1723 as "Jesu, Joy of Man's Desiring." The Moody Blues took that classic piece and added beautiful lyrics to it.

Rainy Christmas Day

Laura Cortese & Dietrich Strause   2022

Laura Cortese & Dietrich Strause   Single (2022)

It's a rainy Christmas day. There are no snowmen, no angels—they've all been washed away. Very somber.

Relax by the Fire

Sacchetto Giuliano & Giordano Trivellato   2016

Christmas Eve   *Traditional Christmas Classics - Relaxing Instrumental Music for Holiday Break* (2016)

Very relaxing Christmas Instrumental.

Remember

Robert Kinkel & Paul O'Neill   2004

Trans-Siberian Orchestra   *The Lost Christmas Eve* (2004)

A children's chorus reminds us to remember a long time ago when there was a night with a gentle falling snow. One would imagine that they would tell us to remember the first Christmas, but there surely wasn't any snow in the desert.

Remember Me

Rory Feek & Tim Johnson   **2017**

Alabama   *American Christmas* (2017)

When you're opening your presents, setting out cookies for Santa, hanging up lights or just gathered around with family at the table, remember me—Jesus. I died on a cross to set you free.

A Ride in the Snow

Rob Tyger & Kay Denar   **2005**

Sarah Connor   *Christmas In My Heart* (2005)

Let's take a long sleigh ride in the snow, no need to know where we're going. The horse knows the way, so we can make love. Very carefree tune.

Ring Out the Bells

Sarah Connor, Max Wolfgang &   **2022**
Nicolas Rebscher

Sarah Connor   *Not So Silent Night* (2022)

Very popular Christmas song of the last couple of years, and for good reason: it is a catchy, happy tune. Ring out the bells and "keep the night rockin' till Santa comes knockin.'" Great description of all the fun things about Christmas.

Ring, Ring the Bells

Leigh Nash, Phil Madeira & John   **2023**
Hartley

Sixpence None the Richer   Single (2023)

Wonderful, rousing song about letting the world know about Christmas. Jesus is born, it's Christmastime. Salvation comes to dwell singing out the Father's love.

Rudolf

Robbie Williams et al   **2019**

Robbie Williams   *The Christmas Present* (2019)

Song about Rudolf, the Red-Nosed Reindeer as he flies through the many skies of the planet to deliver presents. You almost believe you are with the famous reindeer, who hears a choir below, singing "Carol of the Bells." Very well-performed song, capturing excitement.

S-N-O-W

Gavin Slate, Bobby Hamrick, Joy   **2024**
Williams & Jaden Michaels

Jordin Sparks   *Growin' Up Holiday* EP (2024)

Jordin Sparks, the youngest winner of *American Idol* at the age of 17, shares this song about someone ready for a snowman to come back, complete with carrot, buttons, scarf and a hat. She only has one wish on her Christmas list—she wants it to snow, snow, snow. Besides the snowman, she wants to make angel wings and have snowball fights.

Santa Claus Cancelled Christmas

Ria Holzerlandt   **2016**

Ria Lina   *Christmas 4 Adults: A Mother's Lament* (2016)

A frazzled mother lists all the bad things her kids have done and tells them Santa cancelled Christmas for them. If they behave next year, there might be a Christmas then.

Santa Claus You Ought To Go On a Diet

Unknown   **2007**

Pat Boone   *The True Spirit of Christmas* (2007)

Santa got stuck in a chimney last year because his body is built like a barrel of beer. Children can't even find his lap anymore. He has to go on a diet, or his reindeer won't be able to lift the sleigh from the ground.

Santa Forgive Me

Chad Gilbert, Jordan Pundik, Cyrus Bolooki & Ian Grushka   **2021**

New Found Glory   *December's Here* (2021)

Santa, forgive me; forget all the stupid things I did. Please come down my chimney.

Santa Tell Me

Ariana Grande, Savan Kotecha & Ilya Salmanzadeh   **2013**

Ariana Grande   Single (2013)

Very popular Christmas song of the last 10+ years. She asks for Santa's help in her failed relationships. Don't let me fall in love again if he won't be here next year. She's fallen in love on Christmas night but woke up alone on New Year's Day.

Santa Visits Everyone

Jesse Shatkin & Sia   **2017**

Sia   *Everyday Is Christmas (Snowman Deluxe Edition)* (2017)

Great Christmas song by Sia, among others she has brought us. Santa visits everyone, she promises.

Santa Will Find You

Mindy Smith & Chely Wright   **2005**

Mindy Smith   *My Holiday* (2005)

Even if you are far away on Christmas Eve, don't worry—Santa will find you. Nice song, with simple instrumentation.

Santa, Can't You Hear Me

Aben Eubanks & Kelly Clarkson   **2021**

Kelly Clarkson & Ariana Grande   *When Christmas Comes Around…*
                                                           (2021)

Two great superstars of the 21ˢᵗ century combine to produce this great Christmas song about not wanting anything for Christmas except for dreams to come true. They never say what the "dream" is, which is contained in a letter to Santa, but I would guess that it is someone to love. It is clear that it is not something material.

Santa's Almost Here

Florence K., Vince Degiorgio &   **2017**
Ben Riley

Florence K.   *A New Christmas (feat. Stefie*
                                           Shock) (2017)

It feels like Santa's almost here. There is snowfall and city streets are lit up.

Santa's Coming for Us

Greg Kurstin & Sia   **2017**

Sia   *Everyday Is Christmas (Snowman*
                                           Deluxe Edition) (2017)

In my opinion, one of Sia's best Christmas songs. It is a catchy, happy tune, about Santa coming to town and for us. Send all your letters to Santa, telling him your secret wishes too.

The video[133] for this song is very entertaining. It stars Kristen Bell, pretending to mouth the lyrics, hosting a family Christmas party. Guests include her real-life husband Dax Shepard as her husband, JB Smoove as Santa Claus, and Susan Lucci and Henry Winkler as the grandparents. Bell is as cute as can be, playing the perfect housewife, in a model kitchen from the 50s.

Save Some Christmas

Rob Thomas   **2021**

Rob Thomas   *Something About Christmas Time*
(2021)

A man is far away from home and it's almost Christmas. He knows he's late and wants his wife (I assume) to not wait for him, to start decorating and celebrating with friends. But he does ask to save some Christmas for him.

The Season for Romance

Greg Barnhill & Phil Swann   **2002**

Lee Ann Womack   *The Season for Romance* (2002)

A man and woman meet by chance under the mistletoe and slowly develop a romance. The season loves the reason for romance, and it will get you if you give it half a chance.

Shake Up Christmas

Pat Monahan & Butch Walker   **2015**

Train   *Christmas in Tahoe* (2015)

He tells the story of a girl who made a great big wish to fill the world full of happiness. At the same time miles away, a little boy made a wish that the world would be OK. He was happy and wanted to send some of his happiness to the rest of the people of the East and West, and maybe once in a while give his grandma a reason to smile. He wanted to meet a girl one day who also wanted to spread love.

Shooting Star

Caranua & Chuck E Meyers   **2019**

Caranua (feat. Lynn Hilary & Alex   *A Celtic Christmas* (2019)
Sharpe)

She remembers arms that held her tight, belonging to someone who told her the story of a shooting star that brings love to people. She wonders how far that star is.

Shoppin' Around for a Christmas Tree

Bob Rivers   **2002**

Bob Rivers & Twisted Radio   *White Trash Christmas* (2002)

Spoof of "Rockin' Around the Christmas Tree" by Brenda Lee in 1958, with lyrics about the foibles of shopping around for a Christmas tree.

A Silent Night with You

Tori Amos   **2009**

Tori Amos   *Midwinter Graces* (2009)

Young lovers remind her of the glow that she and her lover used to have. Not long ago he said that he just wanted to spend a silent night with her. Radio favorites bring her back to when their love was new. Lost in her daze, he slips past her and says take my hand, nothing has changed; now or then I just want to spend a silent night with you.

The Singing

Pip Lewis   **2024**

Pip Lewis   Single (2024)

Unusual but pretty, subdued song. She's inside a snow globe alone. There is a bad storm in the ornament, but she pays it no mind as she dries off and she's safe inside. It's the singing that really counts; you sit down and pick a song, and it shuffles all day long. In time you might love again, but until then you have to know how to let things come and go.

Sleep Well Little Children

Thiele, Robert, Alan Bergman,   **2008**
George David Weiss & Leon
Klatzkin

Kristin Chenoweth   *A Lovely Way to Spend Christmas*
                                     (2008)

Sleep well little children, every wish will be found under the tree tomorrow morning. The song then segues into "What a Wonderful World" (1967). She then goes back to the original song.

Slow Down Christmas

Jim Brickman, Peter Cincotti &   **2024**
Victoria Shaw

Jim Brickman & Ruben Studdard   Single (2024)

He wants to slow down Christmas this year to enjoy it longer. He wants to hold on to everything dear. Very pretty song.

Small Town Christmas

Aaron Acetta, Rob Thomas &   **2021**
Shep Goodman

Rob Thomas   *Something About Christmas Time*
                              (2021)

Great, festive song about Christmas in a small town when the singer was young. He wants this kind of Christmas again.

Snow

Randy Newman   **2012**

Tracey Thorn   *Tinsel and Lights* (2012)

Snow fills the fields and the little park where she used to go with apparently her former lover. He's gone but the memory lives on. Their dreams are buried in the snow.

Randy Newman is best known for "Short People" (1977), "I Love L.A." (1983), and "You've Got a Friend in Me" (1995) with Lyle Lovett, written for the animated hit *Toy Story*.

I saw Randy Newman perform as a musical guest when I was in the audience of Saturday Night Live *many years ago.*

Snow

Leslie Odom, Jr., Sebastian Kole,   **2020**
Rafael Casal, Theron "Neff-U"
Feemster, Joseph Abate & Kyle
Lawrence Mann

Leslie Odom, Jr.   *The Christmas Album* (2020)

Song with happy beat about a Christmas that is a beautiful bliss. He doesn't need any presents from Santa; the "presence" of his kids is all he wants. So, let it snow. He's just wants to be with his family—where the love is. Nice song.

Snow

Chad Gilbert, Jordan Pundik, Cy-   **2021**
rus Bolooki & Ian Grushka

New Found Glory   *December's Here* (2021)

They made it through just fine this Christmas though a part has died. He will lie in the snow because it makes him feel alright each Christmastime.

Snow Angel

Tori Amos   **2009**

Tori Amos   *Midwinter Graces* (2009)

The Snow Angel will come to the children, and she will stay for a while.

Snowflake

Greg Kurstin & Sia   **2017**

Sia   *Everyday Is Christmas (Snowman Deluxe Edition)* (2017)

She'll catch a snowflake and keep it safe until winter, when it will no longer need her. She loves her snowflake and hopes it won't forget her.

Snowman

Edward Robertson   2004

Barenaked Ladies   *Barenaked for the Holidays* (2004)

The point of view of a snowman. He doesn't know how he fits in. Ever cold, love untold, he doesn't belong. He's paralyzed and just melts away.

Snowman

Greg Kurstin & Sia   2017

Sia   *Everyday Is Christmas (Snowman Deluxe Edition)* (2017)

She's never leaving Mr. Snowman because she's Mrs. Snowman. She wants to go somewhere below zero like the North Pole and hide from the sun. She'll love him forever—till death they'll be freezin.'

The video[134] is an animation styled to look like Claymation. In the video a little girl keeps them safe in a cooler and she drags them to where it is always cold. The snow couple live happily in a snow castle they generate.

Snowy Day

Nathan B. Morris, Shawn Patrick Stockman & Wanya Jermaine Morris   2020

Francesca Battistelli   *This Christmas* (2020)

Short song about a snowy day being the perfect day. It makes you feel so alive. When it snows friends and family come together.

Solemn Christmas

Louise Goulet   2016

Louise Goulet   *Christmas Christmas: Magical Holiday Favorites* (2016)

Beautiful Christmas Instrumental.

Somber Christmas

Chad Gilbert, Jordan Pundik, Cyrus Bolooki & Ian Grushka   2021

New Found Glory   *December's Here* (2021)

It's a somber Christmas because your love is ending. But it doesn't have to be—enjoy it anyway, have fun.

Somewhere in Your Silent Night

Mark Hall, Matthew West & Bernie Herms   2017

Casting Crowns   *It's Finally Christmas* (2017)

Somewhere in your silent night Heaven hears the song your broken heart has cried. But hope is here, for love has come to find you, from God.

The Spirit of Christmas

John Lodge   2003

The Moody Blues   *December* (2003)

Where did the spirit of Christmas go? If you can find it, please let me know.

The Spirit of Christmas Past

Enya & Roma Ryan   2008

Enya   *And Winter Came* (2008)

When tears are in your eyes, don't throw this time away; tomorrow will be Christmas day.

Spirit of the Season

Alan Silvestri & Glen Ballard   2004

Alan Silvestri   *The Polar Express: Original Motion Picture Soundtrack (2004)*

Wonderful song from the classic 21st century Christmas movie *The Polar Express* (2004).

Stay With Me Santa (Mrs. Claus' Christmas Wish)

Jonathan McGowan & Lux Smith   2023

SMITH   Single (2023)

Cute song from Mrs. Claus' point of view. Stay with me, Santa, won't you stay with me?

Still Can't Sleep (on Christmas Eve)

Ed Cash & Franni Cash   2016

Amy Grant   *Tennessee Christmas* (2016)

It's Christmas Eve and she feels like a kid again in anticipation. She still can't sleep on Christmas Eve.

Suite from the Polar Express

Alan Silvestri & Glen Ballard   2004

Alan Silvestri   *The Polar Express: Original Motion Picture Soundtrack (2004)*

Wonderful suite from the classic 21st century Christmas movie *The Polar Express* (2004).

Sure Could Use Some Christmas Around Here

Charles English, Chip Davis, Sam   **2017**
Tate, Teddy Gentry & Janey Street

Alabama   *American Christmas* (2017)

"Half a dozen wars" are still raging, brothers against brothers, families are torn apart, and children are starving. He prays that Christmas comes early this year. The world has gone crazy, and it looks like love has disappeared. It all starts with what we teach our children—not to hate or judge or carry a grudge. Excellent Christmas sentiment.

Sweet Baby Jesus

Carrie Underwood, Brett James &   **2020**
David Garcia

Carrie Underwood   *My Gift* (2020)

She wonders what it was like for Jesus when he was born. Was he cold? Was he scared to death? Did he see tears from his mother's eyes? He could have left us but chose to save us.

Sweet December

Brett Eldredge & Alexis Idarose   **2024**
Kesselan

Brett Eldredge & Kelly Clarkson   *Merry Christmas (Welcome to the Family)* (2024)

I feel the only truth is in your eyes; you are my northern star. Take me home and set me free. Turn on the Christmas tree and put on the classic songs. Your heart's good at making me remember that it's gonna be a sweet December.

Sweet Savior Divine

Thomas Jobmann, Sven Greiner,   **2013**
Helmut Hoinkis & Rebecca Auty

Yvonne Abel   *Christmas All Over the World* (2013)

The story of Jesus in the manger, "sweet savior divine," including his visit from the Three Wise Men.

Text Me Merry Christmas

Adam Schlesinger & David Javerbaum   **2013**

Straight No Chaser (feat. Kristin Bell)   *Under the Influence: Holiday Edition* (2013)

Great statement about the absurdity of modern life and our dedication to cell phones. She asks her Love, who will be far away from home for Christmas, to keep his phone fully charged and text her a Merry Christmas. She only needs "a word or two" to remind her he's still there. A smiley face emoji would be welcome. A Facebook message, tweet, or Snapchat snap won't do. Voicemail is not good, as it is a thing of Christmas past. A selfie would be nice, though.

Thank You

Mark Manio & Scott Hoying   **2020**

Pentatonix   *We Need a Little Christmas* (2020)

His Love helps him get through the year, providing a warm hand and picking him up when he falls, like the snow. He needs his Love's light, smile and gentle laughter, He can't think of the right words to say to his Love, except "thank you." He hopes they share 100 more Christmas days, when their house will be their home.

Thank You Note

Bendik Møller & Salem Ilese Davern   **2021**

Salem Ilese   *Snow Globe* (2021)

The only present she wants is a thank you note, for giving her presence all year long. Her Christmas wish-list fits on a Post-it note.

Thankful

Gloria Estefan, Emily Estefan & Sasha Estefan-Coppola   **2022**

Gloria Estefan, Emily Estefan & Sasha Estefan-Coppola   *Estefan Family Christmas* (2022)

My we always be together as we are tonight on Christmas. We are thankful for our family at Christmas.

That's Christmas to Me

Kevin "K.O." Olusola & Scott Hoying   **2014**

Pentatonix   *That's Christmas to Me* (2014)

There are many examples of what's Christmas to them: a burning fireplace, presents under the tree, waiting for Santa, seeing children play in the snow, mom and dad kissing under the mistletoe, and hanging stockings. But the only gift they will ever need is the joy of family.

That's What Christmas Means

Amy Sky & Anthony Vanderburgh   **2006**

Amy Sky   *The Lights of December* (2006)

Children waiting in their beds, family visiting, giving to those in need—that's what Christmas means.

Think of Christmas

Daniel Crean, Eren Cannata, Justin Tranter & Kennedi Lykken   **2020**

Anne-Marie   *Happiest Season* (2020)

When I think of Christmas, I think of you and me and a classic kiss. She rewrites memories and creates new history, making the season feel new to her—because you're here.

Album is music from and inspired by the Hulu original film *Happiest Season*.

This Christmas

Ingrid Michaelson   **2023**

Ingrid Michaelson   Single (2023)

This Christmas, I'm right where I want to be, holding love close to me, with family and friends, and everything all in-between.

This Christmas

Matthew Dylan Rist, India Anne Parkman & Scarlet Grace Byford   **2024**

Scar   Single (2024)

Unlike many other Christmas songs, this man is happy to be apart from his last love. He wished upon a star that he'd never have to spend another year with her. This Christmas don't come running back to me. You're not the one for me; I'm in love with me. Please don't call my number or show up at my door. I hated all your presents.

This Christmas Day

Gold & Caprio   **2010**

Nicolette Larson   *Stars Come Out for Christmas - Special Edition II* (2010)

Pretty song of a Christmas not being the same without a particular someone.

This Is Christmas

Tasha Layton, Keith Everette Smith & Jeff Pardo   **2021**

Tasha Layton   *This Is Christmas* (2021)

The story of the first Christmas. Our hope has arrived.

This Silent Night

Thomas Jobmann, Sven Greiner,   **2013**
Helmut Hoinkis & Rebecca Auty

Yvonne Abel   *Christmas All Over the World* (2013)

Beautiful song with gentle vocals by Yvonne Abel and wonderful New Age instrumentation about the special silent night Christ was born. The refrain is simple.

'Til the Season Comes Round Again

Randy Goodrum & John Jarvis   **2024**

Amy Grant & Vince Gill   *When I Think of Christmas* (2024)

Family and friends, gather round the table, join hands and remember this moment 'til the season comes round again.

Time for Change

Robbie Williams et al   **2019**

Robbie Williams   *The Christmas Present* (2019)

Time for change is here. Remember the good old days when your parents gave their all to you and send all your loving out into the world. Sing about love and forget about loss. Nice.

Time to Fall in Love

Lindsey Stirling, Jordan Witzi-   **2017**
greuter & Cameron Alexander
Walker-Wright

Lindsey Stirling (feat. Alex Gaskarth)   *Warmer in the Winter* (2017)

Christmas is the time of year to fall in love. He's been trying to fall in love and everyone's looking for someone.

Tinsel and Lights

Tracey Thorn   2012

Tracey Thorn   *Tinsel and Lights* (2012)

She remembers a Christmas with her lover in New York City. Now years have gone by and not everything that has passed has been good. But all those years ago they saw the sights, tinsel and lights, and that's when she fell in love with Christmas once again. Nice song about an enduring relationship that began on Christmas.

Together This Christmas

Maisie Peters & Joe Rubel   2022

Maisie Peters   *Together This Christmas (From the Original Motion Picture Soundtrack "Your Christmas or Mine")* (2022)

Can we be together, babe, this Christmas? Can we have forever?

From the motion picture *Your Christmas or Mine?* (2022).

The Twelve Days After Christmas

Pat Boone   2007

Pat Boone   *The True Spirit of Christmas* (2007)

"The Twelve Days of Christmas" with different lyrics, focused on the twelve days *after* Christmas, which includes things like "wrappings to burn" and "presents to return."

Under the Mistletoe

Aben Eubanks & Kelly Clarkson   2020

Kelly Clarkson & Brett Eldredge   Single (2020)

Popular Christmas tune of the last several years. She wants the love of a particular someone, and wonders if he ever thinks of them as a couple. She's dying to say "I love you" and be wrapped up in his arms.

Underneath the Christmas Lights

Greg Kurstin & Sia   **2017**

Sia   *Everyday Is Christmas (Snowman Deluxe Edition)* (2017)

She used to sit by the Christmas fire with someone, but they are separated now and all she needs tonight is him, underneath the Christmas lights.

Underneath the Mistletoe

Greg Kurstin & Sia   **2017**

Sia   *Everyday Is Christmas (Snowman Deluxe Edition)* (2017)

She's got a crush on someone who she wants to run to her through the white night at Christmastime. She wants him to meet her underneath the mistletoe.

Underneath the Same Sky

Olivia Newton-John, Randy Good-rum & Amy Sky   **2007**

Olivia Newton-John   *Christmas Wish* (2007)

Olivia remembers her childhood in Australia where Christmas is in summer. They would sing carols by the ocean. Underneath the same sky, now that she's a mother, Christmas has another kind of joy for her—giving and receiving to those that are in need. All over the world we are underneath the same sky.

Underneath the Tree

Kelly Clarkson & Greg Kurstin   **2013**

Kelly Clarkson   *Wrapped in Red* (2013)

Newer Christmas classic from just over 10 years ago that gets a lot of airtime. She used to be alone on Christmas day, but now has someone to share it with, and Christmas is no longer cold and gray for her. He's all she needs underneath the tree. This song has been called "an optimistic tune that has Clarkson powering through Darlene Love-style vocals."[135]

Unwrap You at Christmas

Andy Partridge   2018

The Monkees   *Christmas Party* (2018)

The hit group from the 60s never made a Christmas record until about a half-century later. This song is about unwrapping a girl at Christmas. They dream of nothing more. So, they ask Santa to drop her off by the door.

Walk with Me

Unknown   2015

Patty Smyth   *Come on December* (2015)

The winter wind is very cold when there is no-one at your side. But now she is with someone at her side.

Warmer in the Winter

Lindsey Stirling, Evan Bogart &   2017
Brian Phillips

Lindsey Stirling (feat. Trombone   *Warmer in the Winter* (2017)
Shorty)

I just need you by my side, because it's warmer in the winter with you. Swinging song.

Warm on a Christmas Night

Andy Clutterbuck, James Hatcher   2020
& William Coutts

HONNE   *New Christmas Music* (2020)

He's feels so lucky having the one he loves. She can keep him warm on a cold night, warm on a Christmas night. Nice, traditional love song.

We All Go Home for Christmas

Andre O. Mayeux   2007

Juice Newton   *The Gift of Christmas* (2007)

We all go home for Christmas, if only in our hearts. With family and friends all around, the world seems a better place to be. The world seems brighter and all our cares fade.

We All Need Christmas

Rick Savage   2018

Def Leppard   Single (2018)

We all need Christmas and someone to need. Open your heart and say a prayer to light the day for those we've lost along the way.

Def Leppard was part of a new wave of British heavy metal in the early 80s and had their greatest success from then until the mid-90s. This song is very uncharacteristic of their sound then, being very conventional and mellow.

We Could Have This

Ben Folds & Lindsey Kraft   2024

Ben Folds   Single (2024)

Another holiday and we're still here, not quite together yet, but we are growing nearer. Thinking we could have this.

We Need Christmas

Matthew West, AJ Prius, Maddie   2021
Marlow & Taylor Dye

Matthew West   *We Need Christmas* (2021)

We need Christmas now more than ever to bring us together. This world could use a little healing. Our hearts could surely use something to believe in. There are a lot of little things, like singing carols, that make us enjoy Christmas.

We're Going to the Reindeer Games

Sarah Gribeauval   **2023**

Super Simple Songs   Single (2023)

Juvenile-oriented song of a 50s sound with lots of energy about going to the reindeer games and meeting all the reindeer, which they name.

What a Wonderful World (Holiday Mix)

George David Weiss & George Douglas   **2014**

Barry Manilow & Louis Armstrong (sampled)   Single (2014)

Barry Manilow blends an original Christmas song with the classic "What a Wonderful World" by Louis Armstrong in 1967 and sings along with him—virtually.

When Christmas Comes

Mariah Carey & James Poyser   **2010**

Mariah Carey   *Merry Christmas II You* (2010)

The whole world feels a little bit more love when Christmas comes. She only needs her lover to celebrate.

When Christmas Comes to Town

Alan Silvestri & Glen Ballard   **2004**

Matthew Hall & Meagan Moore   *The Polar Express: Original Motion Picture Soundtrack* (2004)

Very pretty song from the 2004 movie *The Polar Express*.

When I Think of Christmas

Amy Grant, Matt Maher & Jason Ingram   **2024**

Amy Grant   *When I think of Christmas* (2024)

Pretty song. There's a feeling she gets at Christmas—the world at peace, love between friends that knows no distance, and a glimmer of hope. And she has memories of what used to be.

White December

Karen Ann Poole, Kylie Minogue & Matt Prime   **2016**

Kylie Minogue   *Kylie Christmas* (2016)

Every year she wishes for a white December. Last year she was snowed in with her lover for a week, and she wants that to happen every year.

White Is in the Winter Night

Enya & Roma Ryan   **2008**

Enya   *Christmas Secrets* (2008)

There is color in specific Christmas things, like green in mistletoe and gold in candlelight. White is in the winter night that everyone remembers.

Who Comes This Night

Dave Grusin & Sally Stevens   **2006**

James Taylor   *James Taylor at Christmas* (2006)

Who came the night of Jesus' birth to visit him in his lowly manger? The shepherds and the kings did come, and the children came to lay their hearts before him.

Why Couldn't It Be Christmas Every Day?

Walter Afanasieff & Jay Landers   **2006**

Bianca Ryan   *Bianca Ryan* (2006)

Why couldn't it be Christmas every day? Riding around with Santa on his sleigh? Just believe in Christmas all the way. We can make December last forever.

This song is also available on the album *Christmas Voices* (2006), an album with various artists.

a	2021	Kristin Chenowith	Happiness is...Christmas!

A Willie Nice Christmas

Kelly Clarkson, Ashley Arrison &   **2013**
Aben Eubanks

Kelly Clarkson   *Wrapped in Red* (2013)

Song with a Hawaiian sound wishing you a really really Willie nice Christmas if you're in Luckenbach [a small Texas town of almost ghost-town status where Willie Nelson made a surprise appearance at the first Luckenbach World's Fair] or Waikiki. May we all stay higher than the angel on the top of the tree. Have a Willie nice Happy New Year, Hanukkah, Feliz Navidad-ukkah, Kwanzaa and Mele Kalikimaka, too.

Winter Dreams (Brandon's Song)

Kelly Clarkson, Ashley Arrison &   **2013**
Aben Eubanks

Kelly Clarkson   *Wrapped in Red* (2013)

Her relationship is so wonderful she wonders if it is a dream. If so, she doesn't want to wake up. She's "swept completely off" her feet.

This song—which features a 50-piece orchestra—was written for Clarkson's then-fiancé Brandon Blackstock.[136] Blackstock, son of her former manager Narvel Blackstock and former stepson of Reba McEntire, was her talent manager. They got married on October 20, 2013. During their marriage, he was her manager. They had a son and daughter but in June 2020, Clarkson filed for divorce from Blackstock, citing irreconcilable differences. The divorce was finalized in March 2022.

In a decision made on November 21, 2023, California's labor commissioner ruled that Blackstock procured a number of deals for Clarkson, including her lucrative role as a judge on *The Voice*, that should have been handled by her talent agents at Creative Artists Agency (CAA). By doing so, Labor Commissioner Lilia Garcia-Brower ruled that Blackstock violated California's Talent Agencies Act (TAA), which bans anyone other than a licensed talent agent from procuring work for artists. All told, Blackstock was ordered to pay back commissions totaling nearly 3 million dollars.[137]

Winter Holidays

Gerald Beckley & Lee Bunnell   2002

America   *Holiday Harmony* (2002)

Nice, calm, easygoing song about the winter holidays and the wonderful things that come with them. Winter holidays fill our hearts with lots of love and cheer.

Winter's Carol

Tori Amos   2009

Tori Amos   *Midwinter Graces* (2009)

Pretty carol about the beauty of winter.

Wintersong

Sarah McLachlan & Pierre Marchand   2006

Sarah McLachlan   *Wintersong* (2006)

The sights of winter are reminders of a lost love.

Pierre Marchand is known for his ongoing collaboration with Sarah McLachlan, having produced all her albums since *Solace* in 1991.

Wrapped in Red

Kelly Clarkson, Ashley Arrison,   **2013**
Aben Eubanks & Shane McAnally

Kelly Clarkson   *Wrapped in Red* (2013)

Very popular Christmas song for the last 10+ years, and rightfully so. She's loved someone from afar every December for years, but never let it show. But this Christmas she's going to risk it all and stands at his door. She is wrapped in red.

Xmas Soul

Brak   **2012**

Daniele Benati   *70s Christmas* (2012)

Very pretty and catchy tune. All she wants for Christmas is love. She doesn't want to sit alone.

Yes I Believe

Justin Hayward   **2003**

The Moody Blues   *December* (2003)

Yes, I believe in a better world and like the rest of us I pray for peace on Earth and a better life with every beautiful day.

You and Me and Christmas

LeAnn Rimes & Darrell Brown   **2018**

LeAnn Rimes   *It's Christmas, Eve - Original Motion Picture Soundtrack* (2018)

Christmastime never really mattered to her but now, as she has someone to hold close, she can't wait to celebrate Christmas—together.

From the movie *It's Christmas, Eve* (2018).

You Don't Have to Be Alone

Alicia Keys & Natalie Hemby   **2022**

Alicia Keys   *Santa Baby* (2022)

You don't have to be alone at Christmas; you should be with me tonight.

You Make Every Day Christmas

Unknown   **2007**

Pat Boone   *The True Spirit of Christmas* (2007)

The Wise Men said that Christmas only comes once a year, but they didn't know you—you make every day Christmas, filled with holiday cheer.

You Make It Feel Like Christmas

Gwen Stefani, Blake Shelton, Michael Busbee & Justin Tranter   **2017**

Gwen Stefani (feat. Blake Shelton)   *You Make It Feel Like Christmas* (2017)

Popular Christmas song performed by then boyfriend-girlfriend couple Gwen Stefani and Blake Shelton, who would later marry, in 2021. Blake sings that Gwen makes it feel like Christmas. Gwen then sings the same about Blake.

You're Here

Ben Glover & Francesca Battistelli   **2012**

Francesca Battistelli   *Christmas* (2012)

The first Christmas, from the Virgin Mary's point of view. He's here, and she's holding him dear. She knows he will be her savior and what he will be doing for humanity, and she is just amazed to look him in the eyes.

Your Hallelujah

Leona Lewis, Jon Levine, Autumn Rowe & Lauren Christy   **2013**

Leona Lewis   *Christmas, With Love* (2013)

Someone needs you and someone loves you, hallelujah. Angels call out and you hear them sing hallelujah. Rejoiceful.

1 Wish

Amanda Ava Koci, Nicholas Oliver Ruth, Peter Fenn, Rory Adams and Sophia Brenan   **2024**

Ava Max   Single (2024)

She's got one wish—that every day could feel like Christmas.

8 Days of Christmas

Beyoncé and Kelly Rowland   **2001**

Destiny's Child   Single (2001)

An updating of "The Twelve Days of Christmas," but with only 8 days.

12 Nights

Erick Serna, Jesse Shatkin & Sia   **2017**

Sia   *Everyday Is Christmas (Snowman Deluxe Edition)* (2017)

Catchy, upbeat song about waiting 12 nights for Santa. As the song progresses, the number of days decrease, until there is only one day left.

ABOUT THE AUTHOR

Steven Mandeli is a software engineer and educator by trade, as well as an actor, comic, and avid writer who has penned books, essays, and screenplays on a variety of topics. He was known as the "little engineer" from an early age, as he was always building something. He grew up in Astoria, Queens, NY, where he attended St. Joseph's Parochial School. Having an interest in engineering, he attended Brooklyn Technical High School, to study electrical engineering. He holds a Bachelor of Science degree in electrical engineering from the Polytechnic Institute of NY (now NYU), a master's degree in computer information systems from the University of Phoenix, and a patent. He worked as an electrical engineer in places like Northrup-Grumman for 15 years, and then switched to software engineering, which he continues doing, in one form or another, to this day. For over 13 years, while also working as an engineer, he taught courses in writing, critical thinking, and information technology.

His brain cluttered with useless trivia, he loves to talk and write about "back in the day." His affinity for puns drives his co-workers crazy, but at least that is better than his singing. He ventured a few decades ago from Queens to Long Island. There he lives with his wife of more than 30 years, his younger daughter, a dog and a parrot. His other daughter moved to Texas and visits sometimes, with her hubby and Steve's beautiful granddaughter and grandson. His life isn't bad, but he yearns to sell a boatload of books and screenplays or be "discovered."

Contact Steve at smandeli1701@gmail.com.

REFERENCES

1 https://gavvie.tripod.com/adeste.html#history

2 https://www.youtube.com/watch?v=IFsDAoCHYiQ

3 https://thecurioussongwriter.wordpress.com/2021/06/04/the-story-behind-ave-maria/

4 http://www.hymnsandcarolsofchristmas.com/History/away_in_a_manger.htm

5 https://secondhandsongs.com/work/47297

6 https://web.archive.org/web/20040124084340/http://www.donelson.org/pocket/pp-031130.html

7 https://www.vox.com/2018/12/19/18138242/coventry-carol-history-plays

8 https://secondhandsongs.com/work/110181

9 http://www.hymnsandcarolsofchristmas.com/Hymns_and_Carols/first_nowell.htm

10 http://www.hymnsandcarolsofchristmas.com/Text/legend_of_s_wenceslaus.htm

11 https://secondhandsongs.com/work/51029

12 https://secondhandsongs.com/work/43698

13 https://www.readersdigest.ca/culture/here-we-come-caroling/

14 https://tradfolk.co/customs/wassailing/wassailing/

15 https://www.pbs.org/wgbh/christmas-tabernacle-choir/the-concert2022/the-holly-and-the-ivy/

16 http://news.bbc.co.uk/2/hi/entertainment/arts_and_culture/7752029.stm

17 https://secondhandsongs.com/work/48785

18 https://www.uuworld.org/articles/came-upon-unitarian-midnight-clear

19 https://www.snopes.com/fact-check/jingle-bells-thanksgiving-carol/

20 https://www.bu.edu/articles/2016/jingle-bells-history

21 https://entertainment.time.com/2012/12/17/yule-laugh-yule-cry-10-things-you-didnt-know-about-beloved-holiday-songs/

22 https://hymnary.org/node/6445#google_vignette

23 https://secondhandsongs.com/work/118981

24 https://www.liveabout.com/what-is-the-nutcracker-march-1007005

25 http://www.hymntime.com/tch/htm/n/o/w/d/nowdayis.htm

26 https://www.liederlexikon.de/lieder/o_tannenbaum

27 https://hymnary.org/text/o_come_o_come_emmanuel_and_ransom#google_vignette

28 https://secondhandsongs.com/work/105993

29 https://www.americamagazine.org/arts-culture/2020/11/19/brief-history-o-holy-night-christmas-hymn-review

30 http://www.hymnsandcarolsofchristmas.com/Hymns_and_Carols/Notes_On_Carols/o_little_town_of_bethlehem.htm

31 https://www.bbc.co.uk/religion/religions/christianity/christmas/carols_1.shtml

32 https://www.billboard.com/culture/lifestyle/mariah-carey-most-recorded-holiday-songs-8061679/]

33 https://www.smithsonianmag.com/smart-news/silent-night-celebrates-its-bicentennial-180971044

34 https://www.dw.com/en/silent-night/a-17295427

35 https://www.bbc.co.uk/religion/religions/christianity/christmas/carols_1.shtml
36 https://www.popvortex.com/music/charts/top-christmas-albums.php
37 https://www.german-way.com/history-and-culture/german-language/german-christmas-carols/still-still-still/#google_vignette
38 http://www.hymnsandcarolsofchristmas.com/Hymns_and_Carols/still_still_still_a ustrian.htm
39 https://parade.com/1136533/jessicasager/twas-the-night-before-christmas-words/
40 http://www.hymnsandcarolsofchristmas.com/Hymns_and_Carols/up_on_the_hous etop.htm
41 https://news.google.com/newspapers?id=hbdaAAAAIBAJ&pg=5456,507145
42 https://web.archive.org/web/20120111142545/http://www.hymntime.com/tch/bio/ h/o/p/hopkins_jh.htm
43 https://news.google.com/newspapers?id=0gpFAAAAIBAJ&pg=1972,4258244&d q=john+henry+hopkins+jr+we+three+kings&hl=en
44 http://www.hymnsandcarolsofchristmas.com/Hymns_and_Carols/while_shepherds _watched_their_fl.htm
45 https://www.thenorthernecho.co.uk/news/4794179.professor-jeremy-dibbles-hymnology-research-reveals-while-shepherds-watched--first-hymn-approved-c-e/
46 https://hymnary.org/text/ah_bleak_and_chill_the_wintry_wind
47 https://www.latimes.com/archives/la-xpm-2004-sep-26-me-gardner26-story.html
48 https://americansongwriter.com/ray-charles-and-betty-carter-baby-its-cold-outside/
49 https://web.archive.org/web/20200523021136/https://www.npr.org/transcripts/572 408088
50 https://performingsongwriter.com/christmas-song/
51 https://www.youtube.com/watch?v=hDsxZWvxZ6E
52 https://books.google.com/books?id=rwRYm1D9CDcC&q=%22Frosty+the+Snow man%22+%22Steve+Nelson%22+%22Jack+Rollins%22&pg=PA30#v=snippet=%2 2Frosty%20the%20Snowman%22%20%22Steve%20Nelson%22%20%22Jack%20 Rollins%22&f=false
53 https://www.youtube.com/watch?v=rZviqskCF4Q
54 https://www.udiscovermusic.com/stories/have-yourself-a-merry-little-christmas-frank-sinatra-song-feature/
55 https://stagedhaze.com/2020/12/09/have-yourself-a-merry-little-christmas-is-2020s-holiday-anthem/
56 https://www.geneautry.com/clubhouse/christmas/geneautry_hcscsong.html
57 https://www.chicagochorale.org/blog/2019/11/5/i-wonder-as-i-wander-an-american-classic
58 https://books.google.com/books?id=4a6oMgT8UsEC&pg=PT54#v=onepage&q&f =false.
Site refers to the book *Stories Behind the Greatest Hits of Christmas*, Andrew Collins Publisher, 2010
59 https://dogwoodjournal.com/the-history-of-the-little-drummer-boy/
60 https://imagesofoldhawaii.com/mele-kalikimaka/
61 https://www.pbs.org/wgbh/christmas-tabernacle-choir/concert-2017/parade-wooden-soldiers/
62 https://hymnary.org/media/fetch/190587

[63] https://arquivo.pt/wayback/20090708151035/http:/www.snopes.com/holidays/christmas/rudolph.asp

[64] https://mymerrychristmas.com/x/the-history-of-santa-claus-is-coming-to-town/

[65] https://the-circuit.greasylake.org/index.php?/topic/139611-the-story-of-santa-claus/

[66] https://www.youtube.com/watch?v=ki1x-d8asq0

[67] http://www.leroyanderson.com/sleigh-ride.php

[68] https://pennsvalleyparish.info/the-story-behind-some-children-see-him/

[69] https://secondhandsongs.com/work/241337/versions#nav-entity

[70] http://www.harryforbes.com/2024/02/babes-in-toyland-victor-herbert.html

[71] https://www.vox.com/21796404/12-days-of-christmas-explained

[72] https://www.bristolpost.co.uk/news/bristol-news/wish-you-merry-christmas-bristol-3678149

[73] http://www.hymnsandcarolsofchristmas.com/Hymns_and_Carols/white_christmas.htm

[74] https://www.youtube.com/watch?v=Xo9z5rkQe84

[75] https://www.youtube.com/watch?v=mMl4Pls41qI

[76] https://www.tricountyindependent.com/story/entertainment/human-interest/2016/12/19/local-history-winter-wonderland-8217/23659254007/

[77] https://www.ascap.com/press/2007/111207_holiday.aspx

[78] https://secondhandsongs.com/work/235936

[79] https://nypost.com/2014/12/13/8-things-you-didnt-know-about-all-i-want-for-christmas-is-you/

[80] https://blogs.loc.gov/music/2022/12/ill-be-home-for-christmas/

[81] https://www.youtube.com/watch?v=jw0ZfyWmkD0

[82] https://secondhandsongs.com/work/124903

[83] https://www.thegospelcoalition.org/blogs/trevin-wax/two-of-my-favorite-christmas-songs/

[84] https://wcsx.com/2023/12/19/tom-petty-christmas-all-over-again-the-story-behind-the-song/

[85] https://www.allmusic.com/album/this-time-of-year-mw0000359840]

[86] https://records.christmas/top-100/

[87] *Christmas Past: The Fascinating Stories Behind Our Favorite Holiday's Traditions* by B. Earl, Lyons Press (2023)

[88] https://www.today.com/popculture/christmas-shoes-worst-holiday-song-ever-1c7689418

[89] https://fee.org/articles/why-the-story-behind-do-they-know-it-s-christmas-is-both-uplifting-and-tragic/

[90] https://web.archive.org/web/20191212201034/https://www.franciscanmedia.org/do-you-hear-what-i-hear-the-story-behind-the-song/

[91] https://007underthemangotree.wordpress.com/2014/12/25/do-you-know-how-christmas-trees-are-grown/

[92] https://www.theguardian.com/culture/2016/dec/19/chris-rea-how-we-made-driving-home-for-christmas

[93] https://www.npr.org/2020/12/14/945401085/50-years-later-feliz-navidad-still-delivers-on-its-bilingual-message

[94] https://www.washingtonpost.com/wpdyn/content/article/2007/12/13/AR2007121302192_2.html

[95] https://www.ft.com/content/6464a160-bd53-11e6-8b45-b8b81dd5d080

[96] https://www.theraineys.org/post/i-heard-the-bells-on-christmas-day

[97] https://www.youtube.com/watch?v=kA5lZZ4-QZ8

[98] https://ucatholic.com/blog/when-the-church-banned-then-unbanned-i-saw-mommy-kissing-santa-claus/

[99] https://www.youtube.com/watch?v=REd9wHlF_oQ

[100] https://www.nytimes.com/2016/12/30/business/retirement/i-want-a-hippopotamus-for-christmas.html

[101] https://archive.ph/20191210101429/https://www.bizjournals.com/jacksonville/stories/2001/08/27/story1.html#selection-2113.0-2555.393

[102] https://www.theneweuropean.co.uk/bert-kaempfert-great-european-lives/

[103] https://www.discogs.com/release/17215687-Various-The-Stars-Come-Out-For-Christmas

[104] https://www.lib.cua.edu/wordpress/newsevents/9949/

[105] https://archive.ph/20191216185922/https://lacrossetribune.com/courierlifenews/news/local/pooler-s-song-dashed-off-for-a-girl-became-a/article_eb1aeb3a-3466-57fa-ac0a-4951ae9b8c31.html#selection-3165.0-3165.40

[106] https://www.songfacts.com/facts/bob-dylan/must-be-santa

[107] https://genius.com/She-and-him-must-be-santa-lyrics

[108] https://www.youtube.com/watch?v=ftzoVer9IcE

[109] https://www.youtube.com/watch?v=lCpXMy5GalI

[110] https://www.andrewlloydwebber.com/news/looking-back-at-requiem-37-years-on/

[111] https://www.youtube.com/watch?v=wnvzwAPqniU

[112] https://www.discogs.com/artist/1655391-Judy-Valentine

[113] https://www.washingtonpost.com/arts-entertainment/2018/12/07/how-thoroughly-depressing-joni-mitchell-song-became-blue-christmas-classic/

[114] https://www.gossipherald.com/amp/17089-brenda-lee-lauds-shania-twain-over-rockin-around-the-christmas-tree-cover

[115] http://www.crlf.de/ChuckBerry/blog/archives/140-Run!-Rudolph,-the-Red-Nosed-Reindeer-and-the-copyright-mystery.html

[116] https://www.musicnotes.com/blog/interview-with-santa-baby-songwriter-philip-springer/

[117] https://www.iwm.org.uk/history/the-real-story-of-the-christmas-truce

[118] https://www.mtishows.co.uk/meredith-willsons-miracle-on-34th-street-the-musical

[119] https://x.com/vas_90s/status/1733354470212325621?lang=en

[120] https://www.legacy.com/ca/obituaries/theglobeandmail/name/janis-orenstein-obituary?id=40497326

[121] https://www.pbs.org/wgbh/christmas-tabernacle-choir/concert-2019/we-need-a-little-christmas/

[122] https://www.youtube.com/watch?v=94Ye-3C1FC8

[123] https://www.theguardian.com/travel/2007/dec/06/bars.top10

[124] https://www.forbes.com/sites/zackomalleygreenburg/2010/12/23/paul-mccartney-continues-to-have-a-wonderful-financial-christmas-time/

[125] https://www.youtube.com/watch?v=ElmsIGT85tI

[126] https://www.youtube.com/watch?v=DudygHca9AY

[127] https://www.youtube.com/watch?v=ByK84WFMaJw

[128] https://villainsong.fandom.com/wiki/Christmastime_Is_Killing_Us

[129] https://www.billboard.com/music/music-news/justin-biebers-mistletoe-brightens-billboard-200-with-no-1-debut-465232/

[130] https://www.totalntertainment.com/music/leona-lewis-announces-christmas-with-love-always/

[131] https://komonews.com/news/local/seattles-lady-a-to-lady-antebellum-we-cant-both-be-lady-a-youll-bury-me

[132] https://www.seattletimes.com/entertainment/music/seattle-singer-lady-a-and-former-lady-antebellum-band-end-lawsuits/

[133] https://www.youtube.com/watch?v=V3EYjVPRClU

[134] https://www.youtube.com/watch?v=gset79KMmt0

[135] https://www.billboard.com/music/music-news/kelly-clarkson-in-the-red-zone-with-wrapped-in-red-the-billboard-cover-5763070/

[136] https://www.billboard.com/music/music-news/kelly-clarkson-in-the-red-zone-with-wrapped-in-red-the-billboard-cover-5763070/

[137] https://www.billboard.com/business/legal/kelly-clarkson-ex-husband-ordered-repay-2-6-million-1235518785/

Printed in Dunstable, United Kingdom